Austerity Management in Academic Libraries

Edited by

John F. Harvey and
Peter Spyers-Duran

The Scarecrow Press, Inc.
Metuchen, N.J., and London
1984

Books Edited by John F. Harvey

The Library Periodical Directory (with Phillips Temple, Betty Martin Brown and
  Mary Adele Springman), 1955 and 1967
The Library College (with Louis Shores and Robert Jordan), 1964
Data Processing in College and Public Libraries, 1966
Comparative and International Library Science, 1977
Church and Synagogue Libraries, 1980
Librarians' Affirmative Action Handbook (with Elizabeth M. Dickinson), 1982
Austerity Management in Academic Libraries (with Peter Spyers-Duran), 1984
Internationalizing Library Education: A Handbook (with Frances Laverne Carroll) (in
  process)

Books Edited by Peter Spyers-Duran

Approval and Gathering Plans in Academic Libraries, 1969
Advances in Understanding Approval Plans in Academic Libraries, 1970
Economics of Approval Plans in Research Libraries, (with Daniel Gore), 1972
Management Problems in Serials Work, (with Daniel Gore), 1973
Prediction of Resource Needs, 1975
Requiem for the Card Catalog: Management Issues in Automated Cataloging, (with
  Joseph Kimbrough and Daniel Gore), 1979
Shaping Library Collections for the 1980s, (with Thomas Mann), 1981
Austerity Management in Academic Libraries (with John F. Harvey), 1984

Library of Congress Cataloging in Publication Data
Main entry under title:

Austerity management in academic libraries.

  Includes bibliographical references and index.
  1. Libraries, University and college—United States—
Finance.   I. Harvey, John F. (John Frederick),
1921–   .   II. Spyers–Duran, Peter.
Z675.U5A88   1984   025.1'1'071173   83-14428
ISBN 0-8108-1648-2

Contents

Introduction

John F. Harvey and Peter Spyers-Duran

Why Was This Book Prepared?

DURING THE 1970s, academic library financial support weakened significantly. The past decade's trend appears to be continuing into the 1980s. Existing general economic problems and the cumulative erosion of the dollar's purchasing power signaled a continuing long-term austerity for these institutions. Severe as the problems may be, few individuals have grasped the full extent of budget deterioration. Most recent American library literature appears to be weak in retrospective analysis of inflation's cumulative effects which have created a considerable budget need arrearage.[1]

Managing austerity requires a creative approach and a formal, comprehensive organizational priority examination. The editors believe that an austerity management handbook can assist local administrators by offering creative ideas and information useful in influencing future academic library programs. This book attempts to document certain recent library fiscal problems. It seeks further to stimulate management thinking. to describe certain approaches which have been used successfully in ameliorating problems, and to encourage service priority rethinking. Guidance to relevant data and literature is provided, also.[2] The book is aimed at all academic librarians, especially managers, and should be useful to higher education administrators and faculty members directly concerned with libraries as well. Special, school, and public librarians may also find something useful here.

Definitions, Assumptions, Research

Management and administration are nearly synonymous and can be defined as referring to library organization and operation. Academic libraries serve post-secondary level educational institutions of all kinds, from small two-year colleges to large comprehensive universities. Austerity is a lean and poor condition, one of sacrificing certain desirable or essential conditions, a limited and unenviable situation where the organization is operating but neither prospering nor giving the service it knows how to give. The term refers primarily to financial condition and its consequences here. Austerity resembles an economic depression, or being ill but not fatally so. Sere, ascetic, stern and forbidding, rigidly abstemious, with enforced or even extreme economy.

The book's usefulness is based on several assumptions which can be explained briefly. One of them is that "good" library service is a vital but unproven academic-institution asset characterizing a "superior" institution. This belief has seldom been subjected to careful analysis, but librarians believe firmly in it nevertheless. Normally, austerity is assumed to be detrimental to service and to counterbalance factors tending to stabilize it. Austerity is assumed to be a basic and enervating condition or force which reflects the national economy's inflation. To reduce its effects, a multiple approach must be used; not just one but several ideas must be tried. The more resourceful managers will survive in better fashion than less imaginative colleagues.

The book assumes continued institutional separation and integrity. American institutions are likely to remain quite independent of each other until austerity's vise becomes very tight. And finally, we assume that this handbook will be useful in easing austerity's stress on persons directly exposed.

Only with close monitoring can librarians understand how various service aspects are affected in stress periods. Accurate, comparable, and comprehensive national tabulations of per full-time equivalent (FTE) student and per staff member analyses, period study over time and consumer price index (CPI) rise information on salary and material expenditures should be made. Careful research is needed about the effects of austerity on the monograph and serial collections, the physical facilities, technical and public service, library use for study and research, and even its effect on campus scholarship and student and faculty learning. The long range effects of the 1970s deprivation should make a revealing dissertation or two. Eventually, such studies may lead librarians to establish new national norms and standards. At the least, we can predict that library austerity literature will grow significantly in coming years. In fact much of 1982 and 1983 literature already reflects the negative and defensive posture of the austere librarian.

Preparation and Acknowledgements

The editors conceived the original book idea, outlined the chapters in fifty pages, secured the publisher's contract, selected potential chapter authors, prepared the invitation letter and author guidance memoran-

dum, corresponded with potential authors, discussed chapter revision
with authors, individually and in conference, edited the resulting papers, and prepared the first chapter, the notes on contributors, and the
index. All chapters were written especially for this book.

The editors would like to thank many persons in Tehran, Nicosia,
Lyndonville, Long Beach, Metuchen and many other cities for assistance. Secretaries Behnaz Behforouzi, Shahzade Hamidi, Foulla
Hadjicharou, Elena Mavridou, and Jane Magill deserve thanks for extensive typing and correspondence. Finally, the chapter authors deserve our warmest thanks for making this book possible.

References

1. However, see Eleanor Francis Brown, *Cutting Library Costs: Increasing Production and Raising Revenues* (Metuchen, N.J.: Scarecrow Press, 1979); Sara Lake,
   Declining Enrollments, Declining Resources (Phoenix: Oryx Press, 1981); *Managing Under Austerity: A Conference for Privately Supported Academic Libraries*, edited by John G. Hayeck (Stanford, CA: Stanford University Press, 1976); *Strategies for Survival: Library Financial Management Today*, edited by Ann Prentice
   (New York: Library Journal, 1978); and *Managing Fiscal Stress; the Crisis in the
   Public Sector*, edited by Charles H. Levine (Chatham, N.J.: Chatham House,
   1980).
2. See *Challenges of Retrenchment* (San Francisco: Jossey-Bass, 1981) for many
   useful approaches and suggestions.

1. The Effect of Inflation on Academic Libraries

John F. Harvey and Peter Spyers-Duran

PRESIDENT JOHN KEMENY of Dartmouth College made the following statement recently:

I am confident that future historians will report that we are now going thru the most prolonged financial crisis in the history of American higher education. . . . We have seen the end of a century of steady growth . . . and have entered what is called a steady state. We have passed the peak of the number of 18-year-olds in the population and there will be a steady decline throughout the eigthties. It has not been a period in which one could think of great new projects to launch. Instead, one is reminded of *Through The Looking Glass* since it takes all the running you can do, to keep in the same place. . . . The major challenge for all our educational institutions has been to maintain quality. I expect there are several more difficult years still to come for higher education. Inflation ran at only a 3% rate in the 1960s . . . but at an extremely high level (in the 1970s). Per student expenditures declined markedly in the 1970s due to inflation and enrollment expansion.[1]

Depressing as this quotation may be, statements like his are common in higher education. Examples of sobering information can be found on every side. Late in the following summer, an issue of the *Chronicle of Higher Education* featured the following brief story:

Over the past ten years, the average faculty salary has risen 72.9% while the Consumer Price Index has gone up 122.7%. Average faculty salary in all ranks in August 1981 was $23,650 but if it had matched the cost of living rise it would have been $29,345 . . . Annual faculty salary increase has failed to match cost of living rise for the past five years. Data were taken from the American Association of University Professors Salary Survey of 2500 colleges based on HEGIS figures.[2]

And finally, a library conference reported the following:

The ARL reported that in the past ten years its member libraries had increased their spending for library material by 91%, but the yearly number of volumes added to their collections had declined by 22.5% (a 1:5.0 ratio). . . . The report said total costs of the research libraries had doubled during the decade as a result of three kinds of financial pressure: (a) inflation in the cost of published material, especially from other countries; (b) rapid growth of information, requiring libraries to acquire a larger number of more expensive materials; and (c) increased demand from faculty members and students for more material and more professional assistance. . . .[3]

This chapter examines the effects of inflation on cost of living, on the federal and state budgets available for social and educational purposes, higher education enrollment, and more. It also examines the changes in 1970s academic library finance in three major parts: personnel, material, and the two combined. Several tables have been prepared to compare Association of Research Libraries (ARL) 1970 and 1981 and NCES LIBGIS (National Center for Education Statistics, Library General Information Survey) 1959, 1969, 1979 academic library data.[4-7] They are fundamental to the discussion and contain data from which various analyses have been made. Chapter discussion will focus primarily on them. Data analysis is simple and direct, and often necessarily crude and weak in the manner of all analyses that depend on not entirely comparable or incomplete data.[8]

This chapter's primary purpose is to describe and analyze the library's fiscal history, not to ascertain all causes nor to discuss all implications. Other useful approaches and analyses exist and can be left to other students. While its conclusions will surprise few readers, its data and analyses are intended to provide more than just personal opinions.

Government and Education Austerity

President Ronald Reagan's 1981 federal government budget slashes cut service expenditures drastically. These cuts occurred in at least two groups: a) those announced soon after Reagan took office in January with the plan to downgrade federal social service expenditures and b) those announced in the Fall on the realization that income would not cover planned expenditures. These reductions cut into previous budget levels substantially in addition to the 9–12 per cent annual Consumer Price Index (CPI) rise then in effect.

The tables of the *Statistical Abstract of the United States* provided the percentage increases in the cost of living or CPI for the typical citizen: 79.5, 1970–78; 101.1, 1970–79; 104.4 from 1969 to 1979; 128.6, 1970–80 and 144.6 for 1970–81.[9] If the base is extended back to 1960, the CPI rise to 1980 equaled 154.2 per cent. The period 1969–1970 is used here as the primary frame of reference because it marked the

beginning of a cost inflationary decade. The CPI figures represent the
level at which the salary budgets, for instance, needed to rise in order
for the 1970 size staff to maintain parity with 1970 dollars. Any smaller
salary increase meant that the staff members' 1980 purchasing power
had been reduced below the 1970 level. Any larger salary raise meant
the opposite, of course.

As an example of inflation's effect on income, in 1980 the federal
government reported median family income *in 1979 dollars* to have
risen only from $18,444 in 1970 to $19.684 in 1979, or 7 percent for
nine years.[10] Two aspects of inflation hit libraries hardest: that affecting staff members' living costs and that affecting library material cost.
Both aspects must be considered.

It should not be thought that 1981 government and service cuts were
new to American citizens. Evidence of austerity in service organizations
had been available for several years. The federal budget as a whole
grew 187 per cent between 1970 and 1980, from $196.6 billion to
$563.6 billion, but inflation reduced the decade's gain to 58.4 per cent.
Table 1 (page 4) shows this picture. Federal education expenditures
followed a similar path in moving from $12.653 billion in 1970 to
$33.897 billion by 1980. However, inflation offset this 168 per cent
advance and left a net gain of 39.6 per cent or 4 per cent per year.[11]

The government's largest library fared better than most but still lost
45 per cent of its impressive budget gain to inflation. Net Library of
Congress budget change 1970 to 1979 is shown in Table 2 (page 5).[12]
Federal aid to academic libraries is shown in Table 3 (page 6) with 1970
dollars worth only 45 cents by 1980. The appropriation sank steadily.
Aid to research libraries rose at the end of this period, however. Thus,
federal budgets of various levels moved ahead during the decade, except for aid to academic libraries, but inflation ate much of the gain
away.

State government varied in confronting austerity. Certain states, such
as Alaska, California, Montana, Louisiana, New Mexico, Oklahoma,
Hawaii, Wyoming and Texas advanced in relatively good fashion as if
prosperity were a permanent condition. In 1981–82 they were expected to spend between $2,712 and $4,156 per FTE student on public
higher education.[13] Other states, such as Massachusetts, Vermont,
Ohio, Minnesota, Michigan, Washington, Colorado, and New
Hampshire retreated sharply or else continued poor support, especially
for higher education.[14,15]

Governor Snelling of Vermont, Chairman of the National Gover-
nors' Association Fiscal Affairs Committee said: "The outlook for state
budgets is bleak."[16] The Committee's report stated that at year-end
1979, state revenue declined by 0.4 per cent in "real" income, while
state spending grew by 2.4 per cent in "real" terms, a 1:6 ratio. He
predicted further that in 1981 state governments might have their
largest deficits. In its December 1981 report, the Advisory Commission

Table 1. U.S. Federal Government Expenditure (in billions)

Category	1970	1980	Increase	Per cent Increase	Per cent Increase Minus CPI %	Per cent Increase Minus CPI % per year
Budget Outlay	$196.7	$563.6	$367.0	187.0	58.4	5.8
Budget Outlay for Education	$12.653	$33.897	$21.244	168.0	39.6	4.0

Source: Adapted from Statistical Abstract of the United States 1980, Tables 223, 431.

Table 2. Library of Congress Total Appropriations and Transfers (in millions)

1961	1970	Increase 1961–1970	Per cent Increase 1961–1970	1979	Increase 1970–79	Per cent Increase 1970–79	Per cent Increase Minus CPI % Increase 1970–79
$24.131	$66.884	$42.753	177.2	$217.799	$150.915	225.1	124.0

N.B.: 1979 = 1978–79, 1970 = 1969–70; each one represents a single fiscal year.

Sources: Annual Report of the Librarian of Congress for the Fiscal Year Ending June 30, 1961 (Washington, D.C.: G.P.O., 1962), p. 113; June 30, 1970 (G.P.O., 1971), p. 125; June 30, 1979 (G.P.O., 1979), p. A25.

Table 3.   Federal Aid to Academic Libraries (in millions)

Category	1970	1980	1983	Change 1970–83	Per cent Change
College	$34.063	$5.000	$1.920	−$32.143	−94.4
Research	1978 5.000	6.000	5.760	1978–83 .760	15.2

Sources: Carol Henderson, "Washington Hotline," *College and Research Library News* 43 (February 1982), pp.
63, 75; W. Vance Grant and Leo J. Eiden, *Digest of Education Statistics 1981* (Washington, D.C.:
NCES, 1981), p. 185.

on Intergovernmental Relations titled its summary, "The Great Slowdown."[17]

Table 4 (page 6) shows state government figures. General Operating Fund change showed a steady increase but not enough to offset inflation, losing at the rate of 4.2 per cent annually. Most institutions felt the tightening vise of financial stringency. They paid the same size staff larger salaries with no production increase.[18] A 16.7 per cent increase occurred in full-time state government employment 1972–77 but also a 65.0 per cent increase in payrolls. Productivity increased 12.9 per cent (federal) during this period.[19] Many budgets were static in fighting inflation and vacated positions frozen. State level education support varied, also. Net decade state school expenditure gain was 42.9 per cent after subtracting CPI (Table 4). Thus, state finance moved ahead through the decade also and at much the same rate as federal finance.

Nineteen seventy-eighty was a belt-tightening decade for most public and nonpublic elementary and secondary school systems, as Table 5 shows. Many systems attempted to retain 1960s financial gains and some of them succeeded. Sunbelt systems often grew and prospered

Table 4.   State Government General Operating Fund Expenditure and Elementary and Secondary School Expenditure (in billions)

Category	1970	1980	Change	Per cent Increase	Per cent Minus CPI %
General Operating Fund	$69.000	$128.854	$59.854	86.7	−41.9
School Expenditure	$15.8	$42.9	$27.1	171.5	42.9

Sources: Adapted from *Statistical Abstract of the United States 1980*, Tables 222, 505; *Statistical Abstract of the United States 1979*, Table 472.

Table 5. Public and Nonpublic Elementary and Secondary Schools

Category	1970	1980	Increase	Per cent Change	Per cent Increase Minus CPI %	Per cent Increase Minus CPI % per year
Enrollment (millions)	52.9	47.9*	−5.0	−9.5	—	—
Expenditure (billions)	$45.7	$107.1	$61.4	134.4	8.0	0.8
Per Student Expenditure	$864	$2,236	$1,372	158.8	30.2	3.0
Average Annual Public School Instructional Staff Member Salary	$8,840	$14,970*	$6,130	69.7	−31.4	−3.1

*1979 figures.

Source: Adapted from Statistical Abstract of the United States 1980, Tables 222, 226, 246.

while North and Middle West systems shrank and suffered.[20] Many systems were blessed with falling enrollment which required fewer teachers and buildings, yet in certain of them, teacher strikes brought higher salary raises and offset other financial gains,[21,22]

Teachers were paid the highest salaries in their careers but could buy less than before, since they suffered a net nine-year loss of 3.1 per cent annually as seen in Table 5 (page 7). While salaries sank, student test scores sank, also.[23,24] Construction, maintenance, and equipment expenditures were often delayed or cancelled. The table shows total decade school system expenditure to have increased by 134.4 per cent, leaving less than a 1 per cent per year net gain over inflation. Due to enrollment decrease, however, per student expenditures rose 3.0 per cent per year after CPI reduction.

Fiscal problems of this kind were reflected in higher education funding, also.[25] Retrenchment evidence was found in many presidents' messages.[26] U.S. NCES data bore out President Kemeny's doleful remarks about needing to run very hard just to stay in place—or, more often, to lose ground less rapidly. After 1960s growth and prosperity, the 1970s were years of enrollment stabilization and cost inflation. The fourfold energy cost increase and the twofold-plus CPI increase were the chief fiscal pressures and they restricted other budget categories. Essential expenses were covered adequately but little else could be afforded.

Table 6 (page 9) shows special categories of higher education enrollment. It makes clear that enrollment gained strongly in the 1960s but at a lower rate in the 1970s, even among graduate students. NCES intermediate projections thru 1988 showed enrollment peaking in 1981 and declining slowly thereafter; other projections showed a much deeper decline in the 1990s.[27]

Table 7 (page 10) shows enrollment and expenditure for universities, two- and four-year colleges, both public and nonpublic, for 1970 and 1980.[28] Institutional expenditure gained only 1.2 per cent per year for the decade and lost by 6.0 per cent per year when per student data is examined.[29] Such a loss was a discouraging showing. Personnel constituted 50 to 70 per cent of all expenditures by 1980 and nonpersonnel categories were increasingly squeezed.[30,31] Higher education suffered more than elementary and secondary levels. Decade expenditures per student increased a net of 30.1 per cent for elementary and secondary, but dropped by 59.8 per cent for higher education. Minter and Bowen identified a slow decline in the percentage of institutional budgets devoted to instruction (and libraries), also.[32] Nonpublic institutions were hit even harder and forced into extensive economy measures. Table 7 shows that nonpublic institutions suffered an after-CPI expenditure loss of 1.6 per cent annually while public higher education moved ahead by 2.6 per cent annually. The per-student annual expenditure contrast was −4.6 to −6.0 per cent nonpublic to public, losses at about the same level, due partly to the modest nonpublic enrollment increase. So, when

Table 6. Higher Education Enrollment in Certain Categories

Category	1960	1970	Increase	Per cent Increase	1979	Increase 1970-79	Per cent Increase 1970-79	Per cent Increase per year 1970-79
Total National Enrollment per Institution (in FTE students)	1,744	3,120	1,376	78.9	3,300	180	5.8	0.6
Total Enrollment in ARL Member Universities per Institution (in FTE students)	—	15,458	—	—	*1981* 23,845	*1970-81* 8,387	*1970-81* 54.3	*1970-81* 4.9
Total National Masters and Doctors Degree Enrollment (in FTE students)	356,000	1,031,000	675,000	189.6	*1980* 1,365,000	*1970-80* 354,000	*1970-80* 32.4	*1970-80* 3.2

N.B.: ARL libraries = 71; NCES libraries = 1951 (1959-60), 2,500 (1969-70), 3,121 (1978-79).

Sources: Association of Research Libraries. *ARL Statistics 1980-81* (Washington, D.C.: 1981), pp. 24-26; *Bowker Annual 1970* (N.Y.: R. R. Bowker, 1970), pp. 14-15; *Bowker Annual 1975* (N.Y.: R. R. Bowker, 1975), pp. 228-29; *Bowker Annual 1981* (N.Y.: R. R. Bowker, 1981), pp. 295; *1981-82 Fact Book for Academic Administrators* (Washington, D.C.: American Council on Education, 1981), Table 98; Kendon Stubbs and David Buxton, comps., *Cumulated ARL University Library Statistics 1962-63 Through 1978-79* (Washington, D.C.: Association of Research Libraries, 1981), Part 6; U.S. Department of Health, Education and Welfare. NCES. *The Conditions of Education Statistical Report* (Washington, D.C.: G.P.O.. 1980). p. 95.

Table 7. Higher Education Enrollment and Expenditure

Category	1970	1980	Increase	Per cent Increase	Per cent Increase Minus CPI %	Per cent Increase Minus CPI % per year
Enrollment (millions)						
Public	5.800	8.786*	2.986	51.5	—	—
Nonpublic	2.120	2.474*	.354	16.7	—	—
Total	7.920	11.260*	3.340	42.2	—	—
Expenditure (billions)						
Public	$15.8	$40.3	$24.5	155.0	26.4	2.6
Nonpublic	$8.9	$19.0	$10.1	113.0	-15.6	-1.6
Total	$24.7	$59.3	$34.6	140.1	11.5	1.2
Expenditure Per Student						
Public	$2,724	$4,587	$1,863	68.4	-60.2	-6.0
Nonpublic	$4,198	$7,680	$3,482	82.9	-45.7	-4.6
Total	$3,119	$5,266	$2,147	68.8	-59.8	-6.0

*1978 figures.

Source: Adapted from *Statistical Abstract of the United States 1980,* Tables 221, 273, 279.

CPI adjustment is made, most institutions suffered net budget reductions while a few had modest increases.[33]

Personnel Austerity

Since academic librarianship is still heavily labor-intensive (a special inflation period problem), it is appropriate to open the discussion with personnel. We will examine enrollment gain against library staff member gain, staff member per student ratio change, and librarian-support staff and student assistant ratios as well as library personnel expenditures and CPI rise in order to learn how inflation affected staffing and service.[34]

Tables 6 and 7 show enrollment for all types of institutions, for ARL institutions and for graduate students.[35] Tables 8 and 9 (pages 11–13) show 1960s and 1970s staff size change. The most notable finding here

---

Table 8.   Association of Research Libraries University Library Personnel Data (N = 71)

Categories	1970	1981	Change	Per cent Change	Per cent Change per year
Professional staff members per ARL library	81.1	81.1	0.0	0.0	0.0
Support staff members per ARL library	147.7	162.4	14.7	10.0	0.9
FTE student assistants per ARL library	62.0	71.3	9.3	15.0	1.4
Total staff members per ARL library	290.7	314.8	24.1	8.3	0.8
Per cent of professional to total staff members per ARL library	27.9	25.8	−2.1	−3.6	−0.3
Ratio of total library staff members to student enrollment	1:53	1:76	−1:23	−43.4	−3.9

Sources: Association of Research Libraries. *ARL Statistics 1980–81* (Washington, D.C. 1981), pp. 9, 11, 13, 15; Kenton Stubbs and David Buxton, *comps., Cumulative ARL University Library Statistic 1962–63 Through 1978–79* (Washington, D.C.: Association of Research Libraries, 1981), Part 5.

Table 9. National Center for Education Statistics Academic Library Personnel Data

Category	1959 (N = 1,951)	1969 (N = 2,500)	Change	Per cent Change	1979 (N = 3,121)	Change 1969–79	Per cent Change 1969–79	Per cent Change per year 1969–79
Professional Staff Members per Library	4.6	8.0	3.4	73.9	7.6	-0.4	-5.0	-0.5
Support Staff Members per Library	4.6	10.3	5.7	123.9	11.1	0.8	7.8	0.8
FTE Student Assistants per Library	3.1	6.9	3.8	122.6	6.3	-0.6	-8.7	-0.9
Total Staff Members per Library	12.3	25.2	12.9	104.9	25.0	-0.2	-0.8	-0.1
Per cent of Professional to Total Staff Members (including FTE Student Assistants) per Library	37.4	32.5	-4.9	-13.1	30.4	-2.1	-6.5	-0.7

Per cent of Professional to Total Staff Members (excluding FTE Student Assistants) per Library	50.1	44.4	−5.7	−11.4	40.5	−3.9	−8.8	−0.9
Ratio of Professional Staff Members to Student Enrollment	1:378	1:390	−1:12	−3.2	1:435	−1:45	−11.5	−1.2
Ratio of Support Staff Members to Student Enrollment	1:378	1:313	1:65	17.2	1:297	1:16	5.1	0.5
Ratio of FTE Student Assistants to Student Enrollment	1:556	1:455	1:101	18.2	1:521	−1:66	−14.5	−1.5
Ratio of Total Library Staff Members to Student Enrollment	1:142	1:125	1:17	12.0	1:132	−1:7	−5.6	−0.6

Sources: Richard M. Beazley, *Library Statistics of Colleges and Universities: 1979 Institutional Data* (Washington, D.C.: NCES, 1981); *Bowker Annual 1970*, (N.Y.: R. R. Bowker, 1970), pp. 14–15; *Bowker Annual 1975*, pp. 228–29; *Bowker Annual 1981*, pp. 298–99.

is that staff size change was small in the 1970s. Total ARL staff rose by less than 1 per cent per year. The NCES reported total staff size to rise by 10.5 per cent per year per library in the 1960s, a very large rise, but to shrink slightly, by 0.1 per cent annually, in the 1970s. Mean 1980–81 ARL size was 314.8 staff members and for NCES libraries was 25.9. So, the 1980 staff picture was little better than 1970 had been in terms of size.

When total staff member per student figures are examined, we see for ARL members that they declined from one FTE staff member (including student assistants) per 53 students in 1970 to 1 for 76 students in FY 1981, an annual loss rate of 3.9 per cent. Table 9's NCES data show that this ratio grew in the 1960s by 1.2 per cent per year for the national data base but declined slightly 1:125 to 1:132, or −0.6 per cent annually, for the 1970s. A special NCES 1968–77 report of academic library trends included an annual per student finding that total staff decreased by 0.7 per cent, a slow decrease.[36] Tables 8 and 9 show that staff size change per enrolled student for both groups was essentially static.

As an additional analysis, we can examine the staff ratio situation from another direction. What was the staff ratio change between librarians and support staff members and student assistants? Tables 8 and 9 show that a slow and modest staff composition change has occurred. The number of librarians per institution rose even more slowly than did the number of support staff members and student assistants. ARL annual 1970s change rate of librarians to support staff and student assistants declined by 0.3 per cent and the corresponding NCES ratios for the 1960s and the 1970s declined consistently by small amounts. The typical ARL library gained no librarian positions while gaining 0.9 support staff members and 1.4 student assistant positions per year.

Retrospectively, for the period 1951–69, Baumol and Marcus found a 1.5 per cent annual reduction in the ratio of librarians to support staff members for their ARL group.[37] In view of their data, we may note that this ratio has apparently been declining for thirty years.[38,39] A 1978–79 survey of large ACRL university libraries found the ratio of librarians to support staff members to student assistants to be medians of 25:50:25.[40] While having certain clearcut benefits, this decline vs. other staff members left students and faculty members with the same number of librarians to depend on for service as in earlier years. Was library productivity maintained in the 1970s with a decreasing librarian to support staff ratio?

That staffing was a common academic library problem was shown in two other recent studies.[41,42] In one, Carpenter studied 1,146 academic libraries (40 per cent of the total) with two-year colleges and larger universities omitted. He concluded: "In sum, for most libraries, it seems fair to say that they are underdeveloped, understaffed and underused. Assuming that the Association of College and Research Libraries (ACRL) standards are reasonable, far greater support for all library functions is required for the great majority of libraries".[43] Carpenter found librarian per FTE student ratio to equal 1:350 and librarian per support staff member and student assistant ratio to equal 1:4 or 25 per cent. More than half of the libraries failed to meet the ACRL standards adequately.[44] More librarians and support staff members were needed to provide adequate service, he concluded.

Now we come to salary expenditure. Table 10 (page 16) shows 1970 and 1981 ARL expenditure, and Table 11 (page 18) shows 1959, 1969, and 1979 NCES library expenditure. Total expenditure was divided by the number of FTE staff members employed to derive crude mean salary levels. These tables can be compared with Table 12 (page 20) showing faculty member salary increase data, 1960–78, also.

For ARL members, salary per staff member rose annually by 10.1 per cent in the 1970s, from $5,543 to $11,682. For NCES data, Table 11 shows that annual salary per staff member rose by 4.7 per cent in the 1960s but by 9.6 per cent in the 1970s, from means of $3,508 and $5,159 to $10,120. ARL salary per staff member increased at a 12.6 to 1 annual rate with staff size and NCES at a 97.0 to 1 annual rate. Both ARL and NCES salary raises were more than offset by the CPI rise. These tables show that much money was expended on salary increases without bringing a significant staff size increase.

Table 13A (page 21) shows that increased enrollments outpaced staffing increases and salary increases when the rise in CPI is subtracted. The data give the personnel situation for both ARL and NCES libraries for this period.

The annual Frarey-Darling-Learmont *Library Journal* placement reports showed academic librarians' mean beginning salaries to rise to the modest figure of $14,035 in 1980.[45] This change represented a 6.5 per cent annual increase for eleven years. When CPI rise was subtracted, however, this salary rise became an annual loss of 4.7 per cent. ACRL university libraries showed a median 1979 salary per staff member of $9,405, 24.2 per cent below the corresponding 1981 ARL figure and 7.6 per cent below the corresponding 1979 NCES figure.[46] And finally, in its special analysis, NCES 1968–77 figures showed total personnel expenditure including fringe benefits as a percent of total expenditures to have increased annually by 0.7 per cent.[47] This figure can be compared with an annual increase for NCES data 1959–69 of −1.1 per cent and for 1969–79 of 1.1 per cent and with an annual 1970–81 ARL increase figure of 0.7 per cent.

When we examine personnel expenditure per student, the ARL figures showed an annual increase of 3.6 per cent, 1970–81. The NCES figures showed an annual increase of 8.9 per cent per student, 1969–79. Although both were strong increases, both were more than wiped out by inflation. Both ARL and NCES groups were paid fewer 1970 level dollars in 1980 than in 1970. This situation led to a somewhat lower living standard

Table 10. Association of Research Libraries University Library Expenditure Data (N = 71)

Categories	1970	1981	Increase	Per cent Increase	Per cent Increase Per Year	Per cent Increase Minus CPI %	Per cent Increase Minus CPI % Per Year
Personnel expenditure per library	$1,704,799	$3,677,561	$1,972,762	115.7	10.5	−30.1	−2.7
Material expenditure per library	1,000,732	2,554,415	1,553,683	155.3	14.1	10.7	1.0
Current serial expenditure per library	626,016*	1,195,013	568,997	90.9	18.2	20.9	4.2
Total expenditure per library	3,063,855	6,859,532	3,795,677	123.9	11.3	−20.7	−1.9
Library personnel expenditure per student	110.28	154.23	43.95	39.8	3.6	−104.8	−9.5
Library material expenditure per student	64.74	107.13	42.39	65.6	6.0	−79.0	−7.2
Total library expenditure per student	198.21	287.67	89.45	45.1	4.1	−99.5	−9.0

Salary per staff member per library	5,543	11,682	6,139	110.8	10.1	−33.8	−3.1
Median library salary per library	9,625	16,578[†]	6,953	77.3	8.6	−23.8	−2.6
Material expenditure per gross annual volumes added per library	9.79	16.33	6.54	66.8	6.1	−78.8	−7.2
Total personnel expenditure as a per cent of total library expenditure	49.80	53.60	3.80	7.6	0.7	—	—
Total material expenditure as a per cent of total library expenditure	30.90	37.20	6.30	20.4	1.9	—	—

*1976 figure. †1979 figure.

N.B.: Library material figures exclude binding and microforms; Material expenditure per gross annual volume added per library assumes a 50–50 division of the material expenditure between monographs and serials. See Theodore Samore, "NCES Survey of College and University Libraries, 1978–79," *Bowker Annual 1981* (N.Y.: R.R. Bowker, 1981), p. 291. But see also, Association of Research Libraries. *ARL Statistics 1980–81* (Washington, D.C.: 1981), p. 6.

Sources: Association of Research Libraries. *ARL Statistics 1980–81* (Washington, D.C.: 1981). pp. 9, 11, 13, 15; Kendon Stubbs and David Boxton, *comps. Cumulative ARL University Library Statistics 1962–63 Through 1978–79* (Washington, D.C.: Association of Research Libraries, 1981), Parts 4 and 5.

Table 11. National Center for Education Statistics Academic Library Expenditure Data

Categories	1959	1969	Change	Per cent Change	1979	Change 1969–79	Per cent Change 1969–79	Per cent Change per year 1969–79	Per cent Increase Minus CPI % 1969–79	Per cent Increase per year Minus CPI % 1969–79
Personnel expenditure per library	$43,145	$126,920	$83,775	194.2	$253,000	$126,080	99.3	10.0	-5.1	-0.5
Material expenditure per library	20,892	85,160	64,268	307.6	144,233	59,073	69.4	6.9	-35.0	-3.5
Current serial expenditure per library	10,446	42,580	32,134	307.6	57,416	14,836	34.8	3.5	-69.6	-7.0
Total expenditure per library	70,382	233,840	163,458	232.2	481,276	247,436	105.8	10.6	1.3	0.1
Library personnel expenditure per student	24.74	40.86	15.94	64.4	76.67	35.99	88.5	8.9	-15.9	-1.6
Library material expenditure per student	11.98	27.29	15.31	127.8	43.71	16.42	60.2	6.0	-44.2	-4.4
Total library expenditure per student	40.34	74.95	34.61	85.8	145.84	70.89	94.6	9.5	-9.8	-1.0
Salary per staff member per library	3,508	5,159	1,651	47.0	10,120	4,961	96.2	9.6	-8.2	-0.8
Salaries as a per cent of total library expenditure	52.8	46.7	-6.1	-11.6	47.2	0.5	1.1	0.1	—	—

Hourly wages as a per cent of total library expenditure	8.5	7.6	−0.9	−10.6	5.3	−2.3	−30.3	−3.0	—	—
Total personnel expenditure as a per cent of total library expenditure	61.3	54.3	−7.0	−11.4	60.2	5.9	10.9	1.1	—	—
Material expenditure as a per cent of total library expenditure	29.7	36.4	6.7	22.6	30.0	−6.4	−17.6	−1.8	—	—
Total library expenditure as a per cent of total academic and general expenditure	3.0	4.0	1.0	33.3	3.8	−0.2	−0.5	−0.1	—	—
Material expenditure per gross annual volume added per library	$2.42	$4.09	$1.67	69.0	$10.41	$6.32	154.5	15.5	50.1	5.0

NB: N = 1,951 libraries in 1959–60; 2,500 in 1969–70; and 3,121 in 1978–79.
Library material figures exclude binding. Personnel figures exclude fringe benefits.
Material expenditures Per Gross Annual Volume Added Per Library assumes a 50–50 division of the material expenditures between monographs and serials.

Sources: Richard M. Beazley, Library Statistics of Colleges and Universities, Trends 1969–77, Summary Data, 1977 (Washington, D.C.: NCES, 1982); Richard M. Beazley, Library Statistics of Colleges and Universities: 1979 Institutional Data (Washington, D.C.: NCES, 1981); Bowker Annual 1970 (N.Y.: R.R. Bowker, 1970), pp. 14–15; Bowker Annual 1975, pp. 228–29; Bowker Annual 1981, pp. 296–99.

Table 12. Median Instructional Faculty Member Annual Salaries in Higher Education

1960	1970	Increase	Per cent Increase	1978	Increase 1970–78	Per cent Increase 1970–78	Per cent Increase Minus CPI % 1970–78	Per cent Increase Minus CPI % per year 1970–78
$6700	$11700	$5000	74.6	$17,800	$6,100	52.1	−27.4	−3.4

Source: Adapted from Statistical Abstract of the United States 1980, Table 286.

Table 13. Library Personnel and Material Deficits

A. *Personnel: Enrollment Gain and CPI Increase vs. Staff Member Gain and Salary Increase*

Annual Enrollment per institution per cent change		Annual staff member increase per library per cent change		Annual staff member per cent salary change per library minus CPI %	
ARL 1970–81	NCES 1970–79	ARL 1970–81	NCES 1969–79	ARL 1970–81	NCES 1969–79
4.9	0.6	0.8	–0.1	–3.1	–0.8

B. *Monographs: Monograph Material Production and Price Increases vs. per Library Volume and Expenditure Increases*

Annual Monograph Production Per cent Change		Annual Monograph Price Per cent Increase	Annual Gross Library Volumes Added Per cent Change		Annual Material Expenditure Per Gross Library Volumes Added Per cent Increase minus CPI %	
Unesco 1970–79	U.S. 1970–79	U.S. 1970–80	ARL 1970–81	NCES 1969–79	ARL 1970–81	NCES 1969–79
4.4	2.8	10.6	–2.1	–3.3	–7.2	5.0

N.B.: Unesco and U.S. title production mean percentage equals 3.6; assumption: Annual Unesco world title price increases equaled U.S. title price increases.

C. *Current Serials: Production and Price Increases vs. Library Title and Expenditure Increases*

Annual Bowker Serial Title Per cent Increase	Annual U.S. Periodical Price Per Title Per cent Increase	Annual Serial Titles Received Per Library Per cent Increase		Annual Current Serial Expenditure Per Library Per cent Increase Minus CPI %	
1969–80	1970–80	ARL 1972–81	NCES 1969–79	ARL 1976–81	NCES 1969–79
5.7	23.2	3.8	4.6	4.2	–7.0

in most cases, to morale problems, and probably to a staff moonlighting increase. Of course, certain individuals were able to beat inflation by securing job promotions and larger base salaries. When these figures are compared with Table 12's faculty salaries we see that CPI rise reduced the salary gain of both to zero or less, but also that faculty members were paid more per service month than were ARL librarians, by 31.2 per cent.

In conclusion, enrollment increased rapidly in the 1960s and more slowly in the 1970s. After a rapid 1960s rise, 1970–80 library staff size experienced very little change. Per student staff size shrank somewhat as the student body outgrew the staff. As a category, librarians were static in size growth and constituted a decreasing staff proportion. After a rapid salary rise in the 1960s, living cost rise outstripped library staff salary rise per person and purchasing power shrank. The emerging picture suggests that the library profession is attempting to retain previous modest gains in staff size and salary, but with little success.

Library Material Austerity

Library material austerity analysis is more complex than personnel austerity analysis. Not only do we have material cost and library material expenditures to consider, but also annual title publication and library additions. Combined quantity and cost increase rates and per student analyses must be considered. We must ascertain this information for both monographs and serials and for both United States and world production if we are to understand the influence of inflation on academic library material and service.

The number of mongraph titles published annually rose in the past twenty years, both in the United States and in other nations. Data from Unesco and U.S. sources document the situation, Table 14 (page 23). Annual hard cover mongraph title publication increased 14.0 per cent in the 1960s and 2.8 per cent in the 1970s in the United States. For the rest of the world, annual monograph publication increased 4.0 per cent in the 1960s and 4.4 per cent 1970–79.

The increase in wealth of material available challenged collection development librarians. Should they try to obtain certain of these titles for their libraries? If so, how could these additions to the already rich flow be justified?[48] Did late 1970s material quality level equal 1960 material quality level? The informal evidence available suggests that the larger recent material volume did not represent a significant quality decline. What proportion was needed? And how could budgeting authorities be convinced to support such additions? Each library needed to find its own answers to these questions.

The number of volumes added averaged 102,171 per ARL library for 1970 but only 78,241 for 1981, a 2.1 per cent annual decline rate.[49] The corresponding NCES figures showed an annual 1960s increase rate of

Table 14. Monograph Production and Prices

Category	1960	1970	Increase	Per cent Increase	1979	Increase 1970–79	Per cent Increase 1970–79	Per cent Increase Per Year 1970–79
Unesco World Estimate of the number of monograph titles published (excluding the United States)	297,000	416,000	119,000	40.1	578,911	162,911	39.2	4.4
United States newly and newly revised monograph production (in titles)	15,012	36,071	21,059	140.3	45,182	9,111	25.5	2.8
United States hardcover monograph price per title	$5.24	$11.66	$6.56	125.2	1980 $23.96	1970–80 $12.30	1970–80 105.5	1970–80 10.6

Sources: *Bowker Annual 1965* (N.Y.: R.R. Bowker, 1965), p. 102; *Bowker Annual 1975*, 1975), p. 180; *Bowker Annual 1981*, 1981), p. 326; *Statistical Abstract of the United States 1980*, Table 1012; *Unesco Yearbook 1981* (New York: Unipub, Inc., 1981), p. VIII–23.

14.1 per cent per library, and a corresponding 1970s loss of 3.3 per cent. Tables 15 (page 25) and 16 (page 26) show these figures which demonstrate similar patterns of 1970s decline.

How did the annual mongraph publication increase rate compare with the annual library volumes added rate? Table 13B shows that academic library expenditures and collection growth lagged behind monograph production growth.

Monographs suffered from price inflation, also. U.S. hardcover monograph prices increased by 10.6 per cent annually during the 1970s. Table 14 shows this change. No figures were available for world monograph price rise. We saw above the degree to which the libraries coped successfully with the monograph quantity increase, and Tables 10 and 11 show the degree to which they coped successfully with the monograph price rise. Nineteen seventies annual volumes added expenditure dropped 7.3 per cent annually for ARL members but rose 5.0 per cent for NCES libraries after CPI subtraction. So, not only did libraries need to cope with a larger publication output but price changes made each item dearer. This double increase—output and price— proved to be very challenging.

Table 13B shows both the extent to which monograph publications increased in quantity and price and the extent to which library acquisitions increased in number of volumes added and in total expenditures. Much the same picture appears when serial title publication is considered.[50–52] Tables 17 (page 27) and 18 (page 28) show these data. Bowker periodical and serial title listings increased in quantity from 58,475 in 1969 to 95,000 in 1980. This change represented a 5.7 per cent increase per year, a strong growth. Much of this growth occurred in the sciences. If Bowker's count can be accepted, then approximately a 62.5 per cent increase occurred in the number of titles available to academic libraries in eleven years. No reliable estimates could be located on world serial production and price increases, but we can assume that Bowker's lists were to some extent internationalized. Again, collection development officers were interested in this growth and its quality. Published evaluations were few but favorable. As with monographs, most libraries tried to add appropriate new titles to their collections.

Table 15 shows the average ARL library to have enlarged its serial title list by 3.8 per cent annually, 1972–79. The annual NCES increase rate was 6.0 per cent per library 1959–69, as Table 16 shows, and 4.6 per cent for 1969–79. How did these rises compare with those for the annual titles available? Table 13C shows that the annual serial acquisitions increase rate fell short by 1.9 per cent for ARL members and 1.1 per cent for NCES libraries of reaching the annual publication increase rate, but parity between these figures was hardly to be expected.

Did the libraries equal in annual serial expenditure the large annual serial price increases? No, they did not. Table 19 (page 29) shows higher institution price rise 1970–79 to have been 161.2 per cent for books

Table 15. ARL University Library Collection Size Data

Category	1970	1981	Change	Per cent change	Per cent change per year
Collection size per library (in volumes)	1,827,129	2,569,295	742,166	40.6	3.7
Gross annual volumes added per library	102,171	78,241	−23,930	−23.4	−2.1
Current serial titles received per library	22,273*	29,899	7,626	34.2	3.8
Collection size per student (in volumes)	118.2	107.7	−10.5	−8.9	−0.8
Gross annual volumes added per student	6.6	3.3	−3.3	−50.0	−4.5
Current serial titles received per student	1.25	1.25	0.0	0.0	0.0
Ratio of gross volumes added to current serial titles received	4.6	2.6	−2.0	−43.5	−4.0

*1972 figure.

Sources: Association of Research Libraries. ARL Statistics 1980–81 (Washington, D.C.: 1981), pp. 8, 10, 12, 14; Kendon Stubbs and David Buxton, comps., Cumulative ARL University Library Statistics 1962–63 Through 1978–79 (Washington, D.C.: Association of Research Libraries, 1981), Part 2.

Table 16. NCES Academic Library Collection Size Data

Categories	1959	1969	Increase	Per cent change	1979	Change 1969–79	Per cent change 1969–79	Per cent change per year 1969–79
Collection size per library (in volumes)	90,580	131,600	41,020	45.3	166,565	34,965	26.6	3.0
Gross annual volumes added per library	4,313	10,400	6,087	141.1	6,923	−3,477	−33.4	−3.3
Current periodical titles received per library	652	1,040	388	59.5	1,516	476	45.8	4.6
Collection size per student (in vols)	51.9	42.2	−9.7	−18.7	50.5	8.3	19.7	2.0
Gross annual volumes added per student	2.5	3.3	0.8	32.0	2.1	−1.2	−36.4	−3.6
Current periodical titles received per student	0.40	0.40	0	0	0.46	0.06	15.0	1.5
Ratio of gross volumes added to current serial titles received	6.6	10.0	3.4	51.5	4.6	−5.4	−54.0	−5.4

N.B.: N = 1,951 libraries in 1959–60; 2,500 in 1969–70; and 3,121 in 1978–79. NCES 1978–79 figures show medians, not means, and therefore are only partially comparable to the NCES means shown for earlier years.

Sources: Richard M. Beazley, Library Statistics of Colleges and Universities, Trends 1968–77, Summary Data 1977 (Washington, D.C.: NCES, 1981), p. 5; Richard M. Beazley, Library Statistics of Colleges and Universities: 1979 Institutional Data (Washington, D.C.: NCES, 1981); Bowker Annual 1970 (N.Y.: R.R. Bowker, 1970), pp. 14–15; Bowker Annual 1975, pp. 228–29; Bowker Annual 1981, p. 289.

Table 17.   United States Serial Production (in titles)

Category Years and Increases	Ulrich	Irregular Serials	Total	Faxon	ARL
1955	16,000				
1963	19,776				
1965	28,000				
1966		14,500			
1969	40,000	(18,475)	(58,475)		
1974		25,000			
1975	57,000				
1980	62,000	33,000	95,000		
1969–80 Increase			(36,525)		
1969–80 Per cent increase			(62.5)		
1969–80 Per cent increase per year			(5.7)		
1981				115,000	104,993
1982		35,000			

N.B.: The figures in parentheses represent extrapolated data.

Sources: Faxon Guide 1981 (Westwood, MA: F.W. Faxon, 1981), p. xxviii; Irregular Serials and Annuals 1966–67 (N.Y.: R.R.Bowker, 1967), p. vii; Irregular Serials and Annuals 1974–75, p. vii; Irregular Serials and Annuals 1980–81, p. vii; Irregular Serials and Annuals 1982–83, p. vii; "1980–81 Ranking of Research Libraries," Chronicle of Higher Education 23 (January 27, 1982), p. 8; Ulrich's Periodicals Directory 1955–56 (N.Y.: R.R. Bowker, 1955), p. v; Ulrich's Periodicals Directory 1963–64, p. ix; Ulrich's International Periodicals Directory 1965–66, (N.Y.: R.R. Bowker, 1965), p. ix; Ulrich's International Periodicals Directory 1969–70, p. vii; Ulrich's International Periodicals Directory 1975–76, p. vii; Ulrich's International Periodicals Directory 1980, p. vii.

Table 18.   United States Serial Indexing Service and
Periodical Prices Per Title

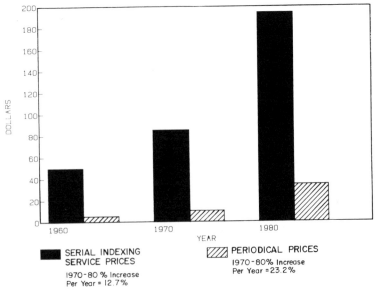

Category	1960	1970	Increase	Per cent Increase	1980	Increase 1970–80	Per cent Increase 1970–80	Per cent Increase per year 1970–80
Serial Indexing Service Prices	$49.99	$85.44	$35.45	70.9	$194.21	$108.77	127.3	12.7
Periodical Prices	5.31	10.41	5.10	96.0	34.54	24.13	231.8	23.2

Periodical prices are based on the group of periodicals indexed in the serial services covered in *Bowker Annual* tables.

Sources: Bowker Annual 1965 (N.Y.: R.R. Bowker, 1965), p. 102, 104–5; *Bowker Annual 1975*, p. 178, 180; *Bowker Annual 1981*, pp. 343–44.

Table 19.   Higher Education Price Indices

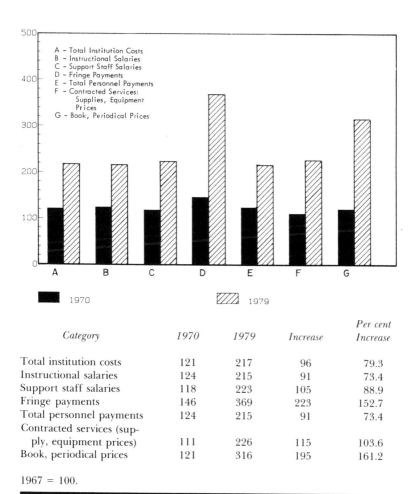

Category	1970	1979	Increase	Per cent Increase
Total institution costs	121	217	96	79.3
Instructional salaries	124	215	91	73.4
Support staff salaries	118	223	105	88.9
Fringe payments	146	369	223	152.7
Total personnel payments	124	215	91	73.4
Contracted services (supply, equipment prices)	111	226	115	103.6
Book, periodical prices	121	316	195	161.2

1967 = 100.

Source: Adapted from *Statistical Abstract of the United States 1980,* Table 284.

and periodicals combined, or 17.9 per cent annually. Periodical price
increase alone for 1970–80 is shown in Table 18 to have been 23.2 per
cent annually. Periodical price rises considerably exceeded those for the
budget items which other university schools and departments customarily ordered. This rise reached 233.7 per cent for American periodicals and caused much trouble for academic librarians. Consequently,
the library suffered more from a steady state budget than did other
campus units. Table 18 shows also an annual 1970–80 price rise of 12.7
per cent for journal index and abstract titles, another serial cost
burden.[53]

These problems presented a challenge which academic libraries met
with strong and determined effort but with only partial success. Carpenter found a majority of the libraries studied to fall short of the
standards for adequacy in material, also.[54]

As an incidental but interesting matter, Tables 15 and 16 provide the
data needed to examine the change in the annual ratio of gross volumes
received to serial titles received. Was there a steady trend toward serials
at the expense of monographs? ARL members 1970–81 added serial
titles at the expense of monograph volumes. NCES libraries 1959–69
increased the monograph-serial ratio while 1969–79 reversed that
trend to correlate with ARL's trend. The ARL ratio dropped by 4.0 per
cent per year, while the NCES ratio dropped by 5.4 per cent annually,
large drops.[55] ACRL library median ratio of monograph volumes added
to current serial titles received was 26,543:7,080, or 3.7:1, slightly closer
to the NCES than the ARL ratio.[56]

What can we discover by examining the ratio of annual material
expenditure to gross volumes added for these libraries? By this time, we
should be well enough informed to predict that this ratio rose sharply in
the 1970s. Tables 10 and 11 show these figures. For ARL university
libraries, the ratio rose by 6.1 per cent annually. NCES annual increase
was even stronger, 15.5 per cent per year. In both cases, expenditure
rose strongly while number of volumes added declined—the libraries
"ran" faster but still lost ground to inflation.

Now we can turn to per-student analyses. Tables 10, 11, 15, and 16
show monograph and serial publication, acquisition, and cost data examined on a per-student basis. Did students benefit from the greatly
increased material budgets of the 1970s? The tables show a mixed
picture on a per-student basis. Monograph publication rate grew more
slowly than the 4.9 per cent annual ARL enrollment increase rate, while
serial publication rate grew somewhat more rapidly than the ARL enrollment rate. In any case, ARL annual collection size per student dropped
by 0.8 per cent during the decade, and per-student ARL gross volumes
added declined significantly, 4.5 per cent annually. Expenditures were
inadequate to withstand inflation's effect.

During the 1960s, NCES libraries lost collection size per student with
an annual decrease of almost 2 per cent, against a strong annual enroll-

ment rise of almost 8 per cent, while annual 1970s NCES collection size
per student rose by 2.0 per cent. The 1960s picture for NCES gross
volumes added annually showed additions rising by 3.2 per cent, while
1970s NCES additions per student declined by 3.6 per cent. So, for the
1970s at least, the picture showed drops in annual gross volumes added
per library in three of four figures, in spite of expenditure increases.
Current serial titles received per student 1970–81 for ARL libraries
remained stationary. For periodicals, this ratio remained stationary
1959–69 for NCES, but for 1969–79 it rose at the rate of 1.5 per cent
annually, a small increase, showing ARL and NCES to have been not far
apart in the 1970s.

Samore confirmed this ratio change.[57] In addition, as further evidence of this trend, Samore found NCES libraries since 1975 to have
consistently increased the proportion of the material budget going to
serials. This trend may have indicated a shift in priorities as well as the
effect of inflation and proliferation.

Let us conclude per-student analysis by examining other library expenditures in Tables 10 and 11. For ARL, annual increase in personnel
expenditure per student was 3.6 per cent, for material it was 6.0 per
cent, and for total expenditure, 4.1 per cent. Nineteen sixties NCES
expenditure rose in the same strong manner, 6.4, 12.8, and 8.6 per cent
respectively. The 1969–79 annual NCES per student expenditure was
8.1 per cent for personnel, 6.0 per cent for material and 9.5 per cent for
total expenditure. In both ARL and NCES, however, inflation wiped out
the 1970s gains. So, the students lost here, also. The special NCES
1968–77 report included several additional annual per-student findings: volumes held increased by 0.4 per cent, current serial titles increased by 3.1 per cent, and total library expenditure decreased by 5.4
per cent after CPI rise was subtracted.[58] In conclusion, for per-student
library progress, the picture was discouraging—inflation's effect on per
student expenditure was significant in all cases.

To review the 1970s decade's changes, we have discovered that
monograph publishing volume grew and that monograph prices grew
at an even faster rate, while library addition of monograph titles and
acquisitions expenditure grew at slower rates. Per student library additions fell or rose slowly while prices rose rapidly. The picture for serials
was the same. Serial title proliferation grew as did serial prices and
library subscription rate and expenditure, but the latter grew more
slowly than did the former. Inflation's effect on monograph and serial
purchasing led to net acquisition losses in most libraries.

Combined Analyses and Conclusions

The analysis of personnel and material may be concluded with various
combinations of these major areas and with a few final remarks. Analy-

ses can be made which reflect other expenditure ratios. How have library salary and wage expenditures changed in relation to material expenditure? Did a trend exist toward raising salaries at the expense of material? Tables 10 and 11 show this picture. For ARL, personnel expenditure as a percent of total library expenditure rose slowly but steadily, 0.7 per cent annually. In spite of more than doubling ARL library expenditure for material during the 1970s, the material per cent of total expenditure rose by only 1.9 per cent annually. The net gap between personnel and material was 1.2 per cent in favor of material.

For NCES in the 1970s, personnel expenditure as a ratio of total library expenditure increased by 1.1 per cent annually, while the corresponding material ratio dropped steadily, 1.8 per cent annually. This yielded a net difference of 2.9 per cent in favor of personnel. The finding was consistent with certain previous findings, but not with ARL figures.[59] The NCES ratio was larger but neither picture was clearcut. For the ACRL university library group, as per cents of total expenditure, 1979 personnel expenditure equaled 51 per cent and material expenditure 36 per cent, as compared with 53.6 per cent and 37.2 per cent for ARL and 60.2 per cent and 30.0 per cent for NCES.[60] These and other findings showed that inflation had both a direct and an indirect effect on material acquisitions, direct through price increases and indirect through forcing large salary increases and thereby squeezing material expenditures.

As a matter of some historical interest, we may consider certain 1950s and 1960s findings here. Baumol and Marcus calculated annual per cent growth rates for 58 university research libraries (ARL) 1951–69.[61] During the eighteen-year period, inflation ran at an annual average of 1.8 per cent. The present study's ARL 1970s findings may be compared with the Baumol and Marcus list, Table 20 (page 33). Only the following factors ran at an accelerated pace in the 1970s: enrollment and librarians as a percent of total staff members (though that trend was down, too). The earlier period was the affluent age of American academic libraries.[62]

The reader may say that the typical library's budget conditions simply reflected those of the parent institution. Often that was true. Table 21 (page 34) shows total library expenditure for five specific years, 1960–80. It shows a gross increase of 1,079.1 per cent, due in part to the increase in number of libraries covered. However, when Tables 7 and 21 are compared, they show 1970 (1971 for libraries) to 1980 higher institutional expenditure to have increased at a somewhat higher rate than did higher institutional library expenditure. After CPI subtraction, the two annual percents were 1.2 per cent for higher education and −1.7 per cent for higher education libraries, a 2.9 per cent difference. From Tables 7 and 21 for 1970–80 per-student expenditure figures, the comparison was −4.6 per cent for higher institutions and −7.9 per cent for their libraries, a difference of 3.3 per cent. This

Table 20.   1951–80 Annual Growth Rate Comparison

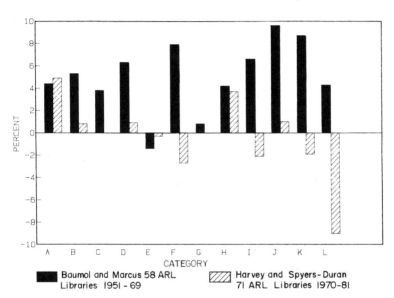

Category	Baumol and Marcus 58 ARL Libraries 1951–69	Harvey and Spyers–Duran 71 ARL Libraries 1970–81
Enrollment	4.4%	4.9%
Total personnel	5.3	0.8
Librarians	3.8	0.0
Support staff members	6.3	0.9
Librarians as a per- cent of total staff	−1.4	−0.3
Salaries and wages	7.9	−2.7
Salaries and wages as a percent of total expenditures	0.8	0.7
Volumes held	4.2	3.7
Volumes added	6.6	−2.1
Book expenditures	9.6	1.0
Total library expenditures	8.7	−1.9
Expenditures per student	4.3	−9.0

N.B.: Annual Consumer Price Index rises have been subtracted from original figures where appropriate.

Source: William J. Baumol and Matityahu Marcus, *Economics of Academic Libraries* (Washington, D.C.: American Council on Education, 1973), p. 7, Table 1.3, selected findings.

Table 21.   Total National Academic Library Expenditure (in billions)

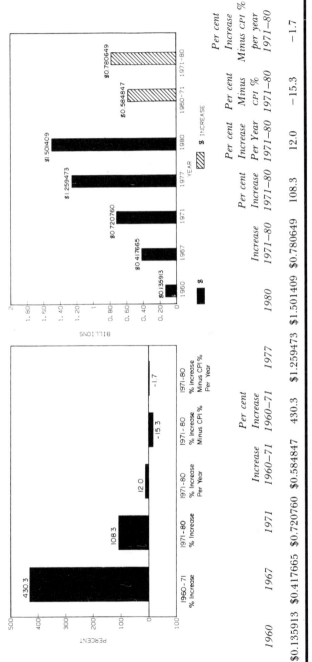

	1960	1967	1971	1977	1980	Increase 1971–80	Per cent Increase 1971–80	Per cent Increase Per Year 1971–80	Per cent Minus CPI % 1971–80	Per cent Increase Minus CPI % per year 1971–80
	$0.135913	$0.417665	$0.720760	$1.259473	$1.501409	$0.780649	108.3	12.0	−15.3	−1.7

Sources: Financial Statistics of Institutions of Higher Education 1959–60 Receipts, Expenditures, Property (Washington, D.C.: U. S. Department of Health, Education and Welfare Office of Education, 1964), p. 53; 1970–71 Current Funds, Revenues and Expenditures, p. 14, 1966–67 Current Funds, Revenues and Expenditures, p. 50, 1976–77 Current Funds, Revenues and Expenditures, p. 4; "College and University Expenditures, 1979–80," Chronicle of Higher Education 23 (September 16, 1981), p. 10.

finding suggests that libraries suffered more from inflation (or some other problem) than did their parent institutions.

In addition, during the 1970s, student enrollment and the number of faculty employed increased, expanding service requirements and academic course offerings, research and graduate programs. At the same time, library collections and staff to serve them remained static or actually decreased.[63-65] Beazley found all types of circulation and reference transactions to have increased, 1977–79, with annual percentages ranging from 0.7 to 5.1 per cent.[66] To take a longer view with quantity and price rises in mind, the library was being squeezed between increasing service demands and rapidly rising living costs on the one hand and inadequate or decreasing net material and salary budget increase ratios on the other hand. Both service and staff suffered in such a no-win situation.

The combined effects of a decade of not-quite-adequate or not-at-all-adequate budgets spelled austerity and retrenchment. And that is what most libraries have had for many years. If a library is in some degree of debt to its theoretically proper 1970 support level, then it has retrenched by that much, whether systematically or haphazardly. Whether the overall deficit means a slight or a severe default may vary greatly, but this chapter considers most deficit situations to represent austerity.

Retrospective recovery chances would seem to be poor.[67] It seems unlikely that libraries will ever obtain the funds needed to recover the 1970s material and salary losses, except in very rare instances, though budgets should continue to rise. Nor should the field necessarily assume that a cyclical situation exists in which the 1970s steady state period is sure to be followed by an upward trend. What falls need not necessarily rebound, at least during our careers. The extent to which current academic library budget levels demonstrate cylical behavior as well as the periods that may exist are unknown, since the earlier Purdue analyses seem no longer to be entirely reliable.[68]

The first signs of a no growth (real growth slowdown in current spending) situation for higher education and its libraries began to be seen in the early 1970s.[69,70] By 1974 a fourth of the private colleges were said to be in financial distress.[71,72] Austerity varied markedly by campus and by state. We could cite certain well supported institutions which had strong budget increases, but still were too weak to meet all title, cost, and CPI rises. Certain institutions at the lower end were forced to close their doors permanently. While austerity can have its positive aspects, many librarians are not yet convinced that the 1970s steady state budgets meant a steady, annual decline in service capability. Table 13 suggests its most negative aspect. Nineteen eighty-three costs are a continuing problem as well as the new threat, the combination of inflation and library unemployment, stagflation.

With continued inflation, the new student generation shrinking by 23 per cent in the eighties, and President Reagan's government reduction program continuing, no upward cycle can be foreseen.[73] In fact, with economic realism, many educators refer to the three "Rs" of the eighties—Reduction, Reallocation, and Retrenchment—as these managers of decline adopt the Cut, Squeeze, and Trim administrative mode.[74] Perhaps a formula would provide an objective way of identifying austerity's local impact.[75]

In conclusion, two recent instances and a quotation may be given which contribute to a pessimistic forecast. The September 16, 1981 issue of *The Chronicle of Higher Education* reported NCES data showing libraries to have received only $1.50 billion of $56.75 billion fiscal 1980 higher educational in tuition expenditure, 2.6 per cent (or 3.8 per cent of educational and general expenditure).[76] Table 21 shows part of this picture. The latter ratio is far below the 6.0 per cent of educational and general expenditure recommended by the ACRL college library standards, in fact only 63 per cent of it. And it is even further below the 7–12 per cent ACRL two-year college standard.[77] Table 11 shows this ratio to have dropped slightly in the 1970s for NCES libraries. Apparently librarians have not convinced their constituency that their services are worth more than they were a decade ago.

The 1981 Council for Financial Aid to Education survey asked academic presidents to list the campus areas critically needing additional corporate support.[78] Only 27.6 per cent of them chose library resources among the first three such areas to be listed. That finding showed the library's priority level. And finally, W. J. Haas, Council on Library Resources: "The hard truth is . . . the funds required to continue to meet traditional needs in traditional ways are unlikely to be forthcoming in anywhere near needed amounts."[79,80]

References

1. John G. Kemeny, "The Ten Year Report By the Thirteenth President," *Dartmouth Alumni Magazine* 72 (June 1980), pp. 22–61.
2. "Faculty Salaries Up 6.7%," *Chronicle of Higher Education* 22 (June 15, 1981), p. 1. See also, "Faculty Salaries Up 8.9% But Fail to Keep Pace With Consumer Prices," *Chronicle of Higher Education* 23 (Nov. 11, 1981), pp. 1, 13.
3. "Libraries Need 'Risk Capital' to Solve Financial Problems," *Chronicle of Higher Education* 23 (November 18, 1981), p. 20. See also, *ARL Statistics 1978–79; A Compilation of Statistics from 110 Members of the Association of Research Libraries*, compiled by Carol A. Mandel and Mary P. Johnson (Washington, D.C.: ARL, 1979), in which four trends were noted: a) libraries increased in size in the past year, b) volumes added rose only 4% while material expenditures rose 11% (a 1:2.75 ratio) c) serial expenditures rose faster than the national inflation rate by 16.3% and d) serials accounted for 54% of material expenditures.
4. The authors are aware of the difficulties of using library statistics, of their lack of comparability, lack of continuity, of regional differences in cost of

living and of the problems of period and ratio analyses. That the data often provide a cruder measure than is needed is often true, but no more accurate data were available to them.

5. The choice of years to be covered in the tables was a difficult one but was limited by the data sets available and by the authors' desire to present the most recent information. The authors regret the lack of exact comparability between the years covered by the ARL and the NCES data. No NCES data were available after 1979, and even so was not comparable in every respect with 1959 and 1969 data.

6. Both ARL and NCES collect data each Autumn, the former from its members and the latter from all American academic institutions. For the most part these data pertain to the previous academic or fiscal year. However, for personnel data, it seems that the reporting time is either the month in which the questionaire is completed or else the end of the previous academic or fiscal year. It is labeled Fall, 1979, for instance, not 1978–79 data, for NCES. ARL personnel data apparently refer to the end of the previous academic year or to the date on which the questionnaire was completed.

7. In tabular and textual presentations, the authors have tried to avoid giving undue weight to CPI rises, but, in doing this, it is hard to avoid pro and con arguments of causation and influence.

8. An example can be provided of the type of thinking used with this paper's data. If annual serial cost increased 10% and serials constituted 33% of library material expenditures, then library material expenditures should rise 3.3% in consequence. If library material expenditures equaled 30% of total library expenditures, then the next library budget proposal should request that expenditures rise by 0.99% to accomodate this serial cost increase.

9. *Statistical Abstract of the United States 1980* (Washington, D.C.: G.P.O., 1980), Table 806. See also, Richard M. Beazley, *Library Statistics of Colleges and Universities, Trends 1968–77, Summary Data, 1977* (Washington, D.C.: NCES, 1982), Appendix A, Technical Note (on CPI vs. HEPI), p. 41.

10. Ibid., *passim.*

11. Advisory Commission on Intergovernmental Relations. *Significant Features of Fiscal Federalism* (Washington, D.C.: 1981).

12. This paper and its tables will use only the fiscal year when listing single fiscal or academic year figures, e.g., 1971–72 becomes 1972 and 1969–70 becomes 1970. However, for NCES personnel counts, the year always refers to the single year in which the count was taken.

13. "State Support for Higher Education," *Chronicle of Higher Education* 23 (February 10, 1982), pp. 1, 8.

14. "Many States Hit By Big Spending Cuts," *Los Angeles Times* (November 16, 1980), pp. 1, 32.

15. David J. Levin, "State and Local Government Fiscal Position, 1981," *Survey of Current Business* 62 (January, 1982), pp. 23–25.

16. "Recession Hurts States. . . . ," *Wall Street Journal* (June 18, 1980), pp. 1, 2, 29.

17. Advisory Commission on Intergovernmental Relations, *op. cit.,* p. 7.

18. U.S. Department of Commerce. Bureau of the Census. Public Employment. Vol. 3 *Compendium of Public Employment* (Washington, D.C.: G.P.O., 1977), p. 1.

19. *Handbook of Labor Statistics* (Washington, D.C.: G.P.O., 1979), p. 230.

20. "Recession Hurts States. . . . ," *op. cit.*, p. 2.
21. "State and Local Government in Trouble," *Business Week* (October 26, 1981), p. 172. Note that Table 4's elementary and secondary school expenditure figures include only the state government contributions, whereas Table 5's school expenditures include funds from all sources—local, state, and national.
22. Richard G. Neal, "The U.S. Teacher Strike Scene, 1978–79," *Phi Delta Kappan* 60 (December 1978), pp. 327–28.
23. See *Standard Education Almanac 1981–82* (Chicago: Marquis, 1982), p. 365.
24. See also, W. John Minter and Howard R. Bowen, "Despite Economic Ills, Colleges Weathered the 70's With Larger Enrollment and Stronger Programs," *Chronicle of Higher Education* 23 (May 12, 1982), pp. 5–7.
25. Minter and Bowen, *op. cit.*, pp. 5–7, especially the concluding section, Intangibles.
26. See L. A. Glenny and others. *Presidents Confront Reality, From Edifice Complex to University Without Walls* (San Francisco: Jossey-Bass, 1976).
27. See *The Conditions of Education Statistical Report* (Washington, D.C.: NCES, 1980), p. 102 and *Challenges of Retrenchment* (San Francisco: Jossey-Bass, 1981), p. 3.
28. Note that certain data sets in Table 7 are not quite comparable and so give slightly different results, as for the public vs. nonpublic institution per-student expenditure. These differences are small and are not significant here, however.
29. Minter and Bowen, *op. cit.*, p. 6.
30. See "Colleges and Universities Face Growing Inflation Peril," *Los Angeles Times* (September 12, 1979), Part 1-B, pp. 3–7.
31. "Cost Differences. . . . ," *Change* 13 (January–February, 1981), pp. 21–27.
32. Minter and Bowen, *op. cit.*, p. 6.
33. See *Challenges of Retrenchment, op. cit.*, Chapter I Challenges of Retrenchment, for a useful discussion.
34. Readers will note the consistent use of per-institution and per-student ratios (means) in this chapter instead of the often preferable use of midpoint and middlemost (median) ratios. This usage is due to the lack of detailed NCES item scores on variables and the need for consistency in data treatment.
35. In using the ARL data, all Canadian institutions were excluded, plus St. Louis University which left ARL in 1972–73. Only 71 members' data are represented in the 1969–70 and 1980–81 figures. This limitation was made to avoid skewing the data with figures from newer, and generally smaller, member libraries. These limitations apply to all tabular and textual material. In a few cases, also, a figure was missing so the number of libraries (N) sometimes varied by 1–4 from the normal 71. It was impossible to follow the same libraries in this way with NCES data.
36. Beazley, *op. cit.*, p. 9. See also, Richard M. Beazley, *Library Statistics of Colleges and Universities: 1979 Institutional Data* (Washington, D.C.: NCES, 1981).
37. William J. Baumol and Matityahu Marcus, *Economics of Academic Libraries* (Washington, D.C.: American Council on Education, 1973), p. 7, Table 1.3.
38. Ibid., p. 73.
39. Beazley, ". . . Trends 1968–77 . . . ," *op. cit.*, pp. 8–9. In fact, in many libraries, in spite of the decrease in the ratio of librarians to support staff members, user service improved in recent years. Among other reasons, this

was due to 1) the increased use of paraprofessionals who were educated in computer data base access, 2) increased resource-sharing programs, and 3) replacement of library personnel who were unable to cope with recent resource-sharing and data base access challenges.

40. Julie A. C. Virgo, Sarah How, and Annette Fern, *ACRL University Library Statistics 1978–79; A Compilation of Statistics from Ninety-Eight Non-ARL University Libraries* (Chicago: Association of College and Research Libraries, 1980), p. 12.

41. Ray L. Carpenter, "College Libraries: A Comparative Analysis in Terms of the ACRL Standards," *College and Research Libraries* 42 (January 1981), pp. 7–18.

42. Raymond L. Carpenter, "Two Year College Libraries: A Comparative Analysis in Terms of the ACRL Standards," *College and Research Libraries* 42 (September, 1981), pp. 407–15. This study is similar to the one cited above, but it concentrated on 1,146 *two* year colleges (40% of the total). Results were similar to those for the previous study but showed even poorer performance.

43. Carpenter, "College Libraries. . . . ," *op. cit.,* p. 18. The authors recognize the many problems associated with library standards' use, hence the presence of Chapter I. However, Carpenter does not necessarily claim reasonableness or validity for the ACRL standards, merely that they can be studied in relation to present service.

44. See the following on university library standards: Kendon Stubbs, "University Libraries: Standards and Statistics," *College and Research Libraries* 42 (November 1981), pp. 527–38.

45. Carlyle J. Frarey, "Placements and Salaries: the 1969 Plateau," *Library Journal* 94 (June 1, 1970), pp. 2099–2103; Carol L. Learmont, "Placements and Salaries 1979: Wider Horizons," *Library Journal* 104 (November 1, 1980), pp. 2271–77; Carol L. Learmont and Stephen Van Houton, "Placements and Salaries 1980: Holding the Line," *Library Journal* 105 (October 1, 1981), pp. 1881–87.

46. Virgo, *op. cit.,* p. 12.

47. Beazley, ". . . Trends 1968–77 . . . ," *op. cit.,* p. 11.

48. Of course, this discussion is based on theoretical considerations, since it is impossible to determine whether any specific title belongs to the base group or to the annual enlargement.

49. Of course, in this crude comparison, volumes added do not equal titles needed, but the two are not compared directly. Instead, per cent increase or decrease is used for these comparisons. Nor do the years covered match exactly or the volumes added consist of monographs only, but more comparable figures were not available. The fact that the base 1970 volume figures differ by so much between production and library volumes added need not concern us here.

50. In certain cases, no publication data could be located for all serials combined so data labeled periodicals was used. And further, it was difficult to locate accurate serial title counts over time. Higher counts could be found for institutions in 1980, but their data extended back only a few years and the composition of the count was open to question.

51. Wherever possible in data collections, the authors have used the gross volumes added figure rather than the net volumes added, have excluded mi-

croforms from volumes added data, have separated serial expenditures from monograph expenditures, and have excluded binding expenditures from consideration.

52. Association of Research Libraries. *ARL Statistics 1980–81*, compiled by Carol A. Mandel and Mary P. Johnson (Washington, D.C.: 1982), p. 16.

53. Charles H. Bellanger and Lise Lavellee, "Towards a Periodical and Monograph Price Index," *College and Research Libraries* 42 (September 1981), pp. 416–24.

54. Carpenter, "College Libraries," *op. cit.*, p. 15.

55. Beazley, ". . . Trends 1968–77 . . . ," *op. cit.*, p. 5.

56. Virgo, *op. cit.*, p. 12.

57. Theodore Samore, "NCES Survey of College and University Libraries, 1978–79," *Bowker Annual 1981* (N.Y.: R. R. Bowker, 1981), p. 291. See also, Beazley, ". . . 1979 Institutional Data . . . ," *op. cit.*, p. 2.

58. Beazley, ". . . Trends 1968–77 . . . ," *op. cit.*, pp. 5, 11.

59. Samore, *op. cit.*, p. 291.

60. Virgo, *op. cit.*, p. 12.

61. Baumol and Marcus, *op. cit.*, p. 7.

62. Richard De Gennaro, "Austerity, Technology and Research Sharing; Research Libraries Face the Future," *Library Journal* 99 (May 15, 1975), pp. 917–23.

63. Samore, *op. cit.*, p. 287.

64. "Libraries Need Risk Capital to Solve Financial Problems," *op. cit.*, p. 20.

65. Minter and Bowen, *op. cit.*, pp. 5–7.

66. Beazley, ". . . 1979 Institutional Data," *op. cit.*, p. 2.

67. Advisory Commission. . . . , *op. cit.*, pp. 7–8.

68. See O. C. Dunn, et al., *The Past and Likely Future of 58 Research Libraries, 1951–80: A Statistical Study of Growth and Change.* Instructional Media Research Unit, University Libraries and Audiovisual Center, Purdue University, W. Lafayette, IN, 1973. And also, DeGennaro, *op. cit.*, p. 917.

69. See F. F. Cheit, *The New Depression in Higher Education. A Study of Financial Conditions at 47 Colleges and Universities* (N.Y.: McGraw-Hill, 1971)

70. Nancy E. Gwynn and Warren J. Haas, "Crisis in the College Libary," *AGB Reports* (March–April, 1981), pp. 41–45.

71. Ibid., p. 42.

72. Advisory Commission. . . . *op. cit.*, p. 8.

73. Kathryn McDonald, "Learning to Finance Learning: A Review Report," *College Board Review*, Number 116 (Summer 1980), pp. 8–11, 129–31.

74. Ibid., p. 129.

75. A theoretical Austerity Identification Formula or Model can be developed which includes the factors that an academic library should monitor to gauge the changes affecting service and budget levels. Its objective is to show the budget changes needed to maintain parity with the personnel and material purchasing power possessed at a particular prior date. Successful austerity management would require that the new budget received at least meet the parity point. Since the variables are normally measured in a variety of units, per cents must be used to obtain comparable results. If desired, the variables can be expressed on a per student basis, then converted to per cents. Each variable should be multiplied by that per cent of the total library budget which is allocated to it or by a factor representing its proper weight. This

multiplication will show the variable's relative importance in this discriminate function formula and in the budget. Factors not normally appearing in the budget, such as enrollment and program changes, must be multiplied by a figure representing their influence on service demands locally.

The formula should contain at least eleven separate variables. Cost of living must be watched since it affects staff living standards directly; monthly government CPI reports provide this information. Monograph title publication rate changes should influence budget preparation, and *Publishers Weekly* reports these data. Monograph price raises will affect the collection development budget, and *Publishers Weekly* and federal sources supply this information. New serial titles of strong use potential must be checked as well as serial price raises. Serial title information can be found in reliable subject journals and in the *Library Journal*. Undergraduate and graduate program changes affect technical and public service and can be monitored through curriculum committee minutes.

Significant changes in both FTE undergraduate and graduate enrollment should be reflected in service adjustments and can be gauged through Registrar's Office reports. Significant research program changes can affect technical and reference service and be monitored thru Research Office reports. Finally, equipment and supply price change rates will affect budget portions, also. These prices can be followed by contact with national library supply and equipment firms and the Buildings and Grounds Department. Incidently, this price rise, 1970–79, was 103.6% for academic institutions, according to Table 19. Other factors could be added to this formula but are usually of little importance.

This is the budget parity model: a% for cost of living (CPI) change per cent, b% for monograph title publication change per cent, c% for monograph price change per cent, d% for serial title publication change per cent, e% for serial title price change per cent, f% for significant undergraduate program change per cent, g% for significant graduate program change per cent, h% for significant undergraduate enrollment change per cent, i% for significant graduate enrollment change per cent, j% for significant research program change per cent, and k% for equipment and supply price change per cent. The series of factors required to identify threats to parity with previous library personnel, material, and service levels is now complete.

The sum of the formula's eleven variables and their multipliers can be called l%, the per cent change needed now to maintain the level of a prior date. The campus library budget change percent actually obtained can be called m%. Then the difference between l% and m% can be called n%, the ratio by which the new budget fell short in meeting cost, enrollment, and program increase demands, or else exceeded them. These budget additions should enable the library to cope with future demands and outside price changes. A few librarians will find it unreasonable to expect compensation for all eleven cost and service increases, but a full statement is useful to clarify the fiscal situation.

76. "College and University Expenditures, 1979–80," *Chronicle of Higher Education* 23 (September 16, 1981), p. 10.
77. Carpenter, "Two Year College. . . . ," *op. cit.*, p. 412.
78. "Pay Called Top Need," *Chronicle of Higher Education* 23 (November 1, 1981), p. 16.

79. See Warren J. Haas, "Managing Academic Libraries; Ways and Means," *College and Research Libraries* 40 (March 1979), pp. 109–19. See also, DeGennaro, *op. cit.,* p. 923 which said much the same thing four years earlier.

80. See also, P. Berman and M. W. McLaughlin, *The Management of Decline: Problems, Opportunities and Research Questions.* Rand Paper Series, P-5984 (Santa Monica: Rand Corporation, 1977).

2. Creative Management in Austerity

Joseph Z. Nitecki

THINKING ABOUT SOMETHING implies either contemplation about the essence of the thing thought about, or a deliberation, that is, making up one's mind about the consequences of such meditation. In this paper, I propose to sketch a thought process that follows each one of the two paths.[1] Austerity should be regarded as a milieu for change. It results from processes that transformed an economy of abundance into one of scarcity. But it also initiates new changes, which either increase or decrease its scope.

I am also proposing that our attitude toward austerity ought to be positive. Although neither positive nor negative thinking will by itself turn scarcity into abundance, a negative attitude will intensify the misery of trying to survive austerity's deprivations while a positive posture will stimulate the search for practical solutions to economic retrenchment. Hence I am deliberately reviewing the concept of library austerity in an optimistic mode and turning the difficulties created by austerity into opportunities for constructive thinking and planning. Even in the most deprived situation, few librarians would abandon their user service responsibilities. Hence, it is very important to replace a passive and custodial approach to resource scarcity with an active and creative approach focused on containment.

Change is so pervasive a phenomenon that perhaps it can be best comprehended by contrast with its opposite, changelessness.[2] If we believe in the status quo, any change brings a dramatic and unexpected interference with a given state of affairs. Thus, for example, when trying to resolve a library service problem as passivists, we would look first to past practice for solutions, since the status quo also implies that the future merely repeats the past. If such a search did not offer a satisfactory answer, probably we would abandon the effort. On the other hand, if we subscribe to the Heraclitean notion of change as a natural process of perpetual transformation from one phase into another, we are also ready to shift from a passive belief in the past to an optimistic faith in the future. We can then better appreciate modern concepts of progress.

Such an approach facilitates discoveries by providing opportunities for working out effective solutions to particular problems. By changing thought patterns and freeing ourselves from a status quo mentality, we not only accept austerity as a necessary consequence of economic change, but are also willing to tackle its problems positively. In the past, "all our institutions and ways of thinking have survived because they were well adapted to an age of rapid growth. If this age is now coming to an end, large adjustments will have to be made in our ways of thinking, in our habits and standards of decision-making."[3]

In general, the extent of optimism is inversely related to the expectations it creates. The less we expect, the more optimistic we may be about the desirable outcome of change. Therefore, it is senseless to plan grandiose expansions in periods of scarcity. However, certain factors determining the degree of success in managing austerity can be controlled by our direct involvement in the change processes themselves. The more we are involved in these processes, the greater will be our opportunities to influence their outcome, thus increasing reasons for optimism. Although we cannot single-handedly eliminate austerity, we can influence its impact on us, to some extent at least.

Nature of Austerity–Driven Changes

The Meaning of Change

Used as a noun, the word "change" is a passive statement of fact. It names an act or a transformation process. Book paper deteriorates, inflationary budgets disappear quickly, and high staff turnover requires continuous training programs. Changes occur constantly, whether acknowledged or not. "Change is inevitable; it is a tide that will not stop. By the very need to survive, an organization must be able to change and adapt to the needs of its users and its staff. . . . The question is: are we as individuals and librarians prepared to meet change in a forceful and dynamic way?"[4]

Used as a verb, "change" stands for an act or process. To change a thing, event, or thought process is to alter a physical object, activity, or mental state into being something other than what it was before. Change implies a cause-effect relationship. For example, poor daily maintenance of a physical plant results in long range deterioration; a reduced acquisition allocation weakens collection growth; and declining resources lead to diminished services.

Yet, even in the same austerity period, different attitudes may result in different change processes. More attention paid to a library's looks can improve its appearance without added cost, prudent selection policies may strengthen the reduced collection's quality, while a redesigned staff organization that eliminates duplication may improve service quality and quantity. Change occurs within a context. Its duration can be anticipated, its effect on operation can be evaluated, and the change itself can be managed.

An effective way of controlling change is by turning it into innovation.[5] This can be done by developing strategies aimed at deliberate alteration of the change process direction. Innovations are usually modifications of existing processes or their products. Library adaptations of microforms, reprography, and automation, as well as cooperative acquisitions and centralized union catalogs are examples.[6] Although not all change involves innovation, all innovation involves change.[7]

Evidence of Austerity

Austerity's impact on academic libraries is already visible but not yet fully apprehended by administrators. We hear about declining student enrollment and sky-high inflation; we worry about deficit budgets, exhausted resources, inadequate space, insufficient staffing, and so on—the list seems endless. Yet, certain librarians cannot accept these facts as manifestations of a new period that requires rethinking managerial styles in order to deal successfully with revolutionary changes. "This may be due partly to our general tendency to deny unpleasant realities, particularly in an age that is so extraordinarily well adjusted to growth and puts such a high value on it."[8]

Certain librarians argue that the present decline is merely a temporary slowdown and that it will soon be changed into an upward movement. They may claim that libraries were never satisfactorily supported by university administrations, thus forcing librarians to complain for as long as one remembers about the lack of sufficient resources. These people forget, however, that in abundant days "it was a poverty of not being able to buy *all* of the additional material they wanted to buy, of not being able to start *all* of the new programs they felt needed starting. . . . It was not, as it tends to be now, decisions of which material to retain and which to cancel, which programs to maintain and which to curtail or abandon."[9] Hence, part of the change now being experienced is psychological in nature. It requires administrators to change their attitudes toward reality from those based on growth and expansion to these assuming no growth or even decline.

The unwillingness or inability to comprehend fully austerity's impact on management creates a discrepancy between the real and the desired world. This discrepancy is responsible for organizational conflicts expressed by managerial unreadiness to deal with anticipated economic changes.

What the library manager needs to recognize is that this new environment exists
and that it requires new and more precise analysis and expression of library
needs. . . . There are ways to save money in libraries, but in the long run the
goals of collection building and services imply spending money creatively. In this
time of uncertainty, it takes a new approach to develop the strategy to support
this creativity.[10]

Attitudes Toward Austerity

Staff and user attitudes toward change processes are critical, since their
support of efforts to manage austerity may determine success. Reasons
for resisting change are many and complex and are often reactions to
personal threats. Bureaucrats, for example, consider that innovations
endanger their own status. Many employees, fearful of job security and
apprehensive of new and unknown working environment factors, become defensive or even hostile to changes. Certain staff members resist
modification of established working patterns by expressing an almost
paranoid fear of persecution in anticipated reorganization. Obviously,
cuts will be accepted more easily if people feel rewarded for cooperation. "It is fools and saints who are known for not resisting uncompen-
sated loss, not the rest of us."[11]

Paradoxes of Austerity

Austerity-driven changes create a number of paradoxes, each one offering an interesting insight into the nature of austerity economics.
Four of them are discussed here.

1) One paradox results from the economies of scale. With reduced
resources and curtailed activities, libraries buy fewer items and pay
more for them per item, thus losing the advantages of volume purchase
discounts. Furthermore, austerity severely limits efforts to improve
productivity by investing in more efficient systems, such as automation.
Levine called this a productivity paradox, "it takes money to save money."[12] Then there is inflation: the same number of dollars buy fewer
books than before, while any saving in operation cost, such as energy
conservation, is negated by the increased price of energy itself.

A different kind of economic paradox is provided by the unique
nature of information which "does not behave like other 'products.' It is
characterized by simultaneity of ownership, difficulty in exclusion and
nondepletability. . . . Information can be sold and retained at the same
time; it is difficult to keep people from using it; and the supply is not
exhausted no matter how many times it is sold."[13] Hence a paradox
exists in determining information's real price. Before automation, that

price was expressed by the relevant serial publication subscription cost or by the appropriate manuscript's market price. Once purchased, a title could be used almost free of charge until replaced by a new edition or new copy.

Today's information retrieval price is per use and depends on such factors as royalties and communication fees. One solution is a charge per service; the other solution, perhaps feasible soon, is to replace infrequently used periodical subscriptions with online retrieval services. Still another automated information retrieval effect is the fact that, with expanding data bases, citations are provided to many more sources than can be found locally. The resulting interlibrary loan activity increase further augments service costs and forces certain lenders to impose new charges.

The need for professional survival requires adjustment from the mentality of affluence to that of austerity. American librarians may choose between following the recent example of the agriculture field by adapting to fast-changing economics or ignoring all change signs and sharing the consequences in the manner that bankrupted the railroads.[14] We must accept the fact that the gradual erosion of university resources changes the library's budgetary role from that of sharing a piece of a pie to sharing the burden of a declining economy.[15]

2) Organizational paradox is expressed by the contrast between the library faculty's singular mission to support its parent institution's program and the highly diversified goals of individual classroom faculty members. With a declining university budget, the discrepancies between these two interest groups' objectives create a competitive environment with ensuing tension.[16]

Librarians' persistent perception of their second-class status within the university further compounds the conflict. This inferiority complex is reinforced in their peers' tenure evaluation process. On certain campuses, library candidates are expected to meet existing scholarly research standards in addition to fulfilling library service criteria. Simultaneously, the deteriorating economy challenges academic traditions of autonomy and freedom and questions faculty immunity from supply and demand laws. Tenure is being challenged and accountability introduced into the vocabularies of unionized professors, researchers, and librarians.

The resulting organizational paradox is the emergence of an expectation lag, expressed in the demand for a somewhat belittled participative management. Librarians ask for the full faculty privileges which are being curtailed for their teaching colleagues and expect more participation in management also though staffing is insufficient to compensate for the hours spent in additional meetings. University libraries cannot be managed by committees or by staff concensus. Individual staff members are insufficiently informed about management issues, do not necessarily have administrative ability, and neither they nor the committee as a whole can be held accountable for the consequences of their action.

One extreme form of participative management, the collegial or faculty system of governance, was developed for academic departments; it works badly there and worse or not at all in libraries. Where it appears to work, it is because those involved have tacitly made concessions to traditional hierarchical systems and to the demands of the environment while preserving the collegial form. A library is not an academic department; it is a service organization and should be so administered. A librarian by any other name is still a librarian and it is time for mature acceptance of that fact.[17]

Two of Levine's paradoxes can also be listed as organizational. One is the paradox of irreducible wholes which "refers to the fact that an organization cannot be reduced piece-by-piece by simply reversing the sequence of activities and resources by which it was built."[18] How, for example, can one reduce collection development officers' activities without at the same time affecting library processes and the workload level in other technical service departments?

The other, a paradox of efficiency, points to the fact that "efficient organizations have a difficult search for more productivity gains because they are likely to have already exhausted most of the easy and obvious productivity improvement strategies."[19] This paradox was illustrated in the days of converting manual to OCLC cataloging. Significant staff savings were achieved mainly in inefficiently organized catalog departments. In well-managed units, automated cataloging improved speed and perhaps quality, but did not reduce staffing significantly.

3) Austerity's psychological paradox rests on the maxim that people do not change as fast as does technology. Human temperaments, tendencies, preferences, and prejudices change slowly and reluctantly, creating a serious adjustment problem. Libraries face the challenge of maintaining staff morale with limited means for rewarding good performance and encouraging innovation, also. And finally, austerity discourages risk-taking through controversial decisions, since the budget provides no margin for experimentation. "Simply put, it just is not as much fun working and managing in a contracting organization as it is in an expanding one."[20]

4) The paradoxes of austerity economics, organizational disequilibrium, and conflicting psychological demands wind up on the administrator's desk as the major ethical dilemma of choosing among incompatible values. Thus, for example, the director may be required to choose between equitable and fair resource distribution among all library departments and the pragmatic necessity to allocate resources only among the most efficient and productive operations. The paradox

lies in the difficult decision to support expansion of the already successful operations at the expense of less efficient ones. Thus, for example, a
fund transfer from technical to public service to subsidize information
retrieval service may support a fast-expanding activity, but at the expense of larger cataloging backlogs.

The ethical dilemma is thus created by a necessity to choose between
equity and overall efficiency in allocating resources. "'Equity' means
the distribution of cuts with an equal probability of hurting all units
irrespective of long term capacity impact. 'Efficiency' means the sorting, shifting, and assignment of cuts to units so for a given budget
decrement they minimize long-term loss to the organization as a whole,
irrespective of their distribution."[21]

The Impact of Austerity on Library Administration

In general, the decline of public organizations

is a symptom, a problem, and a contingency. It is a symptom of resource scarcity . . . creating the necessity . . . to terminate some programs, lower the activity
level of others, and confront tradeoffs between new demands and old programs . . . It is a problem for managers who must maintain organizational capacity by devising new managerial arrangements within prevailing structures that
were designed under assumptions of growth. It is a contingency for public
employees . . . who must sustain their morale and productivity in the face of
increasing control from above and shrinking opportunities for creativity and
promotion.[22]

Obviously, administrative reactions to declining resources can be of
only three kinds: to ignore the decline, to ease its impact on operation,
or to try to eliminate decline by searching for alternatives. Ignoring
austerity's existence is suicidal; when a library is finally forced to absorb
cuts managerial adjustments may come too late. Thus the avoidance
strategy which pretends to ignore the seriousness of the problem must
be rejected.[23]

One can smooth decline by introducing gradual anticipatory adjustments, such as short range goal modification, or one can develop innovative approaches aimed at reaching similar objectives by better methods, such as full automation, for example.

In most cases, however . . . strategies for dealing with decline will be a mixed bag
of tactics intended either to *resist* or to *smooth* decline. . . . No responsible manager wants to be faced with the prospect of being unable to control where cuts will
take place or confront quantum cuts with unpredictable consequences. Instead,
managers will choose a less risky course and attempt to protect organization
capacity and procedures by smoothing decline and its effects on the organization.[24]

	Austerity amplifies:		Strategies to manage austerity
	Internal library weaknesses	External university pressures	
POLICIES	dependence on university mission	university changing priorities	increased goal flexibility
SERVICES	managerial conflicts	environmental deterioration	maintenance of quality of service
PROCESSES	operational deficiencies	declining resources	innovative processes

Figure 1. Impact of Austerity on Library Management

Figure 1 shows austerity to have a direct impact on library policy formulation, on service effectiveness, and on technical processes efficiency. This impact is of two basic types. It brings to the surface internal organizational weaknesses which previously were either insubstantial or were compensated for by the library's strengths in other management areas. Austerity also magnifies external pressures which become more severe than the ones imposed in prosperous periods.

An academic library's primary responsibility is to support the research and educational needs of its university community. This complete dependence on the university mission requires periodic policy revision and updating. In times of severe budget cuts, university goals may change drastically, in a short time, and without warning. To accommodate these changes, such as, for example, elimination of certain academic programs or significant student enrollment reduction, the library must stand ready to readjust its goals. These changes may alter the scope and depth of collections and services but ought not to change the main mission, the very essence of its existence.

In austerity, services are directly affected by internal managerial conflicts created by such factors as indecisive leadership or poor work supervision. Services are further affected by a deteriorating environment. Thus, inefficient university building maintenance increases the plight. In addition, budget retrenchment creates pressures for increased service. Individual colleges with reduced budgets expect library assistance to provide material previously acquired from their own budgets. They also pressure the library for more personalized and decentralized service, while students request longer service hours and more study space, both reduced by insufficient funding.

Unable to protect all activites, the library must concentrate on the good quality services still available. A poorly performed auxiliary service is worse than its elimination, while a seriously curtailed primary service may negate its usefulness. In general, service inefficiency is increasingly visible during overall campus deterioration.

Uneconomical material processing may be tolerated in abundant times, but becomes a liability in austere times. Thus, for example, poor cataloger utilization may not be noticed quickly in normal times, but below-standard cataloging in a department with reduced staff will quickly create backlogs. The only strategy available is to improve performance by introducing policy and procedure innovations. Simplified cataloging or filing rules and cataloging networks may reduce staff shortage problems.

Management of Declining Resources

Creative Management

Changing leadership styles reflect prevailing higher education philosophies. Eighteenth century German librarians were almost exclusively scholarly with a director more interested in his own library use than in management.[25] The more recent bookmen-directors emphasized book acquisition over organization and use. Only recently have managerial skills become a major requirement. In 1960, 90 per cent of Association of Research Libraries (ARL) directors had a doctorate (often in a subject field), but by 1976, only 15 per cent of them had doctorates, although many more such degree-holders were available than before.[26]

Creative decline management requires different managerial skills, increased empathy and compassion for the staff, more realism in assessing library options, and a never-ceasing search for new opportunities.

The skills of managing a declining institution are not only different from but are probably in some senses greater than those required to manage institutional growth. . . . The manager of a declining institution is required to think of more things that haven't been thought of. In a growing institution mistakes are easily corrected; in a declining institution they are not.[27]

The measures that the austerity manager must take are often arbitrary, unpopular, and risky. The economy of decline requires efficient operation which in turn implies strictly enforced deadlines and centralization. Such an approach reduces employee autonomy, imposes more coordination and supervision, and requires higher accountability. Reduced human resource availability forces the manager to optimize staff efficiency and effectiveness. Thus, work quality and quantity become equally important, stressing not only skills but also work habits and attitudes.

These issues become important since the overall quality of service to the clientele is the library's major strength; in austere times these services are the primary mechanisms by which the library can respond to the changing environment.[28] Performance is more difficult to improve for managers who did not apply sound principles and tolerated substandard work in prosperous times. They must resort to "crisis management" before their staff members will accept the new reality.[29]

Planning for Austerity

Planning becomes the most effective defense against austerity's negative impact, since it "is the orderly means used by an organization to establish effective control over its own future."[30] Planning must be logical, comprehensive, and action-oriented. The most important factor is not prediction ability but the mode of thought used. It requires good administrative perspectives, an ability to identify major problems, and a knowledge of the methodology best suiting each situation. Planning should include historical analogies in order to identify past crisis patterns, and it depends on an administrator's ability to make successful implementation decisions. Hence, planning processes are more important than their products.[31]

A word of caution is in order: too much expectation from planning processes will result in disappointment. In austerity, the availability of resources may diminish before plans can be implemented, thus requiring flexibility in adjusting specific objectives to the fast changing environment. The major value of a planning approach is in providing for quick identification and evaluation of contingencies available to the decision maker.

Planning processes can be viewed from three perspectives. Conceptual planning focuses on the long-range mission; it provides an idea to be aimed at. Contextual planning makes adjustments for resources available in a particular library, while procedural planning devises specific actions.[32]

Conceptual planning starts with mission definition. Since the mission is central in institutional perpetuity, it should be formulated as a broad statement of general direction fixed enough to transcend economic changes. The library mission is always defined in terms of support for university research, educational and cultural programs, and activities. The library may be forced to adjust the immediate goals or methods of fulfilling that mission, but the mission itself should not be altered.

This planning tries to answer the president's questions: how do you see the library five years from now? As an expanding black hole of never-ending demands for fiscal increases? Or as a newly emerging information center, requiring less space and material and more automated information access, wherever stored? In effect, conceptual planning reflects the library's philosophy.

In contextual planning, the manager establishes objectives and develops strategy in terms of overall mission, by re-examining operation, clientele, service offered, and austerity impact, together with university administration support of needs. Thus, the library mission is evaluated on its capability to fulfill itself. Contextual planning is still more of an art than a science.

Technical planning establishes specific tactical objectives to implement contextual plans. Such planning must be consistent and accountable in terms of the results obtained from austerity's cuts. Technical planning is based on the assumption that austerity in general and inflation in particular, "can only be fought by improving productivity, by producing more from fewer resources, by working to tighter standards and by seeking, finding, and eliminating unnecessary costs."[33] In technical planning performance standards are essential. "If management does not set standards or does not monitor performance in relation to standards, then it should blame itself, not a deterioration of the work ethic, for poor performance."[34] Technical planning produces engineering blueprints for action.

Conceptual and contextual planning are strategic in nature. They plot long range action courses. Technical planning, on the other hand, develops tactics to be employed in implementing strategic objectives. Strategic planning aims at sweeping and often fundamental changes necessitated by changing conditions, while tactical planning addresses specific problems. Strategy defines the library's future directions. It is formulated after long deliberation and is difficult to change on short notice. Tactics influence immediate decisions on problems at hand, decisions that must be made on the spot and which may be subject to later change.[35]

Decision Processes

"Planning is anticipatory decision making," while decision processes themselves translate planning into action.[36] The best decisions on whether to cut or expand operations are the ones that further the mission by using existing resources most effectively. These decisions always involve choosing from limited resources.

The steps taken normally in the decision process include: 1) defining the problem, 2) determining its nature and the needs served by solving

the problem, 3) identifying and evaluating available options, 4) collecting pertinent information, 5) consulting individuals whom the decision
will affect, 6) the decision itself, and 7) follow-up of the consequences.

Significant in decision-making processes, but especially those imply-
ing cutbacks, is the fairness and legality of proposed action. In order
that no staff members feel punished, changes should be made in full
compliance with university rules and regulations, and decisions must be
made promptly. "There is an increasing need for action . . . there is no
time for perfection . . . decisions must be reversible . . . rigidity must be
eliminated in favor of the '3F' principle: fast, fluid and flexible" . . . in
such a "reactive and adaptive management philosophy . . . simplification is a must."[37]

And finally, decisions cannot be made by staff concensus. The committee approach survived in a growth period since no one was hurt by a
tentatively negative decision. As someone put it, in the days of affluence, "no" merely meant "not yet." In retrenchment, however, the
responsibility for final decisions must be made by an individual administrator, so that "no" is interpreted as "not at all."[38]

Budgeting in Austerity

"Budget is explicit thinking, symbolized numerically. Ideally it includes
only what is requested to implement your plan for your library. The
accountant's techniques can then be used to monitor and control the
program."[39] A budgetary approach can be useful in at least four kinds
of austerity situations: 1) as a political instrument to negotiate operational appropriations; 2) as a managerial instrument to evaluate efficiency in terms of cost-effectiveness; 3) as an economic instrument to
distribute resources according to need; and 4) as an accountant's instrument to determine spending limits.[40]

Among the more obvious methods useful in austerity are: increased
library cooperation in acquisition and collection development activities;
reduced production costs through consolidating certain activities and
automating others, and by decisively eliminating duplicate resources
and staff efforts. An austerity budget should address three questions: 1)
what objectives is the library attempting to meet and what resources are
needed to meet them? 2) Assuming present operation level, where will
the library be in the future, perhaps five years hence? and 3) what
ought the library's objectives and operations be five years from now?
Discrepancies between answers to the last two questions indicate need
for budget restructuring.[41]

Among emerging innovative approaches is the "zero-based budget"
concept which requires annually revising fiscal assumptions before new
allocations are made. This approach is future-directed, involves current

and future project evaluation, allows reviews of underfunded programs and provides political negotiations between competing group interests. It combines consideration of the "intensity of needs" for resources with the impact of these reduced resources on individual library unit activities.[42] A budgetary technique suggested for smaller libraries is the "no-growth" collection development policy. This technique is represented by a "theoretical model of an academic library that does not grow in size, although its contents change from year to year in response to changing reader demand."[43]

Stressful Circumstances

Any work environment change, especially in austere times, is perceived as a sign of organizational instability, which in turn, produces anxiety about job security. Stress created by anticipated but unknown changes can significantly affect operational efficiency. Galbraith referred to it as "the tyranny of circumstance."[44] Managers should recognize stress's impact on staff performance and realize that personnel management is value-intensive, requiring the manager "to view the employee as not just someone assigned to a particular job but as an important resource within the organization, one to be developed to achieve his or her maximum potential."[45]

The extent to which an administrator can cooperate with staff members in overcoming austerity tensions depends on their professional and personal maturity. Austerity brings out the best and the worst in their personalities. Certain individuals are challenged by these obstacles and invent new approaches to reach goals despite limited resources. Others refuse to see the need for cooperative problem resolutions and, instead, try to take advantage of the situation by politicizing and manipulating the changing environment to meet their selfish interests.

In this period the director becomes vulnerable to severe personal criticism under the false pretense of technical or philosophical concerns. Certain directors attempt to soften objections to changes by negotiating with dissidents. Others challenge the critics' motives by appealing to the entire staff's common sense. Choice of method depends on personalities.

Staff Training and Development

The purpose of a staff training program is to identify skill and working habit changes required by the changing environment and to help the individual employee adjust to these requirements. Two important criteria can be used in evaluating training program effectiveness. One is relevance to the library's mission, and the other is effectiveness in accomplishing training program objectives. A well designed program ought to provide improved skill and job requirement matching.

Staff development programs should facilitate both job enrichment by expanding employee responsibilities and job enlargement by increasing individual work assignments. Together, job enrichment and enlargement ought to improve job satisfaction and task performance. Staff development programs should address the needs of the library and its individual employees by relating technical competence norms to the staff's perception of its role in operation.[46]

Understanding Management of Decline

In concluding this discussion, the importance should be reemphasized of accepting the hypothesis that a new management period has begun, a period that is more nearly permanent than any past seasonal economic change. "The recognition by the management of an organization that they are in a condition of decline is fundamental. Then the determination of the cause(s) of decline . . . will allow them to select strategies and tactics for coping with that condition."[47]

Reactions to austerity should be evaluated in terms of "right" and "good" decisions. "Right" decisions result in maximizing needed services and operations and minimizing the value loss that must be surrendered in the change. "Good" decisions are best illustrated by contrasting an honest, direct, and unhypocritical management style with a Machiavellian, manipulative, coercive, and deceptive approach. The former is ends-oriented, the latter means-justified. Certain writers try to avoid the ethical issue altogether by suggesting that "managers should not make value judgements of change—they should make plans to cope with it."[48]

It is unfortunate that we enter this new and unexplored period so poorly prepared. Although fully aware of responsibilities to maintain as many services as possible, we have little experience and technical knowhow to help us fulfill these obligations in austere periods. Therefore, efforts to cope must be limited to a trial and error methodology and austerity management research ought to become a high priority project. "It is important to study the problem of decline in organizations, in order to develop a better data base, to determine better strategies by which decline may be handled, and to develop training programs which will provide administrators with effective skills to manage decline."[49]

Such a library research emphasis will undoubtedly challenge many contemporary library administration tenets. Revising traditional assumptions is necessitated, however, by the powerful combined impact of austerity and new technology on modern operation. It becomes clear that "never has the time been more opportune . . . for shelving old practices and logging new solutions".[50]

References

1. This essay incorporates a review of selected current literature on the concept of austerity as it may apply to academic library management. The review encompasses works footnoted in this section as well as publications listed in the *Bibliography*.

2. Milic Capek, "Change," *The Encyclopedia of Philosophy* (N.Y.: Macmillan and the Free Press, 1967), vol. 2, pp. 75–79.

3. Kenneth E. Boulding, "The Management of Decline," *Change Magazine* 7 (June 1975), p. 8.

4. Sheila Creth, "The Impact of Changing Life Styles on Library Administration," *Southeastern Librarian* 30 (Summer 1980), p. 81.

5. Krishan Kumar and P. K. Jayaswal, "University Librarianship: A Challenge for Change," *Library Herald* 19 (April–September 1980), pp. 30–42.

6. A. L. Kapoor, "Innovation in Academic Library Services," *Library Herald* 19 (April–September 1980), pp. 23–29.

7. Non-librarian managers "are geared to innovation and change, in part because they feel that although not all change involves progress, all progress involves change." Herbert S. White, "Management: A Strategy for Change," *Canadian Library Journal* 35 (October 1978), p. 336.

8. Boulding, *op. cit.*, p. 9.

9. Herbert S. White, "Library Management in the Tight Budget Seventies: Problems, Challenges and Opportunities," *Bulletin of the Medical Library Association* 65 (January 1977), p. 6. Italics mine.

10. Scott Bruntjen, "Librarians in a Time of Uncertainty," *Journal of Academic Librarianship* 4 (July 1978), p. 159.

11. Robert P. Biller, "Leadership Tactics for Retrenchment," *Public Administration Review* 40 (Nov./Dec. 1980), p. 605.

12. Charles H. Levine, "More on Cutback Management Hard Questions for Hard Times," *Public Management Forum* 39 (March/April 1979), p. 181.

13. Marilyn Killebrew Gell, "Supply-Side Economics: Magic or Madness," *Library Journal* 106 (April 15, 1981), p. 833.

14. Boulding, *op. cit.*, p. 9.

15. Robert D. Behn, "Leadership in an Era of Retrenchment," *Public Administration Review* 40 (Nov./Dec. 1980), pp. 603–609.

16. Mary Biggs, "Sources of Tension and Conflict Between Librarians and Faculty," *Journal of Higher Education* 52 (March/April 1981), pp. 182–201.

17. Richard De Gennaro, "Library Administration & New Management Systems," *Library Journal* 103 (December 15, 1978), p. 2480.

18. Levine (1979), *op. cit.*, p. 180.

19. Ibid., p. 181.

20. Ibid., p. 180.

21. Charles H. Levine, "Organizational Decline and Cutback Management," *Public Administration Review* 138 (July/August 1978), p. 320.

22. *Ibid.*, p. 316.

23. Paul Berman and Milbrey W. McLaughlin, *The Management of Decline: Problems, Opportunities, and Research Questions.* Rand Paper Series P-5984 (Washington, D.C.: National Institute of Education, 1970), ERIC ED 147 953.

24. Levine (1978), *op. cit.*, pp. 319–320.

25. Biggs, *op. cit.*, p. 183.

26. White (1978), *op. cit.*, p. 331. This statement should not be interpreted too simplistically. As Harvey noted, it ought not imply "that Ph.D.s are necessarily poorer managers than M.S. graduates. We are now in an era when department and section heads are said to be very competent and to need little help from administrators. I don't necessarily believe that—some are and some are not—but this may have affected the situation. Also, I think many of the new administrators have been chosen for their PR and negotiation abilities rather than other managerial skills. Certain of them may be said to have the "charm" of anonymity and unobtrusive personalities, in contrast to the "leaders" previously in those jobs. One of the most interesting aspects of the situation is that such a change has occurred in no other university administrative position that I know of. I think a close examination of this issue would be interesting" (Letter from John F. Harvey dated July 28, 1982).

27. Boulding, *op. cit.*, p. 64.

28. Thomas W. Shaughnessy, "Library Administration in Support of Emerging Service Patterns," *Library Trends* 28 (Fall 1976), p. 139.

29. Jerry Kinard and others, "The Positive Side of Recessions: Bringing Accountability Back," *Supervisory Management* 26 (February 1981), pp. 13–16.

30. Earl C. Bolton, "Response of University Library Management to Changing Modes of University Governance and Control," *College & Research Libraries* 33 (July 1972), p. 309.

31. North East Association for Institutional Research. *Does IR=Institution Retrenchment? Perspectives on the Role of Institutional Research in a Time of Retrenchment.* Papers from the fourth annual conference (Durham, N.H., October 27, 28 and 29, 1977), ERIC #ED 156058.

32. Francisco R. Sagasti, "A Conceptual 'Systems' Framework for the Study of Planning Theory," *Technological Forecasting and Social Change* 5 (1973), pp. 379–393.
    See also Joseph Z. Nitecki, "An Idea of Librarianship: An Outline for a Root-Metaphor Theory in Library Science," *Library and Culture*, Donald G. Davis, Jr., ed. (Austin: University of Texas Press, 1981), pp. 106–120.

33. Trevor Bentley, "Activity Resource Planning," *Management Accounting* 56 (March 1978), p. 114.

34. Jim Summers, "Management by Crisis," *Public Personnel Management* 6 (May/June 1977), p. 196.

35. American Library Association. LAMA/LOMS Budgeting, Accounting and Cost Committee. *Planning Guide for Managing Cutbacks* (Chicago: American Library Association, 1980), 26 pp.

36. Sagasti, *op. cit.*, p. 386.

37. Michael J. Kami, "Planning in Times of Unpredictability", *Columbia Journal of World Business* 11 (Summer 1976), p. 32.

38. North East Association for Institutional Research, *op. cit.*

39. American Library Association, *op. cit.*, p. 14.

40. Donald G. Frank, "The Library Budgeting Process and Inflationary Pressures: a Perspective," *Texas Library Journal* 57 (Summer 1981), p. 42.

41. Frederick J. Turk, "Cost Behavior Analysis: A Road Map of the Uncertain Future," *Management Controls* 24 (September–October 1977), p. 20.

42. Levine (1978), *op. cit.*, p. 322.

43. Daniel Gore, "Curbing the Growth of Academic Libraries: A 'Clear and Feasible Policy' for Creating the 'No-growth' Collection," *Library Journal* 106 (November 15, 1981), p. 2185.

44. Kurt R. Student, "Personnel's Newest Challenge: Helping to Cope with Greater Stress," *Personnel Administrator* 23 (November 1978), p. 20.

45. Association of Research Libraries. Office of Management Studies. *The Systems and Procedures Exchange Center (SPEC) Flyer no. 75:* "Staff Development" (Washington, D.C.: June, 1981)

46. Charles E. Kozoll and Donald E. Moore, "Professional Growth vs. Fiscal Restraint," *Community College Frontiers* 7 (Summer 1979), pp. 18–22.

47. John W. Brubacher and Mark R. Shibles, "Organizational Decline: Implications for Research." Paper presented at Northeastern Educational Research Association's Annual Conference, October 25, 1979. ERIC #ED 179017, p. 10.

48. Kami, *op. cit.,* p. 26.

49. Brubacher, *op. cit.,* p. 17.

50. Frederick H. Jackson, "The Future of Academic Libraries: The Inevitability of Change," *College Board Review,* no. 117 (Fall, 1980), pp. 6–9. See also *The Economics and Financial Management of Research Libraries,* a report on an exploratory meeting sponsored by the Association of Research Libraries and the Research Libraries Group, Inc., October 14, 1981 (Washington, D.C.: Office of Management Studies/ARL and the Council on Library Resources, 1982), 16 pp.

Bibliography

Association of Research Libraries. *Minutes of the 77th Meeting* (Los Angeles, California, January 17, 1971).

Benge, Eugene J. and the editors of Alexander Hamilton Institute. *Elements of Modern Management* (N.Y.: AMACOM, 1976).

Bennis, Warren G., Kenneth D. Benne, Robert Chin and Kenneth E. Corey, eds. *The Planning of Change* (N.Y.: Holt, Rinehart and Winston, 1976).

Billings, Robert S., Thomas W. Milburn and Mary Lou Schaalman, "A Model of Crisis Perception: A Theoretical and Empirical Analysis," *Administrative Science Quarterly* 25 (June 1980), pp. 300–316.

Bone, Larry Earl, "The Leadership Connection," *Library Journal* 106 (November 1, 1981), pp. 2091–2093.

Borkowski, Casimir, H. David Brumble III and Murdo J. MacLeod, "A Reply to the Kent Study," *Library Journal* 106 (April 1, 1981), pp. 710–713.

Brickman, Sally, "The Academic Library Needs a Planned Communication Program," *Catholic Library World* 53 (October 1981), p. 137.

Burge, Liz, "Change Agents, or Change Victims? An Exploration of the Relevance of an Innovation Diffusion Model for Library Management," *Australian Library Journal* 26 (November 4, 1977), pp. 310–315.

Chirst-Janer, Arland F., "Institutional Mission in an Era of Retrenchment: Stephens College," *Liberal Education* 66 (Summer 1980), pp. 161–168.

Cohen, Aaron and Elaine Cohen, "The Quiet Revolution of the Campuses," *Chronicle of Higher Education* 23 (November 25, 1981), p. 56.

60   Nitecki

Cyert, Richard M., "The Management of Universities of Constant or Decreasing Size," *Public Administration Review* 38 (July/August 1979), pp. 344–349.

De Gennaro, Richard, "Libraries & Networks in Transition: Problems and Prospects for the 1980's," *Library Journal* 106 (May 15, 1981), pp. 1045–1049.

Drucker, Peter F., *The Age of Discontinuity: Guidelines to our Changing Society* (N.Y.: Harper & Row, 1969).

Duffy, N. M., "Top Management Information: Perspectives in a Changing World," *South African Libraries* 48 (April 1981), pp. 145–149.

Euster, Joanne R., *Changing Patterns in Internal Communication in Large Academic Libraries.* Occasional Paper No. 6. (Washington, D.C.: Office of Management Studies, ARL, 1981).

Fores, Michael and Arndt Sorge, "The Decline of the Management Ethics," *Journal of General Management* 6 (1981), pp. 36–50.

Gapen, D. Kaye, "Simplification of the MARC Format: Feasibility, Benefits, Disadvantages, Consequences." Unpublished manuscript, under contract for the ARL Task Force on Bibliographic Control, 1981.

Gore, Daniel, "The View from the Tower of Babel," *Library Journal* 100 (September 15, 1975), pp. 1599–1605.

Groff, Warren H., *Key External Data Required in Strategic Decision-Making: A New Role for Management Systems,* 1980. 17 p. ERIC #ED 201 295.

Gwinn, Nancy E. and Warren J. Haas, "Crisis in the College Library," *AGB Reports* 23 (March–April 1981), pp. 41–45.

Holtz, Virginia and Paul Olson, "Planning for Meaningful Change in Libraries and Library Networks: A First Step," *Medical Library Association Bulletin* 64 (October 1975), pp. 376–381.

Johnson, Edward R. and Stuart H. Mann, *Organization Development for Academic Libraries: An Evaluation of the Management Review and Analysis Program* (Contributions in Librarianship and Information Science, No. 28) (Westport, Conn.: Greenwood Press, 1980).

Kemper, Robert E. and Richard E. Ostrander, *Directorship by Objectives* (Littleton, Colo.: Libraries Unlimited, 1977).

Klinger, Donald E. and John Nalbandian, "Personnel Management by Whose Objectives?" *Public Administration Review* 38 (July/August 1978), pp. 366–372.

Lancaster, F. Wilfrid, "The Future of the Librarian Lies Outside the Library," *Catholic Library World* 51 (April 1980), pp. 388–391.

Levine, Arthur, "Wanted: New Leaders for America's Colleges," *Chronicle of Higher Education* 23 (September 2, 1981), p. 33.

Lewis, Carol W. and Anthony T. Logalbo, "Cutback Principles and Practices: A Checklist for Managers," *Public Administration Review* 40 (March/April 1980), pp. 184–188.

Lippitt, Ronald, Jeanne Watson and Bruce Westley, *The Dynamics of Planned Change: A Comparative Study of Principles and Techniques* (N.Y.: Harcourt, Brace & World, 1958).

Lucas, Henry C., *Implementation: The Key to Successful Information Systems* (N.Y.: Columbia University Press, 1981).

Lundberg, Susan O., "A Delphi Study of Public Library Goals, Innovations, and Performance Measurements," *Library Research* 3 (Spring 1981), pp. 67–90.

McDonald, Kathryn, "Learning to Finance Learning," *College Board Review*, No. 116 (Summer 1980), pp. 8–11, 29–31.

McGrath, William E., *Development of a Long-Range Strategic Plan for a University Library*. The Cornell Experience: Chronicle and Evaluation of the First Year's Effort (Ithaca, N.Y.: Cornell University Libraries, 1973).

Merikangas, Robert J., "Leadership by Non-Administrators in Academic Libraries," *Journal of Library Administration* 4 (Winter 1980), pp. 21–39.

Miner, John B. and Norman R. Smith, "Can Organizational Design Make Up for Motivational Decline?" *Wharton Magazine* (Summer 1981), pp. 29–35.

Nelson, Charles A., "Ways to Exert Planning Leverage on a Future Rife with Surprises," *Management Controls* 24 (September–October 1977), pp. 2–3.

Nyren, Karl, "ACRL in Minneapolis: Options for the 80's," *LJ/SLJ Hotline*, No. 33 (October 12, 1981), pp. 1–8.

Palmer, Vernon E., Edwin E. Olson and Nancy K. Roderer. *Methods of Financing Interlibrary Loan Services* (Washington, D.C.: ARL, 1974).

Peterson, Marvin, W., "Faculty and Academic Responsiveness in a Period of Decline: An Organizational Perspective," *Journal of the College and University Personnel Association* 31 (Spring 1980), pp. 95–104.

Prentice, Ann E., *Strategies for Survival: Library Financial Management Today*. LJ Special Report # 7 (N.Y.: Library Journal, 1978), 56 p.

Schiller, Anita, "Shifting Boundaries in Information," *Library Journal* 106 (April 1, 1981), pp. 705–709.

Schwerin, Ursula C., "Institutional Mission in an Era of Retrenchment: New York City Community College, CUNY," *Liberal Education* 66 (Summer, 1980), pp. 169–176. Also published by ERIC #ED 188 694 (Prepared for Annual Meeting, American Association of Colleges, Phoenix, Arizona, January 10–12, 1980)

Stevenson, Mike, and Dan Walleri, *Program Evaluation in the Era of Retrenchment: The Role of Institutional Research in a Community College* (Gresham, Oregon: Mount Hood Community College, 1978), ERIC #ED 164 044.

Stueart, Robert D., "Great Expectations: Library and Information Science Education at the Crossroads," *Library Journal* 106 (October 15, 1981), pp. 1981–1992.

Wayne State University. *A Proposed Working Definition for Reorganization of the WSU Library System; Working Paper No. 5* (Detroit: University Libraries, Wayne State University, January 4, 1972), 5 pp. ERIC #ED 058 886.

Zipsie, Josephine, "Choosing Strategies for Change," *Wisconsin Library Bulletin* 75 (November–December 1979), p. 278.

3. An Interlibrary Coordination Extension Program

Thomas C. Harris

ADVANCING TECHNOLOGY and worsening economic conditions are causing significant changes in the academic library environment. Consequently, a new institution is emerging which promises to reshape the academic library's image. Furthermore, it is becoming apparent to many theorists and practitioners that this metamorphosis is causing increasing concern about coordinating interlibrary activity and redefining theory.

The Emerging Institution

The emerging institution to which I refer is already known to many as a network, to others as a cooperative, to some as a consortium and to a few as an information analysis center. A major problem in discussing interlibrary coordination, however, is in dealing clearly with networking terminology and perception. Network, the term so often used, is also used to describe certain of its activities. Why librarians have not accepted the term, consortium, instead of network, to describe the organization is a puzzle, but I would like to suggest its appropriateness. Webster's suggestion that a consortium may also be defined as an association seems to fit well with current network development. In this case, we may accept Webster's consortium or association description:

An enduring and cooperating social group whose members have developed organized patterns of relationships through interaction with one another . . . an interdependent system of (organization).[1]

Straton defined consortia even further:

A consortium is an entity created by two or more independent institutions that voluntarily choose to create an organization with all the requisites of an independent institution—namely, organizational mission, domain, staff, resources, and procedures. The consortium is created to serve their mutual interests. The work of the consortium is controlled through the governing involvement of the participating institutions. Despite this continual control, the consortium develops an identity separate from, but dedicated to the sponsoring institutions.[2]

I have chosen to nominate the term consortium in order to reconcile two schools of thought. My labels for them are Method School and Organization School.[3]

The *Method School* suggests a computer capability emphasis as an essential element. The term, network, therefore, describes the organizations that provide benefits through computers and other electronic communication means. The method used to facilitate the service which is rendered dominates and is used to identify the organization in terms of its working relationship, goal, and objectives. Therefore, emphasis is placed on governance, organization, and goals. Whether or not computers are used depends on goal-related factors.

The *Organization School* suggests that organizational structure and purpose are as essential to interlibrary activity success as are computers and other technology forms. Some may point out that the current concern level for interlibrary activity did not develop through traditional cooperative means, but rather through computer development. While a desire existed to share resources, the lack of tools for working together effectively obstructed organization benefits. With the advent of the computer and mini-computer, interlibrary activity is both desirable and feasible.

Others point out, however, that previous interlibrary activity also lacked purpose before recent technological advances. As long as libraries had adequate resources (a term that few have attempted to quantify), collaboration attempts were provincially interpreted and implemented. Inasmuch as academic libraries reflect economic conditions, the library value of computer technology and the interlibrary consortium increases in direct proportion to economic crisis development.

The reverse of this phenomenon is also apparent, however. As funds become readily available, interlibrary coordination need wanes. Straton wrote

One of the main observations of this study is that consortia are temporary organizations. With their own special mission, domain, resources, and identity, consortia have the ability to become their own entities without ties to sponsoring organizations. However, given their vulnerability to unique environmental pressures and their initial control by sponsoring organizations which are motivated by strong financial and institutional self-interests, consortia are limited in their ability to create the institutional independence to become their own entities.[4]

Ethic

A program to extend interlibrary coordination is also concerned with the ethic and thought quality associated with information theory. Therefore, the emerging institution in reshaping thought into new theories that support managerial, communication, and delivery processes is performing a vital change process role.

In this context, coordination may be likened to choreography, since its purpose is to bring into harmonious action the composition, arrangement and application of systemwide ideas as well as the administration of several libraries working together in common purpose. The verb coordinate means to bring [something] into common action, movement, or condition: *to regulate and combine in harmonious action.*[5] It also suggests that coordinating is the work of several bureaus.

A curious combination of circumstances involving tool (computer) development and economic conditions is providing both the means and purpose for advancing new library and information ideas. The emerging new-idea-advocating institution that I call the Interlibrary Consortium has among its attributes many described in the information analysis centers (think tanks) recommended by the 1963 U.S. President's Science Advisory Committee [Weinberg Report].[6]

That Report saw the information analysis center as an important information system rationalization. The Committee recommended that such centers function primarily as technical institutes, not as libraries, to be led by scientists and engineers developing new ideas and foundations for future decisions. This is what I see in an interlibrary coordination extension program: a planned continuing library institution development, pointed as much toward furthering information theory analysis as toward information maintenance, identification, and delivery.

To this end, the COSATI (Committee on Scientific and Technical Information) definition fits well:

An information analysis center is a formally structured organizational unit specifically (but not exclusively) established for the purpose of acquiring, selecting, storing, retrieving, evaluating, analyzing, and synthesizing a body of information in a clearly defined specialized field or pertaining to a specified mission with the intent of compiling, digesting, repackaging, or otherwise organizing and presenting pertinent information in a form most authoritative, timely, and useful to a society of peers and management.[7]

Interlibrary coordination extension includes pragmatic processes as well as theory development. The observation, however, pertaining to the consortium's value in this environment relates to the differences existing between traditional libraries and interlibrary consortia. Writing about the information analysis center, a type of institution possessing desirable consortia-related attributes, Carrol and Maskewitz discussed three organization orientations: discipline, mission, and large scale phenomena data oriented.[8] Each one of them may be defined further according to data sources or functions or even by development stage. Thus, there can be, for example, clearinghouses for newly emerging fields, archival repositories for old fields, and organizations identified by their products and services. Certain centers may exist only to produce a journal while others focus on computer technology. The differences between institutions focused on information and on library service are important. Carrol and Maskewitz pointed out these differences by comparing COSATI's and Cottrell's definitions. They noted that COSATI's definition (quoted above) is similiar to Cottrell's (quoted below) with an interesting difference:

A scientific information center is an organization, staffed mainly with scientists and engineers, which first indexes and then compiles, analyzes, evaluates, condenses, extrapolates and/or synthesizes information in a given area as integral steps in a comprehensive information acquisition, storage, retrieval, and dissemination process for the benefit of the scientific community to which they belong.[9]

Cottrell defined information analysis centers as serving the scientific community, while the more comprehensive COSATI definition saw them as serving a society of peers and management as well. This definition may serve also as an interlibrary consortium model and an interlibrary coordination extension program. The COSATI definition suggested concern for both theory and application.

The rationale supporting the emerging consortium trend resides within the academic library model's traditions. Old reasons and values are weighed against new abilities to meet new social, academic, and market needs; thus, we have the reshaping of subsequent ideas and institutions. As an institution the academic library maintains the organization's self-interest in order to hold its self identity. Consortia extending interlibrary coordination, on the other hand, are articulating a new identity, broader in purpose and scope and serving the larger community.

Value conflicts occur when the same people are required to function in managerial modes across different organizations. This may suggest that successful consortia are the result of conflict issue solutions. Straton found second-level managers did not coordinate consortium work as well as they coordinated their own institution's work.[10] Adler and Hlavacek pointed out that the much needed objective approach to joint venture work was provided by managers outside the participating organizations.[11] All of these researchers—Straton, Adler, and Hlavacek—made the case that conflict existed most often where organizations insisted on equal management representation. Inter-institutional conflicts were resolved by selecting consortia managers from outside the parent organizations.[12] It is apparent, therefore, that organizational conflicts must be anticipated and clearly identified at initial consortium organization and anti-conflict processes developed and implemented. If the organization's own identity is so important, why are consortia established?

Consortia are found in one of two situations: one in which the participating organizations are losing control over their environments (a situation that results in changes in the basic character of the organization) or one in which the organization wants to expand in areas where it does not have sufficient resources.[13]

The fact that organizations (academic libraries) do not change is firmly established in the literature. Katz and Kahn's theory, called the "steady state of dynamic homeostasis," suggested that forces constantly keep a system in balance.[14] In addition, to support this theory:

If the organization cannot expect a restoration of the status quo ante without effort on its part, it will maintain [an] intensified search while seeking to find the most effective response to this change. Other things being equal, it will select the response that involves the least profound change in its structure. Thus, it will prefer responses requiring it to change only its rules, and it will prefer the latter to those that necessitate shifts in institutional structure. Only in the most drastic situations will it alter fundamental purposes.[15]

The slowing Gross National Product growth, the consequent capital formation problems and continuing energy and material shortages increase product and service innovation risk.[16] Library stability becomes more difficult when economic relationships become less predictable. In such an environment, new product and service development slackens and the conservative library loses innovative vitality. Hence an alternative institution or process must be sought in order to continue library development.

Organization

Most effective among the interlibrary consortia types is the corporate model. It requires no surrender of local program responsibility for action. Instead it requires the member to actualize a specified amount of decision-making authority. The contract binding the local organization to the consortium describes the criteria upon which the organization is obliged to act. The corporate interlibrary model's advantage is that the local organization is responsible and accountable for its own program development and should provide effectively for local needs. Decisions and actions are focused on local program requirements and interpretations. Each organization moves freely within its own orbit. (See Figure 1.)

CORPORATE MODEL INTERACTION

INTERLIBRARY CONSORTIA

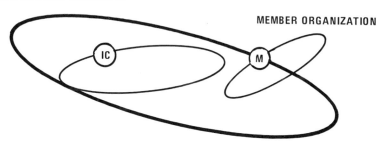

Figure 1.

BUREAUCRATIC MODEL INTERACTION

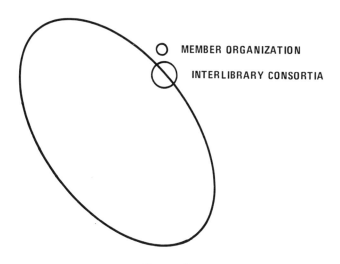

Figure 2.

An example of this consortium form is shown by the relationship between the Chancellor's Office, California State University (CSU) and the nineteen libraries. The Chancellor's Office is the controlling agency holding library directors (and campus Presidents) responsible and accountable for certain specified tasks, while coordinating certain systemwide library functions required by California law and Trustee regulation. The headquarters staff administers policy in coordination with CSU Board of Trustees regulations by utilizing the consultative process.

CSU was created legislatively. Its libraries form a system that is a corporate consortium. Webster makes no distinction between voluntary and involuntary. The verb, to cooperate, means to work together with others to a common end or for mutual and often economic benefit.

The bureaucratic model is less effective among interlibrary cooperative types. In the bureaucratic format, the larger organization takes control of the smaller local units which therefore experience an identity loss. The governing body assumes full responsibility for local program decisions and actions. One of the chief bureaucratic model criticisms relates to its decision-making motives. Since major policy decisions are made at some distance from local service needs and local organizations have lost their identity, policy-makers lose touch with the practical applications of library services and products and long-range theoretical goals tend to dominate decisions at the expense of current solutions to meet immediate needs. Each member organization is a satellite, always within the force of the bureaucratic pull. (See Figure 2.)

Fundamental to all programs associated with interlibrary coordination are five basic questions:

1. What is to be achieved?
2. Who is to be involved?
3. How shall it proceed?
4. What will be the effect?
5. Is it worth doing?

Encompassed within the answer to each question is the identification of a basic part of the interlibrary program. These questions need to be applied to the whole as well as to each part and function of interlibrary activity continuously. The boundary of interlibrary activity lies solely within the identification of the goal to be achieved by those involved, their willingness and ability to proceed, the effects on themselves, clients and proprietors, and the final evaluation.

The suggestion to extend a program of interlibrary coordination assumes that, through the composition, arrangement, and application of mutually beneficial regulations or laws, some good will result. It assumes a need and desire to work together in a coordinated and regulated fashion. The resulting good derived is to be sufficient to justify the expense of initiating, developing, and maintaining the organization and the program. It must also provide psychic compensation in the form of *satisfaction* achieved by also reaching goals other than economic. These are efficient working relationships, product and service reliability, and overall high program quality. These must be identified as functional goals apart from product or service goals. Psychic goals are equally as important to the success of interlibrary coordination as the program goals themselves.

Motive

Consortia are often described as voluntary organizations. Around this concept, however, revolve notions regarding cooperation and coordination. For example, Grupe suggests cooperation exists when institutions volunteer to work together, and coordination exists when a third party becomes involved and directs that the institutions *will* work together.[17] Coordination is not to be confused with interlibrary cooperation or activity, although it is hard to imagine or discuss one without the other. The two terms, nevertheless, are often used synonymously. Each of the two distinctly different terms may also mean different things to different people.

A controlling agency, for example, may espouse interlibrary cooperation while planning intrasystem coordination. Of course, shades of differences may exist also.

Present conditions are too complex to suggest need for a third party to insist on interlibrary coordination. The initiation and development of interlibrary consortia was inevitable. Currently important issues are such development's fecundity and growth speed. Belief in choice is illusionary. Choice exists in selecting the consortium that provides best for local needs. Often geography, governance, economics, and theory determine the selection in advance. Library theorists are discovering that the same motives exist for desiring as for requiring such development. Interlibrary consortia of any kind result naturally from the impact of advancing technology and economic pressure.

An experience record and, subsequently, a body of knowledge have shown that motives for interlibrary consortia development are to

1. Provide efficient library service.
2. Expand resources.
3. Receive technological benefits.
4. Develop ideas or concepts.
5. Implement cost-effective solutions to relieve economic pressures.
6. Escape political criticism.

Some students may argue that voluntary organizations predicated on cooperation rather than coordination are strengthened by members

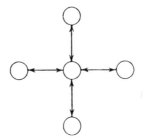

Figure 3.

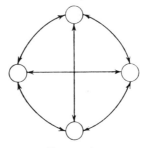

Figure 4.

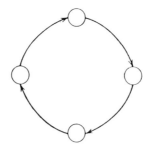

Figure 5.

deeply committed to their objectives and that formal organization is unnecessary. While this may be true, on the other hand, a problem contributing to many poor decisions is the decision's political and self-interest nature; it is made to keep specific members in the fold in order to reach certain other objectives. This leads to weak compromises such as those associated with coalitions and confederations. The voluntary organization type lacks the commitment akin to desperation required by the fireman whose escape route is cut off. He must act imaginatively or perish.

An interlibrary coordination extension program requires such a commitment. There can be no truly responsible, accountable decision-making process when members are not bound to stay, participate, and contribute toward achieving the organization's purpose. Rouse and Rouse described four common network configurations central to this discussion which contribute toward their understanding.[18] They include the star, distributed, ring, and hierarchy types, and to my mind represent the traditional network models.

In the *star model* (see Figure 3) the central organization provides services to the outlying units; no communication exists between outer units.[19] The *distributed model* (see Figure 4) represents a decentralized organization of units.[20] Each unit can freely provide for, receive, and communicate with every other unit. The *ring model* (see Figure 5) represents a decentralized work flow organization in which work enters one unit and moves on to the next until process completion.[21] Communication and services pass in one direction. This may be referred to as a peer or priority model. Rouse and Rouse cautioned against assuming that these models represent the only laterally structured network forms.[22] The organizations possess roughly equal responsibility in member business and their activity is called interlibrary cooperation. The ring model, therefore, may represent a format which requires members to seek service from peer libraries in a specific pecking order. An interlibrary coordination extension program assumes much more than supporting interlibrary service traffic. It requires a comprehensive model fitting the COSATI definition. The final Rouse and Rouse model (see Figure 6) is the *hierarchical* structure.[23] It displays, for example, the National Library of Medicine network model structure.[24]

None of these four examples, however, deals with decision-making, problem-solving, and planning. They are static organizational models existing in similar forms and demonstrating the status quo. The emerging interlibrary consortia do not fit the old models. They are not units situated among other organizations of equal responsibility and function. They are independent entities, sophisticated organizations, energetic, sustaining other systems, and operating at a high level. The model is dynamic. Instead of resisting change, the interlibrary consortium is constantly moving and affecting organizations which come within its influence. Therefore, an energy model form seems appropriate.

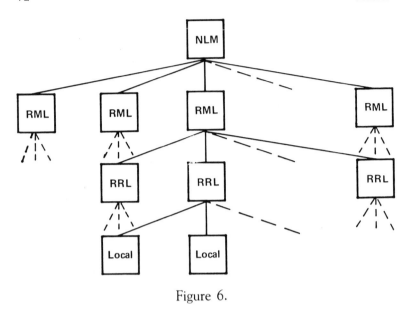

Figure 6.

(See Figures 7 and 8). The *energy model* (Figure 8) demonstrates both energy and interaction. Each element orbits about its respective area and interacts with other elements while influencing and being influenced as they come into proximity.

Interlibrary consortia are not without decision-making problems. Indeed, such problems are almost identical with those of cooperating organizations. Issues are strongly influenced by political self-interest objectives. An important difference, however, lies in the fact that each coordinated type member is totally bound by the final decision, and the decision itself is presumably directed toward group good based on each objective's merits and the overall goal. Such decisions are usually strongly binding and possess a legal and statutory nature. Success is more predictable through this kind of support.

Interlibrary Goals Are Decision-Bound

Ultimately, the decision process will lie with one or more persons authorized to act for the members. While review mechanisms will undoubtedly surround the decision-making process, the goals reached will depend on the ability to make decisions and carry them through. Since not everyone will support each decision, decision-makers are required to enforce decisions. This decision-making process test is a focal point upon which interlibrary coordination is balanced.

Extending interlibrary coordination also means surrendering some

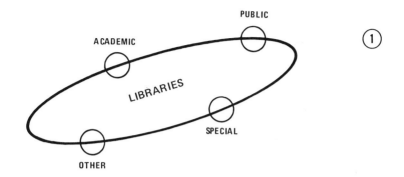

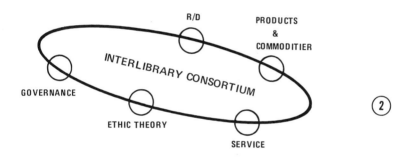

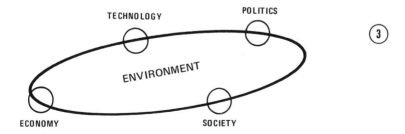

Figure 7.

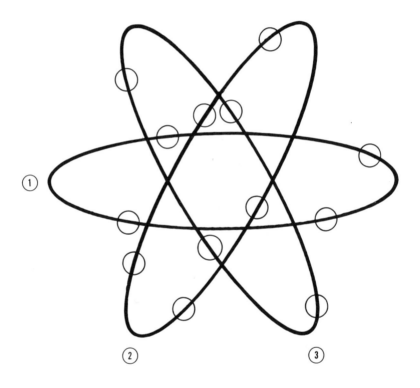

Figure 8.

local autonomy. Just how much autonomy is to be surrendered depends on many factors. What is to be achieved will often determine how much must be surrendered. Commitment, responsibility, and accountability are the important interlibrary coordination factors. Interlibrary decisions must always be tailored to the consortium's mission and goals statement. Considerations to assure decision success are, for example:

1. A precise definition of the consortium.
2. Initial and future participant contribution.
3. Initial equity position and clauses for modifying it.
4. Performance clauses and measurement criteria.
5. Governance structure composition and function.
6. Gain and loss distribution and handling.[25]

Interlibrary Goals Are Intellectually Bound

Different environments contribute toward developing different values and different priorities. Not only is it difficult to identify goals, but it is more difficult for individuals within groups to agree on the arrangement of priorities of such goals. Whereas it may be shown that group decisions are not necessarily better than the decisions made by individuals, groups offer opportunities to intellectualize, discuss, and confront issues with colleagues and clients. While this is not an exclusive group function, it guarantees a broad stage for developing ideas and analysis. What is to be achieved is bound by the members' ability to initiate and identify their thoughts about goals, to assign priorities to them, and to be imaginative and innovative. Thinking beyond traditional means, creating new goals, as well as discovering new ways to reach old goals, are in large part a responsibility associated with extending interlibrary coordination.

Interlibrary Goals Are Market Bound

The market activity of buying and selling library services and commodities is a major business of interlibrary consortia. The consortia which have the authority for representing a number of libraries and are empowered to negotiate contracts for library services and commodities also act as brokers. A program to extend interlibrary coordination recognizes the increasing need for libraries to use brokers to obtain necessary library services and commodities at lower prices than could be obtained by the individual members.

Straton discovered that market conditions will influence the number of consortia and their characteristics.[26] Studies in the banking, automobile manufacturing, petroleum, and chemical industries showed that intensive technology consortia were more enduring because of the markets in which they operate.

One of the most tenuous relationships exists between the member and the interlibrary consortium. A commitment to another based only on economics makes for a frivolous and brief relationship. The consortium that loses contact with the market will also lose member commitment, and may result in a separation. A comprehensive collegial involvement between the two (consortium and member) will contribute toward a relationship with more than materialistic objectives. Commitment to each other often leads to success. An interlibrary coordination program assumes that the desire, responsibility, and need to build an ethic is stronger than immediate self-interest. Members must contribute as much as the consortium.

Economics

Economic factors have led to the development of interlibrary consortial activity. Several of the most important reasons given for joining interlibrary cooperatives are:

- The rising rate of inflation.
- Current and anticipated reductions of library budgets.
- Changes among publishers, dealers, and service agents affecting costs.

The rising rate of inflation needs little commentary. For institutions where built-in inflation adjustments exist as part of the budget planning, appropriation, and allocation process, the task is easier. There, management's main task is to keep the balance of cost stable so that one category of costs cannot overwhelm the mean inflationary activity for that area. Library directors saw this problem type develop early in the 60's, hence the rise of cooperatives focused on union listing and interlibrary periodical lending.

Budget reductions motivated librarians to seek alternative means through cooperatives for maintaining service levels in austerity. Some have grasped this as a time to turn adversity into advantage by focusing cooperative activity on enhancing services and products as well. Difficulties are seen to develop, however, since state level controlling agents view approval for instituting enhancements as an issue separate from planning to maintain current service levels. Without prior approval for identified enhancements, unlikely in an austere environment, library expense reduction through cooperative contracts is viewed as reasonable.

Librarians are moving toward greater cooperative activity involvement to reduce costs. In the process, they are discovering ways to enhance current service level and reduce annual cost increase rate. Unfortunately, we have others demanding current level spending reduction without reference to enhancements or future cost levels except as they relate to current activity definitions. This behavior is understandable. Time and lack of clear information constraints restrict decision-makers' ability to evaluate all relevant demands and resources. Budget process identification of long-range goals and priorities is discouraged, since it introduces conflict among organizations otherwise agreeable to specific action courses.[27] We need to explain widely *why* library service and products should be enhanced, how it can be done, and at what cost and benefit, a story that should emerge from interlibrary consortia.

Drake indicated that labor costs were a major problem.[28] She supported her statement with an example citing Big Ten university library budgets. With no annual labor productivity increase, these libraries required an increasing portion of university budget appropriations from the mid-1960s thru the 1970s, a trend that must be reversed if libraries are to survive the austere 1980s.[29] Evidence of reversal, that greater productivity is possible without labor force increase, is beginning to emerge.

This is demonstrated, for example, in the California State University systemwide library development program and may be traced in the history of the CSU library services staffing formulas which show that since the CSU Board of Trustees approved the library automation project in 1972/73, the staffing formulas associated with the technical processing cost centers were reduced from 1.0 full-time equivalent position for each 850 volumes added to 1.0 FTE position for each 1,160 volumes added, a reduction of 25 per cent. Put in another context, this has resulted in a cumulative reduction since 1972/73 of 602.8 technical processing positions or $8,201,237 by June 1980.[30] This may be viewed as a classic example of technological economies of scale resulting in lower unit costs associated with computer-supported cataloging functions. In this isolated example the investment of $918,000 was more than justified.

The same level of returns is not to be expected for other capitalizations and applications of advanced library technology. It is apparent, however, that it will become increasingly necessary to identify where the return on an investment will be realized and in what terms. Presumably such will be equated at some point in dollars and compared to the traditional cost. There may even be controversy over the manner in which the return on an investment is evaluated and where the return value is assessed. Ultimately, it will come down to dollars and cents. An example of this may be found in the circulation cost center. The CSU automation circulation support program is costing approximately $3.5 million to implement. Of this amount, approximately $1.6 million was required to convert holdings information into machine readable form.[31] In view of the fact that the 19 CSU campuses range in size from

2,300 full-time equivalent students to 24,500, one may conclude that it is not likely that a return on the investment will be realized in the circulation cost center at the smaller campuses. Drake pointed out that libraries have high fixed costs which must be paid regardless of the output level or book use.[32] Therefore, to be cost effective in the cost center to which technology is applied, the new fixed cost must be no more than the traditional fixed cost. Five and possibly six of the nineteen CSU academic libraries will operate automated circulation systems that are not locally cost effective in the circulation cost center. Fortunately, however, assessment does not rest entirely on local or exclusive cost center criteria. A program to extend interlibrary coordination develops the institution and ethics to reconcile such issues.

Many academic libraries serve institutions that are too small to allocate sufficient funds to enable them to implement advanced library technology. In fact, many academic institutions are too small for their libraries to operate in areas where the economy of scale is to their advantage. The answer to this problem lies with the development of the interlibrary consortium. When a library such as described above is an integral part of a larger organization, the criteria which justify a large capital investment are measured against a broader base. The 19 CSU libraries function much like a corporate consortium; the return on the investment of automated circulation is justified by a systemwide population of over 231,000 FTE students. Thus, when compared to the traditional costs for providing circulation services systemwide, the scales balance. Additional returns are realized in such other cost centers as, for example, capital construction.

Technological Advances

Technological advances in support of the organization, storage, manipulation, and delivery of information are revolutionizing library service. Primarily, however, the impacts from library automation are being felt in the application areas affecting internal library operations. This is demonstrated by the rapid development of catalog, circulation, and acquisition support. The reference applications of bibliographic searching, along with greater sophistication and interconnection with other applications, promise even further functional enhancements. The total electric library is very close at hand, providing someone pays the electric bill. The theoretical and academic problems, however, have not yet been solved. Information cannot be described and analyzed and categorized with sufficient accuracy to avoid the redundancy in academic research, a long sought after goal of information transfer.

Librarians are not seen as active participants in the procurement of information. They don't produce information. They are viewed as housekeepers, organizers, or managers of information responsible and accountable for the advances made in the technology affecting its management. In addition, it is logical to assume that they are also responsible for the institutions developed to manage information, as well as being the curators and architects of the surrounding ethic.

Technological advances and economic conditions are responsible for the development of modern library consortia. The consortia rose amidst modern technology and current economic conditions that changed the environment surrounding academic libraries. Informal cooperation generally associated with interlibrary lending gave way in the 1970's to a much more substantial form of cooperation. Technological advances provided libraries with new tools to cope with rising service and economic demands in the cataloging, circulation, acquisition, and reference functions. A new era for interlibrary consortia began in 1971 with the establishment of OCLC. No longer were loan and resource sharing the principal reasons for interlibrary activity. Informal agreements were replaced with business contracts while promises of cost effectiveness were increasingly supported. OCLC provided libraries with a working model. It redefined the meaning of interlibrary cooperation in terms of *coordinated* activity. Three elements of library development were brought together:

- Technology,
- Economics, and
- Coordination

Barbara Evans Markuson described this time as the beginning of a social revolution wherein libraries cannot return to the conditions as they existed only a few years earlier.[33]

During this same period, the nation's economy turned significantly downward impacting library funding and affecting almost every part of the library. A review of the literature as well as current events shows a national trend to prohibit deficit spending, limit taxes, and reduce the number of public employees.[34]

The effect this will have on academic libraries if alternative methods are not implemented is difficult to assess clearly. Miriam A. Drake, in her article, "The Economics of Library Networks,"[35] cites evidence to suggest that in less than ten years or by 1990 the annual proportional level of state support for education will drop by approximately ten per cent. That is to say, where now approximately 43 per cent of the state's expenditures are directed toward education, only 33 per cent will be so directed ten years later.[36] An information-dependent society simply cannot and will not be well served by traditional methods. The questions that come to mind are: How will academic libraries be affected by the predicted economic crises, and what can be done about it? The answers to these two important questions should be closely related to the alternatives chosen to counter austerity.

Are the effects of an economic recession to be deflected by technology or by organization in the form of the interlibrary consortia? An interlibrary coordination extension program recognizes that the two alternatives are inseparable. The interlibrary consortium's "time has come." The modern library consortium cannot exist without networking supported by technology. The consortium represents the leading edge of library practice and theory. Markuson suggested[37] two economic assaults could destroy networking, and I would include the consortium as well, because without networking the current coordinated model ceases to exist. She said in effect that the first crisis would have to be so severe as to eliminate totally library funding, and I believe we need to act as though this would not occur. The second crisis would set into motion severe reductions in library budgets. The second crisis is already upon many libraries and their funding will likely fall faster than the economy. Undoubtedly, the consortium will survive current austerity stresses because individual library austerity will enlarge and strengthen consortia.

References

1. *Webster's Third New International Dictionary of the English Language Unabridged* (Springfield, Mass.: G. & C. Merriam Company, 1976), p. 485.
2. Richard Straton, *Organizational Characteristics of Consortia in Intensive Technology Industries.* (Ph. D. dissertation, University of Southern California, August 1982), p. 150.
3. Brenda White, "Cooperatives and Networks: A Preliminary Survey and Suggested Sources of Information," *Networks for Networkers*, ed. Barbara Evans Markuson and Blanche Woolls (N.Y.: Neal-Schuman, 1980), pp. 320–21.
4. Straton, *op. cit.*, p. 62.
5. Websters, *op. cit.*, p. 501.
6. U.S. President's Science Advisory Committee. *Science, Government and Information: The Responsibility of the Technical Community and the Government in the Transfer of Information* [Weinberg Report] (Washington D.C.: USGPO, 1963).
7. U.S. Federal Council for Science and Technology. Committee on Scientific and Technical Information (COSATI) Panel on Information Analysis Centers. *Proceedings* (Gaithersburg, MD and Springfield, Virginia: National Technical Information Service Publ., 1967), p. iii.
8. Bonnie Carrol and Betty F. Maskewitz, "Information Analysis Centers," *Annual Review of Information Science and Technology*, ed. Martha E. Williams (N.Y.: Knowledge Industry Publications, 1980), Vol. 15, p. 151.
9. W. B. Cottrell and G. S. Simpson Jr., *Proceedings of the First Ad Hoc Forum on Scientific and Technical Information Analysis Center Managers, Directors and Professional Analysts* (Conf. 651131) (Oak Ridge, Tennessee: U.S. Atomic Energy Commission, Division of Technical Information, National Technical Information Service, 1945).
10. Straton, *op. cit.*, p. 179.
11. Lee Adler and James D. Hlavacek, *Joint Ventures for Product Innovation* (N.Y.: Amacom, A Division of American Management Association, 1976), p. 26.

12. Ibid., p. 27.
13. Straton, *op. cit.*, p. 157.
14. Daniel Katz and Robert L. Kahn, *The Social Psychology of Organizations* (N.Y.: John Wiley and Sons, 1978), p. 26.
15. Anthony Downs, *Inside Bureaucracy* (Boston: Little, Brown, 1967), p. 174.
16. Adler, *op. cit.*, p. 37.
17. Fritz H. Grupe, *Managing Interinstitutional Change* (Potsdam, N.Y.: Associated Colleges of the St. Lawrence Valley, 1975), p. 15.
18. William B. Rouse and Sandra B. Rouse, *Management of Library Networks, Policy Analysis Implementation and Control* (N.Y.: Wiley, 1980), pp. 20–26.
19. Ibid., p. 21.
20. Ibid., p. 22.
21. Ibid., p. 23.
22. Ibid., p. 25.
23. Ibid., p. 26.
24. Louise Darling, "Changes in Information Delivery Since 1960 in Health Science Libraries," *Library Trends* 23 (November 1974), pp. 31–62.
25. Adler, *op. cit.*, p. 25.
26. Straton, *op. cit.*, p. 27.
27. A. Wildavasky, "Comprehensive vs. Incremental Budgeting in the Department of Agriculture," *Administrative Science Quarterly* 10:3 (December 1965), p. 321.
28. Miriam A. Drake, "The Economics of Library Networks," *Networks for Networkers*, ed. Barbara Evans Markuson and Blanche Woolls (N.Y.: Neal-Schuman, 1980), pp. 211–243.
29. Ibid., p. 222.
30. William Mason and Thomas C. Harris, "Library Staffing Formulas in CSUC Libraries," A report to the Joint Legislative Budget Committee (Long Beach: The California State University and Colleges, 1981), p. 9.
31. The California State University and Colleges, *The Trustees Library Development Program, Trustee Support Budget, FY 1977/78–1981–82*, (Long Beach, CA.). An annual document, unpublished and unpaged.
32. Drake, *op. cit.*, p. 222.
33. Barbara Evans Markuson, "Revolution and Evolution: Critical Issues in Library Network Development," *Networks for Networkers*, ed. Barbara Evans Markuson and Blanche Woolls (N.Y.: Neal-Schuman, 1980), pp. 5–6.
34. Adam Clymer, *Tax Revolt: An Idea Whose Time Has Come* (New York: Times National Economy Survey, June 7, 1979), p. 3.
35. Drake, *op. cit.*, p. 219.
36. Norman C. Saunders, "The U.S. Economy to 1990: Two Projections for Growth," *Monthly Labor Review* 101 (December 1978), pp. 36–46.
37. Markuson, *op. cit.*, p. 7.

4. Revitalization of Academic Library Programs Through Creative Fund-Raising

Peter Spyers-Duran

THE CHOICE between operative poverty and relative affluence may be determined by the academic library's ability to increase outside support level. "Outside support" includes any enhancement received beyond the institutional library budget. It can take many forms: gifts in funds or material, monetary contributions, volunteer programs, and grants. This chapter will discuss support sources and suggest practical methods of increasing outside funding level. Almost all American and Canadian academic libraries enjoy some degree of outside support. Its extent is difficult to estimate, however. The only information available is found in specific categories such as foundation and federal government grants. Parent institution operating budgets have provided the largest percentage of library funds in the past. As these funds have decreased, an accompanying erosion has impacted the material budget beyond other expense categories. Table 1 shows the academic book and periodical price index to have outpaced that for salaries, services and supplies. Dollar erosion exerted both a short- and long-term effect on ability to meet institutional needs. Before short-term solutions can be addressed, the extent of additional funds needed to restore equilibrium must be calculated. A National Commission on Libraries and Information Science (NCLIS) report estimated that academic libraries needed to supplement their $1 billion expenditure level with an additional $621 million (or $134,473 per library) to achieve minimum service level.[1]

Each library must evaluate its circumstances before developing an outside support program. Realistic and almost achievable goals should be established and adjusted in subsequent years. After four to five years of effort a library may show a respectiable amount of outside support which can be helpful in fighting austerity. "There is no doubt that most academic libraries are hard pressed financially," Haas said. He continued:

Table 1. Higher Education Price Indexes: 1965 to 1980

[1967 = 100. For years ending June 30. Reflects prices paid by colleges and universities]

YEAR	Index, total	Average annual percent change	PERSONNEL COMPENSATION				CONTRACTED SERVICES, SUPPLIES, AND EQUIPMENT					
			Total	Professional salaries	Nonprofessional salaries	Fringe benefits	Total	Services	Supplies and materials	Equipment	Books, periodicals	Utilities
1965	91	43	89	89	94	78	96	95	96	95	91	100
1970	121	59	124	121	118	146	111	113	106	111	121	104
1975	166	86	166	154	166	241	169	150	161	154	220	203
1980	238	99	232	202	243	409	261	202	239	216	364	409

Source: U.S. Bureau of the Census, Statistical Abstract of the United States, 1981, Washington, D.C., 1981, p. 164.

83

How are libraries accepting the gradually tightening belt? In some cases the approach is to maintain a myth of business as usual, which in fact means erosion in salaries and collections and a subtle deterioration of overall library performance. Others will face up to the problem by cutting hours, consciously reducing acquisitions in specific areas, and hedging on the quality of binding. But such actions simply defer the day of reckoning and that is clear to those that are responsible for providing the funds.[2]

Eaton offered academic librarians a positive approach to the age of austerity:

What is the university librarian to do under these circumstances? He should certainly not be expected to apologize for the fact that libraries cost money; he is no more responsible for this than the graduate dean is responsible for increases in the research budget. He should continue to look for ways to reduce costs through such means as relying on other collections for highly specialized materials, using cataloging information developed by the Library of Congress . . . and experimenting with other cooperative ventures. He should hope that his institution will scrutinize its academic program to bring it in line with anticipated resources. Also, he should consider the possibility of raising some money from outside sources for library support.[3]

Institutions appear to guard information jealously about outside support activities. Certain private institutions are concerned about competition or the protection of privacy. Publicly funded institutions may fear that publicity will result in institutional appropriations being reduced in some proportion to the outside funding received. It is common for a state legislature to announce that a tuition increase beyond the approved level in publicly assisted universities will result in legislative support reduction, dollar for dollar. While raising tuition may be the easiest way to generate additional funds, it is also the least imaginative.

Fund-Raising

Librarians have long been noted for their willingness to promote book gifts and encourage Friends of the Library support organizations. Eaton shares this viewpoint:

It is probably fair to say that the typical university librarian's attitude toward fund-riaising is that this is a responsibility which belongs primarily to others—the development office, the president and the board of trustees. The librarian has been willing and, in many cases, eager to work at the job of acquiring gifts of books, and he has devoted his time to friends of the library organizations in the hope of obtaining both collections and annual income from dues. But in seeking cash gifts he has hesitated to take the initiative, preferring to leave this job to others. When the development office suggests the names of prospective donors, the librarian responds by proposing appropriate projects. He may know a few donors who are keenly interested in the library and whose devotion is such that he feels free to approach them when special needs arise. But toward other prospects his role has been a passive one, influenced perhaps by the view that a librarian who devotes his time aggressively to raising money is straying outside his field. In some universities the development office has apparently encouraged this view, hoping to keep all fund-raising activities under tight central control.[4]

Exceptions to Eaton's generalizations have existed primarily among privately funded universities and colleges, but interest has been rising in many other institutions during the past decade. Further, several university school and departmental libraries have active fund-raising programs. American fund-raising has been elevated to professional status in recent years, to sophisticated persuasion, the skillful art of asking for a gift. A library interested in seeking significant outside support, as opposed to token donations, must carry out careful planning and preparation.

How do library staff members become familiar with productive fund-raising principles? A good start is to initiate a program to educate the key staff members in the fund-raising process. The bibliography provides a basic fund-raising reading list.[5] Reading should be followed by workshop attendance and discussion with other library fund-raisers, if possible. Workshops are given frequently in many cities by various commercial and public organizations.

During the staff development period, the library's fund-raising goals and plans should be discussed with the campus chief academic officer, development officer, president, and others. They can offer valuable suggestions and guidance. Coordination will minimize duplication and the embarrassment that occurs when the college president approaches a prospect for a $1 million gift, only to be told that she has just given the librarian a $10,000 contribution.

When the staff development period is finished, the Director must institute a planning process. An organization plan's success depends on management's ability to define *what* is desired, *why* it is desired, and by *whom*. A plan helps to achieve realistic goals in an orderly and timely manner. Clearly defined goals with deadlines for accomplishment help to avoid confusion and diversion.[6]

Development Team

The library's Development Team is a relatively new concept. The Director must establish a rational team size and type to achieve the desired results. The team must be motivated, educated, trained, and given specific contact assignments. The saying "it takes money to make money" applies here. Many libraries willing to invest in fund-raising staff have been pleased with the results. Lynden found among private university libraries:

Half of the libraries visited have designated an individual on their staff who is concerned with fund-raising. Two of the six are full-time staff members whose sole responsibility is fund-raising. The other four include an Assistant Director for Special Collections who is paid one-third by the Development Office; a half-time Assistant to the Director; a faculty member who works three quarter time; and a full-time position concerned with copyright, legal suits and governmental relations as well as fund-raising. In many institutions the Development Office has discouraged such a position. However, in all cases where the library had such a position there was close coordination with the university development office, and in one instance, the Library Development Officer is a librarian who spent an internship of two and a half years in the University Development Office prior to beginning work in the library. According to its proponents, use of library fund raisers has been most successful because library staff are best able to relate library conditions and expectations to potential donors. As one director put it: "Fund raisers cannot be as enthusiastic and knowledgeable as librarians."[7]

The Lynden survey described the growing trend to address fund-raising in an organized manner. It also depicted the staffing pattern and commitment in larger institutions. A number of state-supported institutions have followed this trend, among them, California State University, Long Beach.

Consultant

Since fund-raising is a specialized field, professional services should be considered. When and for what purpose should a library engage a professional consultant or fund-raising firm? Whenever the organization feels that an outside expert's advice is required. Most fund-raising efforts of $100,000 or more will benefit from outside advice. The consultant's role is not to raise money but to help the library raise it. A consultant is normally retained to perform one or more of these functions:

1. Conducting studies. The most common fund-raising study is a sophisticated form of market research. Sometimes called a feasibility study, it is designed to determine whether, in fact, the institution's specific long-and/or short-term development goals can be achieved.
2. Providing campaign management. Once it has been decided to conduct a campaign, professional counsel may be retained to manage the major portion of the campaign. This service typically includes provision of a full-time resident director and part-time supervision by an officer of the firm.
3. Consulting. Frequently in the period prior (which may also include the study period) or subsequent to a capital campaign, an organization requires professional fund-raising consulting services on a per-diem basis. These services

may focus on virtually any or every aspect of the institution's development efforts. Consulting is typically provided by an officer of the firm who works with the institution's administration, including the development officer and staff and related volunteers, usually trustees.[8]

The consultant or fund-raising firm should be selected by a careful screening process. The consultant's cost is secondary to what he/she can be expected to deliver. For this reason reputation and evidence of past performance must be evaluated. The consultant must gain a thorough grasp of the institution and the library.[9] In the selection process membership should be checked in the American Association of Fund-Raising Counsel (AAFRC). AAFRC members adhere to a fair practice code:

1. Member firms will serve only those nonprofit institutions or agencies whose purpose and methods they can approve. They will not knowingly be used by any organization to induce philanthropically inclined persons to give their money to unworthy causes.

2. Member firms do business only on the basis of a specified fee, determined prior to the beginning of the campaign. They will not serve clients on the unprofessional basis of a percentage or commission of the sums raised. They maintain this ethical standard also by not profiting, directly or indirectly, from disbursements for the accounts of clients.

3. The executive head of a member organization must demonstrate at least a six-year record of continuous experience as a professional in the fund-raising field. This helps to protect the public from those who enter the profession without sufficient competence, experience or devotion to ideals of public service.

4. The Association looks with disfavor upon firms which use methods harmful to the public, such as making exaggerated claims of past achievements, guaranteeing results, and promising to raise unobtainable sums.

5. No payment in cash or kind shall be made by a member to an officer, director, trustee, or adviser of a philanthropic agency or institution as compensation for using his influence for the engaging of a member for fund-raising counsel.[10]

In spite of consultants' availability, most academic libraries depend on local campus resources, but this may change as fund-raising becomes a natural program administration extension.

Annual Giving

Fund-raising employs three major designs to mobilize voluntary giving: annual giving, major gifts campaign, and special events. Annual gift campaigns stress the recurring need for income and can be set at any level. Typically, donors receive certain privileges, such as a one-year library card, a newsletter, and invitations to lectures, programs, open houses, and social events. These "perks" are geared to the level of the gift received and that can range from $5 to $10,000 or more. Pledges may be solicited which commit the donor to a minimum gift for a specific number of years.

Motivation is "the essential ingredient in generating substantial private philanthropy."[11] If a program is to be successful, the fund-raiser must motivate constituents not only to give but to give at increasingly higher levels. This need to motivate people is the basic premise for creating special gift clubs. Many librarians have fostered elements of this concept through Friends of the Library groups.[12]

Major Gifts

Unless it has a well established annual gift program, a library may not yet be ready to move into a major gifts campaign. Annual giving is the foundation for future major gifts. Academic institutions regularly soliciting varied gifts receive contributions from the same donors almost habitually. Major gift campaigns have better success when the appeal is made to an already "primed" donor group. It is also likely that certain small donors will become major contributors as the result of long-term institutional association. Of course, this association must be properly maintained over the years to keep interest level high.

At least four steps are necessary catalysts in a successful major gift campaign. First, prepare a comprehensive statement explaining the need for the major gift. If the campaign is to raise funds for a new library building, for example, compelling reasons must be presented to support facility construction. Second, conduct a random sample survey of students, faculty, alumni, trustees, and knowledgeable friends regarding need perceptions. If the majority react negatively, the major gift campaign may run into difficulty.

Third, after positive survey feedback, select the major gift campaign chairperson. This individual should be a respected community or campus member and, preferably, a generous campaign donor. The fourth step requires the institution to assess the need for an outside consultant. It is important to involve past donors and Friends of the Library members in the drive.

Special Events

Special events provide limitless opportunities for libraries interested in raising money or generating goodwill. Since special events create an additional staff workload, it is especially desirable to use outside volunteer help and the Library Friends. Examples of special events are lecture series, exhibit series, book reviews, dinners, and open houses. Innovative ideas, such as a library-sponsored tour of China or the Caribbean, have been offered successfully. Several useful fund-raising books are available also.[13-16]

Foundation Grantsmanship

Librarians seriously committed to fighting austerity and creating opportunities beyond institutional support level should not overlook foundation grants. A grant is "a requested subsidy from a public or private source for a specific purpose."[17] One must understand the difference between a gift and a grant. A gift is given by an individual or a family and is associated with emotional philanthropy, demonstrated need, or personal vanity. An example would be funds given to the library in memory of a family member, sometimes designated for use in a specified subject area. Personal vanity is evidenced when the donor requests his or her name on a bookplate or even on a building if warranted by a large gift.

Most grants are based on formal proposals submitted to granting agencies. They are given in support of program enhancement, experimentation, or innovation. Usually, grants are evaluated by trustees or a committee, making grantor and grant seeker interaction quite impersonal.

A foundation is a well-funded organization with a program objective to aid the educational, social or charitable activities maintained by other non-profit organizations. It may be private and non-governmental, or governmental and tax-supported. The Ford Foundation is an example of a private fundation, while the National Science Foundation is a governmental grant-making body.

The standard reference work on the larger private foundations is *The Foundation Directory*.[18] Smaller foundations number 19,000, and brief entries for them are found in the *National Data Book*.[19] They are often overlooked by librarians. In addition, the *Chronicle of Higher Education* lists grants to libraries regularly. The Foundation Center reported the average 1980 grant to range from $48,603 for the larger to $3,443 for the smaller foundation.[20]

Buckman gives an interesting historical overview of libraries as grant recipients:

[T]he total amount given for libraries and related activities—slightly more than $202 million—is larger than expected. On the other hand, the total amount of federal grants appropriated for libraries during the period 1957–72 was about $1.3 billion, according to the American Library Association. Thus foundation support was hardly negligible, but amounted to less than one-sixth of the funds from federal sources. Many of the foundation grants were for special purposes, and not open to general application; for example they were limited to certain localities or had other qualifications attached to them. Federal grants were necessarily administered on a broad, egalitarian basis.

On the average, foundations gave about $15 million a year for libraries, which is about 1 percent of total foundation giving for all purposes for a given year. If total foundation giving for "education" (broadly defined) is used as a base, all gifts to libraries amount to about 2 percent of the total.

It is encouraging to note that there is a fairly steady upward curve with respect to the number of grants to libraries within the United States.[21]

Figure 1 shows foundation giving for libraries to have remained at 2 per cent of the total disbursed during 1980 (See Appendix I for a sample 1981 grant list). The infusion of federal grants appropriated to libraries during the 1970's has now been vastly reduced. For this rea-

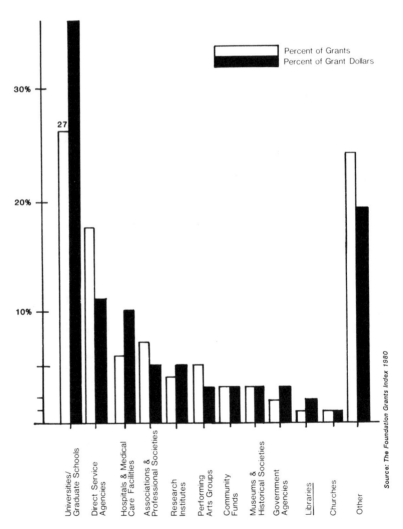

Figure 1. Grant Recipients

son, foundation funding faces enormous competition, but foundations lack the resources to pick up the slack left by discontinued federal funds. No more than one request in ten may receive funding.

"In the competitive world of academic grant-seeking, good ideas are not enough," wrote Perry.[22] Foundations look for three "basic" qualities when reviewing grant proposals: "the significance of the problem being addressed, the quality of the proposed solution, and the track records of the people in the project."[23]

Even when these qualities are present, the proposal will fail if it falls outside the foundation's interests. The need to study the foundation thoroughly before preparing a grant request cannot be over-emphasized. "Grant seekers must do their homework," wrote Thaler.[24] The foundation must be researched and identified as the one most likely to be interested in the proposal.

Thaler identified the following points to be researched:

a. The *correct name* of the foundation, key individuals and contact persons.
b. A *brief foundation history*. Information about where, when, and why it was incorporated.
c. The *purpose* is needed to help match the proposal with the correct foundation.
d. The size and number of *grants* made in a recent year. This information can show whether or not the proposal will seem reasonable in terms of past funding levels.
e. *Geographical limitations,* if any. Certain foundations restrict giving to specific areas. Review the past giving pattern in case of doubt.
f. The *key decision makers*. It is helpful to know who they are and their special interests.
g. *Prior gifts or grants* to the institution may impact on the proposal. The grant writer should know their circumstances and outcome. If there was no prior grant, the grant record to similar institutions may be helpful to know.[25,26]

The Foundation Center

Information basic to all grantseekers is available through the Foundation Center's publications and services. The Center's functions and operation mode are as follows:

The Center gathers and disseminates factual information on the philanthropic foundations through programs of library service, publication, and research. It has organized a nationwide network of foundation reference collections for free public use. These collections fall within three basic categories. The four reference libraries operated by the Center offer the widest variety of user services and the most comprehensive collections of foundation materials, including all of the Center's publications, books, services and periodicals on foundations and philanthropy, and foundation annual reports, newsletters, and press clippings. The New York and Washington, D.C. libraries contain the IRS returns for all currently active private foundations in the U.S. The Cleveland and San Francisco libraries contain the IRS records for those foundations in the midwestern and western states, respectively. The cooperating collections generally contain IRS records for only those foundations within their state, although they may request information or copies of other records from the New York library.[27]

A list of 105 cooperative collections is given in Appendix II. The Foundation Center assists in chosing the appropriate foundation by publishing useful reference books. It makes available the directories, grant indexes, and guides, listed in Appendix III.

Additional Center services are available exclusively through a membership program called The Associates which is open to any individual or organization for a $250 annual fee. Services include:

   a. Access to reference specialists who retrieve requested information. The membership fee includes ten calls or two and a half hours of reference work per month. Additional service is charged at a $25 per hour rate.
   b. Access to computerized foundation files. This service includes subject search copy of COMSEARCH Printouts. Seventy nine subject categories are useful in identifying the foundations most likely to be interested in a given proposal.
   c. Associates can request on-line computer searches custom designed to satisfy specific needs. The search can encompass all 22,000 plus foundation listings, including the smaller and lesser-known local sources. A member may request specialized information, such as a list of foundations which have made 1981 grants of $1,000 or more for California library building renovation. Computer searches tapping commercial data bases such as DIALOG and SDC may be made for a fee, also.
   d. Perhaps the most valuable part of the Associates program is early access to the most current Foundation information, not available otherwise.

Before submitting a grant proposal, the depth of research needed must be determined. In this respect, there is no substitute for grant-seeker experience, patience, and persistence. The researcher must understand thoroughly the variables in the grant application process. Grants are not necessarily given to proposals submitted through normal channels. For example, a foundation may be seeking a university to implement one of its own ideas or it may decide to support a new interest field or another specialized field. Or the foundation may invite a proposal based on certain ideas that emerged during grantseeker discussions with staff members. Although foundation criteria for funding proposals may vary, the proposal's relevance to the foundation's interest is paramount. Grant proposal writing is an art which must be mastered through reading, study and practice.

Corporate Grantsmanship

There are two corporate funding program types. One is the corporate foundation which, like other foundations, is subject to Internal Revenue Service regulations. In such foundations, company executive influence may be strongly reflected. The second type is a corporate philanthropic activity often referred to as a "contribution program." In 1980, U.S. corporations gave $696 million to higher education.[28] Corporations rarely publicize their contribution programs, but many corporations give 50–60 per cent of their contributions to the local United Way and other charities.[29]

While not all corporations adhere to the same contribution guidelines, often they reflect the same "principle of usage." For instance, corporations tend to support those universities from which they recruit employees or those that engage in research relevant to their industry. This "usage" principle may also apply to the campus library. The fundraiser may capitalize on the corporation by allowing its employees to use the library. Often an encounter with corporation employees, such as chief engineer or legal counsel, in the library can provide the contact needed for an introduction to the corporate giving director.

Larger corporations may use top management committees to decide general contribution policy which is then carried out by the appropriate department—public relations, public affairs, corporate relations, community affairs, or corporate communications. In smaller corporations, contribution decisions may be made by the president or the board of directors.

Only 20 per cent of U.S. corporations participate in "corporate giving." For this reason alone this area has a growth potential for library program support. "Very few colleges and universities are putting enough emphasis on corporate support," explained Grenzebach.[30] After analysing 1,561 institutions, Grenzebach concluded that few campuses had anyone with a suitable background in corporate profit-making objectives and complex marketing problems assigned to corporate fund-raising. To overcome this deficiency he suggested a six-prong action:

a. Appoint an aggressive individual with the ability to effectively present and articulate the college or university's case.
b. Target the corporations most likely to support the programs presented.
c. Cultivate the corporate prospects before they are solicited. Arrange a campus visit for key corporate officers, bring

them to the library and demonstrate how it can help the corporation.

d. Present a simple and direct proposal, one that is realistic and within the institution's ability to implement the stated objectives.

e. Following the donation, reward the corporation in various ways: provide follow up information about project results and recognize the philanthropy publicly.

f. Recognize the corporate officers who made the gift possible.

Most corporate giving patterns are conservative. Some prefer only minimal publicity for the contribution. A publicly held corporation must consider stockholders' interests. Typically, philanthropic programs are not a high company priority. Companies want their giving to have impact in the communities where their own employees reside. Corporations also maintain a low contribution profile because they fear an influx of requests. It may be easier to approach a corporation than a foundation. A plant manager may be the appropriate local contact person if no local corporate office is nearby.

Companies can also be abundant goods and services sources. A company may provide advice in an area that a library would normally have under outside contract. The loan of a computer programmer to establish a simple mini-computer accounting system, or a draftsman to assist with a rare book room remodelling project are service donation illustrations. Creative corporate solicitation should include both cash and gifts in kind.

Corporate Employee Gift Matching

Nearly 700 corporations support educational programs by matching employee gifts, up to a specified dollar level. The Council for the Advancement and Support of Education (CASE) serves as the national college and university clearinghouse for information on corporate gift-matching programs. These programs are designed to encourage employees to support higher institutions. The program assures that some portion of the corporate support dollar reaches those educational institutions which hold significant employee interest. Most corporate executives like the matching gift's "challenge" aspect since the beneficiary is involved in the fund-raising effort.

Most families have members currently or formerly enrolled in a college or university. While a non-college educated employee may not personally feel motivated to give to a relative's college, that employee may appreciate the corporation's higher education assistance. The best known library matching gift program is an early one—that of Andrew Carnegie of public library fame.[31]

Alumni associations have long known matching programs' stimulating effects. However, two misconceptions need to be clarified: the first is that only alumni associations can be involved in them. That is untrue; libraries can also participate. A joint alumni office/library program can produce attractive results. The second is that an employee can support only an institution attended previously. This, too, is untrue. Any college or university can be named the gift beneficiary.

A library may also conduct its own independent matching gift campaign. Advise Friends of the Library members, external library card holders, and past donors that their future library contributions can be doubled if their employers will match their gifts. Local bookstores, printers, binders, and publishers of all kinds may be interested in participating. A descriptive article in the library's newsletter or a promotional mailer to the audience can start the program. However, an independent program must not lead to poor coordination and communication with other appropriate campus offices. The Library's fund raiser will find the Council for Financial Aid to Education (CFAE) publication series useful here.[32]

Friends of the Library Organization

U.S. library development is closely tied to private gifts, both in publicly and privately supported institutions. Harvard and Yale demonstrate this tradition.[33] However, the organized "Friends of the Library" movement is a recent development. Harvard is credited with establishing the first university library Friends group in 1925.

By 1930 there were emulative friends groups at Columbia, Yale, Princeton, and Johns Hopkins, and the number grew substantially during the next four decades. While the process of growth has been substantial, it has undergone fluctuations; there has been a fairly high mortality rate among friends groups. The number swells during periods of poor library funding. . . .[34]

Gwyn found that 28 per cent of the Friends groups had been established after 1970. "It seems that many libraries, feeling financial pressures, are looking for ways to supplement their budgets".[35] Surprisingly, only 56 per cent of the academic libraries surveyed had Friends groups. Should an academic library establish a Friends group? Mixer wrote:

The question indicated above could well be asked (in fact should be asked) by the college librarian and college president at any collegiate institution which has not as yet established a Friends group. The answer to the question may well turn out to be "yes"—not only for benefits that can accrue internally for the college but also because institutions are under some obligation to help in the locating and the preserving for scholarly use of rarities which are part of the nation's heritage.[36]

Gwyn revealed academic library Friends group objectives:

Thirty-seven university libraries responded to this question. Sixty percent said that both fund-raising and developing support for the library were purposes of their groups, and two mentioned advising the administration as well. Developing support for the library (25 percent), fund-raising (9 percent), and acquiring funds and gifts for special collections (30 percent), were given as sole objectives. Other objectives mentioned were "promote culture," "promote town-gown relations," and "sponsor exhibits and lectures."[37]

It is clear that Friends groups carry on diverse activities and require leadership and direction. The library administration must guide and direct this group's energies in the areas appropriate for effective library development. Often this means providing secretariat service for the group, usually located in the special collections department. The Friends can be expected to be especially active in assisting with the special collections exhibit program. Friends officers may wish to participate in American LIbrary Association Friends activities.[38]

The Friends of the Free Library of Philadelphia have developed a seven-point checklist applicable to any proposed activity. At least one of the following criteria must be met: "Raise money, spotlight library services, spotlight library needs, gain new members, serve the community, engender community spirit or influence political action."[39] An academic library can employ these criteria quite well. Evaluating proposed activities based on predetermined criteria is useful in keeping the group on its desired track.

Friends organizations have another beneficial function in publicly supported institutions. Gift acceptance by the Friends organization rather than the library itself can mean the difference between being locked into inflexible regulations or being free to use the gift for the greatest benefit. For example, certain state university libraries cannot sell state-owned property. Gifts which they accept become state property and are subject to state agency red tape. Gifts held by the Friends are exempt from these regulations. Consequently, certain gifts no longer useful may be sold.

The California State University/Fullerton Library demonstrates such support versatility. Here the Friends operate the Library's public coin-operated copy machines. The revenue realized from the machines is used to supplement institutional library support. Were the copy machines owned by the library (and therefore by the state), the revenue generated would be severely limited or even lost to the library. In addition, an active Friends group can serve as a conduit to other community individuals with a library support interest. Not to be neglected are local book collector's clubs which may meet in the library's special collections department. Adelphi University has hosted the Long Island Book Collector's Club in recent years.

Gift and Exchange Program

A substantial material gift program must function on at least two levels. The first is the unusual or highly valuable gift. In most instances, these items represent a notable library addition. Often academic libraries announce such gifts in *C&RL News*. Lesser or mixed gifts comprise the second level. They may or may not be added to the collection. Unwanted items may be sold and the proceeds used to purchase needed items. As the critical contact person for donors, the gift and exchange librarian should be involved with the Friends group. Gift solicitation and fund-raising are closely related activities. The special collections or gift and exchange librarian should prepare a list of community persons and institutions with collections of correspondence or printed material of research and library interest.

The gift and exchange librarian may be asked for advice in finding a knowledgable appraiser or for tax guidance on charitable deductions. The library's acceptance policies greatly influence gift volume and flow. Many libraries have the policy that gift material is accepted with the understanding that upon receipt it is owned by the university which reserves the right to determine retention, location, and disposition. This "no strings" policy provides library protection. The ability to sell, exchange, or add gift material is an important component in the library's total effort to maximize outside support usefulness.

Many librarians believe that a gift should not be accepted unless the library intends to keep most or all of it. This approach, however, presents several problems. A librarian must be available to review all proposed gifts when they are offered. This may cause inconvenience because gift offers are unpredictable and most donations have a sense of urgency associated with them. The donor wishes not to deal with a librarian who will chose only a few items and then leave the rest; rather, she/he wants the entire gift taken.

A selective gift acceptance policy makes it difficult to maximize Friends memberships to solicit material gifts. An attorney normally in a position to solicit library gifts through wills will seldom recommend a library with a "pick and choose" acceptance policy. Such a library will be by-passed, *even* for valuable donations. Donors simply assume that the library will turn them down and, fearing rejection, they will go elsewhere. A liberal gift acceptance policy may result in modest being followed by valuable gifts. Donors should be praised for their thoughtfulness and invited to join the Friends group. The donation of even a small gift can turn eventually into a major support program.

Lane presented a chapter on disposing of unwanted material in which he recommended considering sale, exchange, give-away, or throw-away.[40] Sale may be to a book dealer, the general public, student body, or other libraries. The Friends group may assist with book sales. Libraries have reported sales events yielding $200 to $5,000. Several libraries maintain a lobby or browsing area "sale" shelf for student use, Stanford University and California State University/Long Beach, being among them. This shelf provides a steady income and encourages students to own and even collect books.

"Exchange is a useful way to dispose of duplicates as well as other unwanted material such as books in subject areas not collected by the library."[41] Libraries concerned with international acquisition will find many interested exchange partners.[42] Costly procedures can make the exchange program difficult to justify economically, however.

Giving away unwanted material is widely practiced. Because space costs money, librarians should consider reducing unnecessary and excessive material storage by exchange or discard. Many libraries do not discard material because they fear a public outcry if discovered. Third world colleges and domestic prisons and community service agencies have become popular disposal places. The throwaway category can also yield income if the material is suitable for recycling.

Volunteers

Few libraries use volunteers to supplement regular employees to the same extent as hospitals and YMCAs. Perhaps one reason is that part-time students represent an inexpensive and readily available labor force. Another reason is that campuses and their libraries are viewed as a major student employment source. The federal government has reinforced this notion with its Federal Work Study Program. However, as work study funds diminish and campus budgets shrink, it is realistic to consider volunteers.

A library considering volunteer use must examine the commitment closely. Their recruitment, training, and supervision will require time and patience from the paid staff. Certain volunteers do not want a mundane task; if interest is not matched by an appropriate assignment, the volunteer may drop out. After all, his/her primary reward comes from enjoying the designated work. Before developing a large scale volunteer program, a library should consider the necessary investment and the potential payoff. Certain retired library staff members may be interested in volunteer work.

A wide range of volunteer work assignments can be made, for example

    a. Public service areas: desk attendant, information assistant
    b. Clerical service: typing, telephone service
    c. Public-relations: newsletters, publication design
    d. Special collections processing and material solicitation
    e. Computer programming
    f. Fund-raising
    g. Advisory board service

Volunteer use for fund-raising and advisory board functions is widely accepted. However, resistance and confrontation can develop as plans mature for volunteer use elsewhere. Most full-time employees regard volunteers as inferior and undependable. Hospitals separate nurses and volunteers. Unions sometimes object since volunteers replace paid workers. Clearly defined and articulated policies regarding the volunteer's role are necessary to eliminate undue concern, resistance, and confrontation.[43,44]

Utilizing Free and Inexpensive Material to Fight Austerity

United States government documents, state documents, books, newspapers, and many journals can be obtained with little or no acquisition cost from sources known to most librarians. Foreign consulates and embassies are often willing to donate useful current information about their country, also. Subject matter may range widely, but propaganda aimed at U.S. audiences must be avoided. Useless material may be minimized by a carefully structured negotiation about what is available.

This can best be achieved by writing a formal letter to the embassy or consulate cultural affairs officer. Describe academic programs that would benefit from material available from the officer's country, and invite the officer to lunch with the president and other administrators to discuss a range of cultural exchange opportunities that the institution would like to pursue. The cultural officer is a broker between the local institution and the foreign institutions concerned with disseminating information, performing arts, music, literary material, etc. The Los Angeles Canadian Consulate and California State University/Long Beach, have such a program. Following library visits the consulate arranged to deposit a Canadian Broadcasting Corporation music recording collection there. Canadian lecturers and performers are guided to the campus, also.

Surplus Property

Federal government excess property can be a valuable source of free or inexpensive items. Typewriters, office machines, telecommunications equipment, computers, calculators, desks, storage units, and vehicles are just a few of the items available. Of course, item availability may not coincide with immediate institutional need, so long-range planning and patience are required for surplus property program participation. Property condition may range from worn out to brand new. A persistent manager is likely to find many useful bargains offered.

The Federal Property and Administration Services Act of 1949, as amended, constitutes the basis for the surplus property program and is administered by the General Services Administration (GSA), specifically, the Federal Property Resources Services (FPRS).[45] A library can obtain surplus items by participating in regional GSA office competitive bid property sales or in the GSA property donation program. A library interested in receiving sales catalogs and announcements should file a mailing list application with the nearest FPRS office (See Appendix IV).

Each state has one or more GSA surplus distribution centers which handle donations to qualified public or private non-profit tax-exempt institutions, including all colleges and universities. "FPRS allocates surplus property among the states on a fair and equitable basis and each state provides for the fair and equitable distribution of surplus property to eligible donees within its bountries."[46] Most states charge a service and handling fee for property issued. Surplus property is distributed by all government levels, including cities and counties.

One of the most promising private developments in the surplus industrial resources area is the establishment of the National Association for the Exchange of Industrial Resources (NAEIR). It solicits manufacturers for donations based on requests filed by member academic institutions. During 1982 NAEIR expects to receive and distribute $10 million worth of merchandise donated by businesses.[47] A not-for-profit organization, NAEIR charges an annual membership fee, and members pay shipping charges, also. Since NAEIR does not pay transportation, certain companies deliver their gifts directly to the receiving institution. The Association sends members an occasional inventory list and also fills requests for specific equipment or supply items. In 1981 it began publishing a quarterly newsletter that lists items available enabling members to exchange information and supplies among themselves.[48]

Service Fees

External user services have become an identifiable financial burden. The principle of open access to free information and the primary obligation to provide service for the parent institution's students and faculty have been in an economic conflict of increasing proportions during the 1970s. Many librarians have been forced to evaluate the wisdom of diverting resources from the primary responsibility to benefit the outside community. A 1980 ARL library survey revealed that

. . . 61 out of a total of 64 institutions responding had written formal policies for external user access and service. Fully 70%, or 45 libraries, had modified their policies within the past five years. A minority of the respondents, 19 institutions, indicated that they had instituted some kind of user fee during the past five years. Only eight libraries, however, had actually reduced external user privileges, while 23 had increased their services to outside individuals and groups. Thus it appears that rather than curtailing services, most libraries prefer to continue serving outside users and to avoid fees if possible.[49]

It is unclear why any academic library supported by tuition-based income would prefer to provide free service to outside users. Assuming
that a typical library received 5 per cent of the general educational
budget, mostly tuition-based, if the tuition is $4,000 per year, for exam-
ple, the library receives about $200 of it. Based on these figures, it
would seem that a $200 outside user fee would be reasonable. An
increasing number of librarians is examining the full costs of these
services. A subsequent ARL survey listed a

... total of six services that frequently involve user fees: online searching, current awareness, interlibrary loan, photoduplication, microform duplication, and
external user borrowing. Among the 60 respondents, seven indicated that they
charge for all the services listed, and all respondents charge for at least two of the
services. . . From the data available, it appears that academic libraries prefer to
charge for selected services only, and judging by the fee schedules, they have not
normally operated on a full cost recovery basis.
In addition to the fee schedules for borrowing, interlibrary loans, copying and
online searching, some research libraries have imposed fees for special services
designed to meet particular demands. In such cases services are added on a full
or partial cost recovery basis. Examples of such services are the delivery of
library material to campus locations and selective dissemination of information.
In response to external user requests, research libraries have imposed relatively
large individual fees for full access and borrowing privileges. Most recently,
special service units designed to provide corporate and special user groups with
research resources for a fee have been started.[50]

Thus the trend has been established and the service cost will be borne
by users. Enterprising administrators may discover that certain new
services, such as database searches, computerized interlibrary loans,
translation service, and literature searching service, can become revenue sources. This revenue may be important to the library's ability to
continue to provide quality service to the outside user and to upgrade
the skills of personnel assigned to the task. Most corporations are more
concerned about getting quality library service when they need it than
about the fee paid. An Association of American Universities report
described academic library corporate interdependence:

Research libraries support research not only in the academic community but also
in business and industry. A number of corporations are quite explicit about the
extent to which they depend on the collections of research libraries in their area;
many have planned the location of their business with nearby library facilities in
mind. Many industries maintain their own special libraries, but they tend to be
limited to current materials; the maintenance of large retrospective collections is
simply too expensive to be practical, given their limited use.
Some corporations are critical of the limitations which research libraries have
imposed on corporate use of their collections. Although many research libraries
have worked out agreements with nearby corporations for corporate payment of
fees for library services, these are not universal, especially where the library's
facilities are already strained by services to students and scholars.[51]

Certain libraries beset by rising costs and shrinking revenues have turned to contract services in such diverse areas as interlibrary loan and computer library software development. Newcomer to this arena is Library Resources Corporation of America (LRCA) currently operating libraries with federal government contracts. It has announced expansion into the academic library area.[52] The corporation has announced a series of regional seminars on alternative funding methods. Their purpose is to offer survival guidance in today's financial environment.[53]

Conclusion

We have discussed a wide range of academic library outside support possibilities. The innovative manager will size up all opportunities and then make an implementation decision. Each institution's pattern of program adoption will be unique. However, there can be little doubt about the need for combined creative and competent financial management. Many role models exist to demonstrate its possibility. Indeed, the future holds many exciting possibilities for increasing outside support level sufficiently to supplement strained budgets.

References

1. *Our Nation's Libraries: An Inventory of Resources and Needs* (Washington, D.C.: National Commission on Libraries and Information Science, 1978).
2. Warren J. Haas, "Managing Our Academic Libraries: Ways and Means" (Paper presented at the First National Conference of the Association of College and Research Libraries, Boston, November 8–11, 1978).
3. Andrew J. Eaton, "Fund-Raising for Academic Libraries," *College and Research Libraries* 31 (September 1971), p. 352.
4. Ibid., p. 353.
5. Patricia S. Breivik, ed., *Funding Alternatives for Libraries* (Chicago: American Library Association, 1979).
6. Ibid. The chapter on planning gives an excellent review, pp. 11–25.
7. Frederick Lynden, "External Fund-Raising for Book Funds (A CLR Fellowship Report)," in: *ARL SPEC Kit Number 48* (Washington, D.C.: Association of Research Libraries, 1978).
8. George A. Brakely, *Tested Ways to Successful Fund-Raising* (N.Y.: American Management Association, 1980), p. 154.
9. Thomas E. Broce, *Fund-Raising, the Guide to Raising Money from Private Sources* (Norman, OK: University of Oklahoma Press, 1979), p. 190.
10. "Fair Practice Code," American Association of Fund-Raising Counsel, 500 Fifth Avenue, New York, N.Y. 10036.
11. Robert D. Sweeney, *Raising Money Through Gift Clubs* (Washington, D.C.: Council for Advancement and Support of Education, 1982), p. 1. Strong on motivation ideas.

12. Edwin R. Leibert, *Handbook of Events for Nonprofit Organizations* (N.Y.: Association Press, 1972). Contains a wealth of tested ideas.
13. Joan Flanagan, *The Grass Roots Fund-Raising Book* (Chicago: Swallow Press, 1977). A handbook with dozens of suggestions.
14. Lisa Pulling, *The KRC Desk Book for Fund-Raisers: With Model Forms and Records* (New Canaan, Conn: KRC Development Council, 1980).
15. William Cumerford, *Fund-Raising, A Professional Guide* (Fort Lauderdale, FL: Ferguson E. Peters Co., P.O. Box 21587, 1978).
16. Broce, *op. cit.*, This book emphasizes academic institutions.
17. William J. Hill, *Successful Grantsmanship* (Steamboat Springs, CO: Grant Development Institute, 1980).
18. *The Foundation Directory* (N.Y.: The Foundation Center, 1981).
19. *The Foundation Center, National Data Book* (N.Y.: The Foundation Center, 1979)
20. *Foundation Directory, op. cit.*, p. viii.
21. Thomas R. Buckman and Sherry E. Goldstein, "Foundation Funding," in: Patricia S. Breivik, ed., *Funding Alternatives for Libraries* (Chicago: American Library Association, 1979), p. 102.
22. Suzanne Perry, "Getting a Foundation Grant Takes More Than a Good Idea," *Chronicle of Higher Education* 25 (October 20, 1982), p. 25.
23. Ibid., p. 25.
24. Roger F. Thaler, "What You Need to Know in Researching Foundations," *New Directions for Institutional Advancement* 11 (1981), pp. 19–24.
25. Ibid., p. 24.
26. Barbara V. Smith and Mark A. Smylie, "Further Resources and Readings," *New Directions for Institutional Advancement* 11 (1981), pp. 79–90.
27. *Foundation Directory, op. cit.*, p. xxvii.
28. Source: *Statistical Abstract of the United States, 1981* (Washington, D.C.: Government Printing Office, 1981), p. 163.
29. *The Handbook of Corporate Social Responsibility: Profiles of Involvement* (Philadelphia: Human Resources Network, 1975).
30. John Grenzebach, "Getting in Gear: How to Organize for Maximum Support," *Case Currents* 7 (November 1981), p. 22.
31. Scott Bennett, "Library Friends: A Theoretical History," in: Donald W. Krummel, *Organizing the Library's Support: Donors, Volunteers, Friends* (Urbana, IL: University of Illinois, 1980), p. 25.
32. CASE represents 1900 academic institutions and is located at 1 Dupont Circle, Washington, D.C. 20036. CFAE is a non-profit service organization concerned with stimulating voluntary support of higher education, especially by the corporate community, and is located at 680 Fifth Avenue, New York, N.Y. 10019.
33. Edward Holley, "The Library and its Friends," in: Donald W. Krummel, *Organizing the Library's Support* . . . (Urbana, IL: University of Illinois, 1980), p. 9.
34. Paul Mosher, "Friends Groups and Academic Libraries," in: Donald W. Krummel, *Organizing the Library's Support* . . . (Urbana, IL: University of Illinois, 1980), p. 69.
35. Ann Gwyn, "Friends of the Library," *College and Research Libraries* 36 (July 1975), p. 272.

36. Charles W. Mixer, "A Friends of the Library Group for My College?" *College Library Notes for the College President* 31 (Summer 1971), p. 1.

37. Gwyn, *op. cit.*, p. 273.

38. The ALA Library Administration and Management Association (ALA LAMA) Public Relations Section Friends of the Libraries Committee has an active program. In addition, the Friends of Libraries USA is a national organization devoted to developing Friends activities. Its secretariat is located at ALA LAMA, 50 E. Huron Street, Chicago, IL 60611. It publishes the *Friends of the Library National Notebook*, a quarterly newsletter.

39. H. Barret Pennell, ed., *Find Out Who Your Friends Are: A Practical Manual for the Formation of Library Support Groups* (Philadelphia: Friends of the Free Library of Philadelphia, Inc., 1978), p. 49.

40. Alfred H. Lane, *Gifts and Exchange Manual* (Westport, Conn: Greenwood Press, 1980).

41. Ibid., p. 10.

42. *Handbook on the International Exchange of Publications* (Paris: Unesco, 1978).

43. Eva Schildler-Rainman, *The Volunteer Community* (Fairfax, VA: NTL Learning Resources Corporation, 1975), p. 19.

44. Virginia Gates, *Helping Hands, the Key to Success* (Chicago: YMCA, 1979). An excellent source book for a volunteer manager.

45. "Utilization and Disposal of Personal Property, General Services Administration," *Federal Register* 42 (October 1977), entire issue.

46. *The United States Government Manual 1981/82* (Washington, D.C.: Office of the Federal Register, GSA, 1981), p. 549.

47. "Industrial Surplus Finds Outlet Via Exchange," *Crain's Chicago Business* 5 (September 13, 1982), p. 4.

48. National Association for the Exchange of Industrial Resources (NAEIR). Information flyer received November 1982. The address is 550 Frontage Road, Northfield, Illinois 60093.

49. "External User Services," *ARL SPEC Kit Number 73* (Washington, D.C.: Association of Research Libraries, April 1981), p. 2.

50. "Fees for Services," *ARL SPEC Kit Number 74* (Washington, D.C.: Association of Research Libraries, May 1981), p. 2.

51. Robert Rosenzweig, *The Research Universities and Their Patrons* (Berkeley: University of California Press, 1982), p. 80.

52. "New Corporation Offers to Run Libraries on Contract," *Library Journal-Hotline* 11 (September 6, 1982), p. 2.

53. "Alternative Methods for Funding Libraries," *Library Journal-Hotline* 11 (November 8, 1982), p. 3.

Appendix I. *Selected Foundations that Contributed to Academic Libraries during 1981*

Name of Foundation	Amount Received	Name of the Recipient	Purpose of the Grant
Benedum	$100,000	Carnegie-Mellon University	Development of enhanced energy & environmental research library/information system.
Bingham	$ 25,000	Radcliffe College	Archival processing project at Schlesinger
Bremer	$ 85,000	College of Saint Benedict	Renovation of college library
Carnegie Corp. of New York	$ 15,000	Association of Amer. Univ.	Support of task forces on major issues facing research libraries
Cary Charitable Trust	$ 26,513	Yale University	Accession of Carl R. Rollins collection on history of printing·
Clark	$ 75,000	Drew University	Library renovation & building program
Dana	$300,000	Hamilton College	Renovation of James Library building
Davis	$ 50,000	Reed College	Toward renovation & expansion of library
	$ 35,000	Northwestern University	Assist in Funding core collection of Joseph Schaffner Library
	$ 50,000	Hampden-Sydney College	Acquisition of periodical backfiles for library
	$ 50,000	Grinnell College	Library acquisitions
Edison	$ 15,000	Upsala College	Library Enhancement Prog.
Exxon Education	$200,000	Tuskegee Institute	Support activities of Carver Research Found. to improve library of traditionally black college.
Ford	$ 11,152	Cornell University	Preparation of bibliography of university's collection of documents on Vietnam War.
	27,000	University of Washington	Building enlargement, acquisition, & computerization of East Asian serial publications for library.

(continued)

Appendix I. *Continued*

Name of Foundation	Amount Received	Name of the Recipient	Purpose of the Grant
Ford (*cont.*)	$ 15,665	University of San Carlos	Publications, library acquisitions, & fellowship aid.
Gannett	$ 10,000	Hartwick College	24-hour study room in renovated library
	$ 20,000	Saint Thomas Aquinas College	Toward cost of library & gymnasium
	$ 5,000	National Judicial College	Book purchases for law library
	$ 5,000	Kings College	Library addition
Hearst	$ 20,000	Saint Francis College	Library renovation
	$ 15,000	Saint Lawrence University	Addition to Owen D. Young Library
	$ 20,000	Brandeis	Library acquisitions
	$ 30,000	Bentley College	Expansion of library facilities
Joyce	$ 5,000	Southern Ill. University	Support acquisition of Freedom of the Press collection
Kaiser	$ 62,000	U.C.—Berkeley	Development of Henry J. Kaiser Archives
Kellogg	$522,352	State Univ. of New York	Expand cooperative comprehensive library educational info & referral networks for adult learners.
Kresge	$250,000	Wittenberg University	Expansion & renovation of Thomas Library
	$150,000	Bentley College	Renovation & expansion of library
	$300,000	Denison University	Renovation & expansion of W. H. Doane Library
	$300,000	Teachers College	Renovation & expansion of library
	$200,000	Colgate University	Construction of addition to library

(*continued*)

Appendix I. *Continued*

Name of Foundation	Amount Received	Name of the Recipient	Purpose of the Grant
Kresge (*cont.*)	$1,000,000	Brown University	Renovation of John Hay Library
	$150,000	Saint Meinrad College	Construction of library
	$200,000	Saint Joseph's University	Construction of library-learning resources center
	$350,000	Atlanta University Center	Construction of joint library
	$100,000	Siena Heights College	Construction of library addition
Pitcairn-Crabbe	$ 15,820	Carlow College	Conversion of Grace Library holdings to Western Penn. Buhl Network automated circulation system
Lilly Endowment	$250,000	Indiana Univ.	Acquisitions for library
Mellon	$500,000	Atlanta University	Cataloging and training activities associated with consolidation of library collections of Center's six constituent institutions into single central library
	$185,000	Johns Hopkins University	Programs to train preservation apprentices and provide instruction & services to other institutions.
	$110,000	University of Michigan	Costs of converting to machine-readable selected bibliographic records for American Studies monographs in library

(*continued*)

Appendix I. *Continued*

Name of Foundation	Amount Received	Name of the Recipient	Purpose of the Grant
Mellon (*cont.*)	$ 90,000	Harvard University	Permanent endowment for Center for Hellenic Studies in Washington, D.C.
	$ 15,000	Association of Amer. Univ.	Costs to develop a strategy for problems of the nation's research libraries
Northwest Area Foundation	$ 11,905	Eastern Oregon State College	Computer software library
Sloan	$ 9,000	University of Michigan	Software development project
	$ 78,000	Amherst, MA Five Colleges	Development of computerized system
Whitaker	$ 25,000	York College	Supplemental support for construction of Life Sciences Bldg. annex & library improvements
Woods Charitable Fund	$ 50,000	Concordia Teachers College	Challenge grant for library addition

Source: DIALOG–Foundation Grants Database, October 1982.

Appendix II. The Foundation Center

Reference Collections Operated by The Foundation Center

The Foundation Center, 888 Seventh Avenue, New York, New York 10106; 212-975-1120

The Foundation Center, 1001 Connecticut Avenue, NW, Washington, D.C. 20036; 202-331-1400

The Foundation Center, Kent H. Smith Library, 739 National City Bank Bldg., 629 Euclid, Cleveland, Ohio 44114; 215-861-1933

The Foundation Center, 312 Sutter Street, San Francisco, Calif. 94108; 415-397-0902

Cooperating Collections

ALABAMA

Birmingham Public Library, 2020 Park Place, Birmingham 35203;
205-254-2541

Auburn University at Montgomery Library, Montgomery 36193;
205-279-9110

ALASKA

University of Alaska, Anchorage Library, 3211 Providence Drive, Anchorage
99504; 907-263-1848

ARIZONA

Phoenix Public Library, Social Sciences Subject Department, 12 East
McDowell Road, Phoenix 85004; 602-262-4782

Tucson Public Library, Main Library, 200 South Sixth Avenue, Tucson
85701; 602-791-4393

ARKANSAS

Westark Community College Library, Grand Avenue at Waldron Rd., Fort
Smith 72913; 501-785-4241

Little Rock Public Library, Reference Department, 700 Louisiana Street, Little
Rock 72201; 501-374-7546

CALIFORNIA

California Community Foundation, 1644 Wilshire Boulevard, Los Angeles
90017; 213-413-4042

San Diego Public Library, 820 E Street, San Diego 92101; 714-236-5816

Santa Barbara Public Library, Reference Section, 40 East Anapamu, P.O. Box
1019, Santa Barbara 93102; 805-962-7653

COLORADO

Denver Public Library, Sociology Division, 1357 Broadway, Denver 80203;
303-573-5152

CONNECTICUT

Hartford Public Library, Reference Department, 500 Main Street, Hartford
06103; 203-525-9121

DELAWARE

Hugh Morris Library, University of Delaware, Newark 19711; 302-738-2965

FLORIDA

Jacksonville Public Library, Business, Science, and Industry Department, 122
North Ocean Street, Jacksonville 32202; 904-633-3926

Miami-Dade Public Library, Florida Collection, One Biscayne Boulevard,
Miami 33132; 305-579-5001

GEORGIA

Atlanta Public Library, 1 Margaret Mitchell Square at Forsyth and Carnegie
Way, Atlanta 30303; 404-688-4636

HAWAII

Thomas Hale Hamilton Library, University of Hawaii, General Reference
Department, 2550 The Mall, Honolulu 96822; 808-948-7214

IDAHO

Caldwell Public Library, 1010 Dearborn Street, Caldwell 83605; 208-459-3242

ILLINOIS

Donors Forum of Chicago, 208 South LaSalle Street, Chicago 60604;
312-726-4882

Sangamon State University Library, Shepherd Road, Springfield 62708;
217-786-6633
INDIANA
Indianapolis-Marion County Public Library, 40 East St. Clair Street, Indianapolis 46204; 317-269-1733
IOWA
Public Library of Des Moines, 100 Locust Street, Des Moines 50309;
515-283-4259
KANSAS
Topeka Public Library, Adult Services Department, 1515 West Tenth Street,
Topeka 66604; 913-233-2040
KENTUCKY
Louisville Free Public Library, Fourth and York Streets, Louisville 40203;
502-584-4154
LOUISIANA
East Baton Rouge Parish Library, Centroplex Library, 120 St. Louis Street,
Baton Rouge 70802; 504-344-5291
New Orleans Public Library, Business and Science Division, 219 Loyola
Avenue, New Orleans 70140; 504-586-4919
MAINE
University of Southern Maine Center for Research and Advanced Study, 246
Deering Avenue, Portland 04102; 207-780-4411
MARYLAND
Enoch Pratt Free Library, Social Science and History Department, 400
Cathedral Street, Baltimore 21201; 301-396-5320
MASSACHUSETTS
Associated Grantmakers of Massachusetts, 294 Washington Street, Suite 501,
Boston 02108; 617-426-2608
Boston Public Library, Copley Square, Boston 02117; 617-536-5400
MICHIGAN
Alpena County Library, 211 North First Avenue, Alpena 49707;
517-356-6188
Henry Ford Centennial Library, 16301 Michigan Avenue, Dearborn 48126;
313-943-2337
Purdy Library, Wayne State University, Detroit 48202; 313-577-4040
Michigan State University Libraries, Reference Library, East Lansing 48824;
517-353-8816
University of Michigan-Flint, UM-F Library, Reference Department, Flint
48503; 313-762-3408
Grand Rapids Public Library, Sociology and Education Dept., Library Plaza,
Grand Rapids 49502; 616-456-4411
Michigan Technological University Library, Highway U.S. 41, Houghton
49931; 906-487-2507
MINNESOTA
Minneapolis Public Library, Sociology Department, 300 Nicollet Mall, Minneapolis 55401; 612-372-6555
MISSISSIPPI
Jackson Metropolitan Library, 301 North State Street, Jackson 39201;
601-944-1120
MISSOURI
Clearinghouse for Mid-continent Foundations, Univ. of Missouri, Kansas City,

Law School, Suite 1-300, 52nd Street and Oak, Kansas City 64110;
   816-276-1176
Kansas City Public Library, 311 East 12th Street, Kansas City 64106;
   816-221-2685
Metropolitan Association for Philanthropy, Inc., 5600 Oakland, G-324, St.
   Louis 63110; 314-647-2290
Springfield-Greene County Library, 397 East Central Street, Springfield
   65801; 417-869-4621
   MONTANA
Eastern Montana College Library, Reference Department, Billings 59101;
   406-657-2337
   NEBRASKA
W. Dale Clark Library, Social Sciences Department, 215 South 15th Street,
   Omaha 68102; 402-444-4822
   NEVADA
Clark County Library, 1401 East Flamingo Road, Las Vegas 89109;
   702-733-7810
Washoe County Library, 301 South Center Street, Reno 89505; 702-785-4190
   NEW HAMPSHIRE
The New Hampshire Charitable Fund, One South Street, P.O. Box 1335,
   Concord 03301; 603-225-6641
   NEW JERSEY
New Jersey State Library, Governmental Reference, 185 West State Street,
   P.O. Box 1898, Trenton 08625; 609-292-6220
   NEW MEXICO
New Mexico State Library, 300 Don Gaspar Street, Santa Fe 87501;
   505-827-2033
   NEW YORK
New York State Library, Cultural Education Center, Humanities Section,
   Empire State Plaza, Albany 12230; 518-474-7645
Buffalo and Erie County Public Library, Lafayette Square; Buffalo 14203;
   716-856-7525
Levittown Public Library, Reference Department, One Bluegrass Lane, Levit-
   town 11756; 516-731-5728
Plattsburgh Public Library, Reference Department, 15 Oak Street, Plattsburgh
   12901; 518-563-0921
Rochester Public Library, Business and Social Sciences Division, 115 South
   Avenue, Rochester 14604; 716-428-7328
Onondaga County Public Library, 335 Montgomery Street, Syracuse 13202;
   315-473-4491
   NORTH CAROLINA
North Carolina State Library, 109 East Jones Street, Raleigh 27611;
   919-733-3270
The Winston-Salem Foundation, 229 First Union National Bank Building,
   Winston-Salem 27101; 919-725-2382
   NORTH DAKOTA
The Library, North Dakota State University, Fargo 58105; 710-237-8876
   OHIO
Public Library of Cincinnati and Hamilton County, Education Department,
   800 Vine Street, Cincinnati 45202; 513-369-6940

Toledo-Lucas County Public Library, Social Science Department, 325 Michigan Street, Toledo 43624; 419-255-7055, ext. 221
OKLAHOMA
Oklahoma City Community Foundation, 1300 North Broadway, Oklahoma City 73103; 405-235-5621
Tulsa City-County Library System, 400 Civic Center, Tulsa 74103; 918-581-5144
OREGON
Library Association of Portland, Education and Documents Rm., 801 S.W. Tenth Avenue, Portland 97205; 503-223-7201
PENNSYLVANIA
The Free Library of Philadelphia, Logan Square, Philadelphia 19103; 215-686-5423
Hillman Library, University of Pittsburgh, Pittsburgh 15260; 412-624-4528
RHODE ISLAND
Providence Public Library, Reference Department, 150 Empire Street, Providence 02903; 401-521-7722
SOUTH CAROLINA
South Carolina State Library, Reader Services Department, 1500 Senate Street, Columbia 29211; 803-758-3181
SOUTH DAKOTA
South Dakota State Library, State Library Building, 322 South Fort Street, Pierre 57501; 605-773-3131
TENNESSEE
Resources Center for Non-Profit Agencies, Inc., 502 Gay Street, Suite 201, P.O. Box 1606, Knoxville 37901; 615-521-6034
Memphis Public Library, 1850 Peabody Avenue, Memphis 38104; 901-528-2957
TEXAS
The Hogg Foundation for Mental Health, The University of Texas, Austin 78712; 512-471-5041
Corpus Christi State University Library, 6300 Ocean Drive, Corpus Christi 78412; 512-991-6810
Dallas Public Library, Grants Information Service, 1954 Commerce Street, Dallas 75201; 214-748-9071, ext. 332
El Paso Community Foundation, El Paso National Bank Building, Suite 1616, El Paso 79901; 915-533-4020
Houston Public Library, Bibliographic & Information Center, 500 McKinney Avenue, Houston 77002; 713-224-5441, ext. 265
Funding Information Library, Minnie Stevens Piper Foundation, 201 North St. Mary's Street, Suite 100, San Antonio 78205; 512-227-4333
UTAH
Salt Lake City Public Library, Information and Adult Services, 209 East Fifth South, Salt Lake City 84111; 801-363-5733
VERMONT
State of Vermont Department of Libraries, Reference Services Unit, 111 State Street, Montpelier 05602; 802-828-3261
VIRGINIA
Grants Resources Library, Ninth Floor, Hampton City Hall, Hampton 23669; 804-727-6496

Richmond Public Library, Business, Science, & Technology Department, 101 East Franklin Street, Richmond 23219; 804-780-8223
WASHINGTON
Seattle Public Library, 1000 Fourth Avenue, Seattle 98104; 206-625-4881
Spokane Public Library, Reference Department, West 906 Main Avenue, Spokane 99201; 509-838-3361
WEST VIRGINIA
Kanawha County Public Library, 123 Capitol Street, Charleston 25301; 304-343-4646
WISCONSIN
Marquette University Memorial Library, 1415 West Wisconsin Avenue, Milwaukee 53233; 414-224-1515
WYOMING
Laramie County Community College Library, 1400 East College Drive, Cheyenne 82001; 307-634-6853
CANADA
The Canadian Centre for Philanthropy, 12 Sheppard Street, 3rd Floor, Toronto, Ontario M5H 3A1; 416-364-4875
MEXICO
Biblioteca Benjamin Franklin, Londres 16, Mexico City 6, D.F.
PUERTO RICO
Consumer Education and Service Center, Department of Consumer Affairs, Minillas Central Government Building North, Santurce 00904
VIRGIN ISLANDS
College of the Virgin Islands Library, Saint Thomas, U.S. Virgin Islands 00801; 809-774-1252

Appendix III. Foundation Center Publications

Publications of The Foundation Center are the primary working tools of every serious grantseeker. Copies of all publications are available for examination free of charge at any of the regional collections. Publications may be ordered from The Foundation Center, 888 Seventh Avenue, New York, NY 10106; please include prepayment and complete shipping address. For additional information or to place credit card orders, call toll free 800-424-9836.

Source Book Profiles is an annual subscription service offering an in-depth picture of the 1,000 largest foundations, breaking down each one's giving patterns by subject area, type of support, and type of recipient.
Series 4 (1981)—$200 annual subscription—
ISBN 0-87954-037-0.
Series 3 (1979–80)—$200 set of 500—
ISBN 0-87954-024-9.

Foundation Grants Index Annual lists the grants of $5,000 or more awarded to nonprofit organizations by over 400 major U.S. foundations. The volume is arranged alphabetically by state and foundation name.
Annually in April.
ISBN 0-87954-040-0. $30

National Data Book, 5th Edition, lists the over 22,000 currently active grantmaking foundations in the U.S. in one easy-to-use volume arranged by state in descending order by their annual grant totals. A separate alphabetical index to foundation names is also included.
  2 volumes. Annually in January.
  ISBN 0-87954-039-7. $45

Corporate Foundation Profiles includes comprehensive analyses of over 200 of the nation's largest company-sponsored foundations, with full subject, type of support, and geographic indexes. Summary financial data is provided for more than 300 additional corporate foundations.
  1980. 512 pages.
  ISBN 0-87954-038-9. $50

Foundation Grants to Individuals, 2nd Edition, is the only publication devoted entirely to foundation grant opportunities for individual applicants. The second edition provides full descriptions of the programs for individuals of about 950 foundations.
  2nd edition, 1979. 236 pages.
  ISBN 0-87954-025-7. $15

COMSEARCH Printouts are computer-produced guides to foundation grants published in the annual volume of The Foundation Grants Index arranged in easy-to-use subject and geographic listings. *COMSEARCH: Subjects* includes 68 separate subject listings of grant information which can be ordered as a complete set on microfiche or by the particular subject area of interest. *COMSEARCH: Geographic* lists grants awarded to recipients in each of ten states and two cities. A new series, *COMSEARCH: Special Topics,* includes four computer printouts drawn from the Center's specialized databases.
  Series published annually in May; full list of categories available on request.

Foundation Fundamentals: A Guide for Grantseekers is a comprehensive, easy-to-read guidebook written by Carol Kurzig. All of the facts you need to understand the world of foundations and to identify foundation funding sources for your organizations.
  1980. 148 pages.
  ISBN0-87954-026-5. $4.95.

Directory of Evaluation Consultants, edited by Richard Johnson, Exxon Education Foundation, this directory lists over 400 individuals and organizations available to provide evaluation services to all types of agencies and organizations.
  1981.
  ISBN 0-87954-035-4. $8.95

Conducting Evaluations: Three Perspectives: a collection of three thought-provoking essays which explore the issues involved in evaluation from the viewpoint of the granting agency, the grant recipient, and the professional evaluation community.
  1980.
  ISBN 0-87954-0362. $2.95

Foundations Today: Current Facts and Figures on Private Foundations: this pamphlet
presents a brief overview of the general characteristics of foundations, current
fiscal status of foundations, and trends in foundation giving.
1981.
22 pages. $1.50

Philanthropy in the United States: History and Structure: this pamphlet by F. Emerson
Andrews describes the history of philanthropy in the U.S. with emphasis on its
present structure and dimensions. It describes the various types of foundations,
the fields which have most benefited from foundation giving, and the effect of
increased governmental scrutiny.
35 pages. $1.50

Appendix IV. GSA Regional Offices

1. Post Office and Courthouse, Boston, MA 02109 (Connecticut,
   Maine, Massachusetts, New Hampshire, Rhode Island, Vermont).
2. 26 Federal Plaza, New York, NY 10007 (New Jersey, New York,
   Puerto Rico, Virgin Islands).
3. 7th & D Streets, SW, Washington, DC 20407 (Delaware, District of
   Columbia, Maryland, Pennsylvania, Virginia, West Virginia).
4. 1776 Peachtree Street, NW, Atlanta, GA 30309 (Alabama, Florida,
   Georgia, Kentucky, Mississippi, North Carolina, South Carolina,
   Tennessee).
5. 230 South Dearborn Street, Chicago, IL 60604 (Illinois, Indiana,
   Michigan, Minnesota, Ohio, Wisconsin).
6. 1500 E. Bannister Road, Kansas City, MO 64131 (Iowa, Kansas,
   Missouri, Nebraska).
7. 819 Taylor Street, Fort Worth, TX 76102 (Arkansas, Louisiana,
   New Mexico, Oklahoma, Texas).
8. Denver Federal Center, Bldg. 41, Denver, CO 80225 (Colorado,
   Montana, North Dakota, South Dakota, Utah, Wyoming).
9. 525 Market Street, San Francisco, CA 94105 (Arizona, California,
   Nevada).
10. GSA Center, Auburn, WA 98002 (Idaho, Oregon, Washington).
    Alaskan area: P.O. Box 11632, Anchorage, AK 99510.
    Hawaiian area: Federal Building, 300 Ala Moana Blvd., Honolulu,
    HI 96813.

5. Intra-Campus Coordination and Austerity Management

Frederick C. Lynden and Thomas W. Leonhardt

A PROGRAM in intra-campus coordination is a logical but often over-looked means of cutting costs through library use of campus facilities, services, and personnel. The skill that one can find in the local college or university community can be surprising. Mason tells the story of finding a national lighting expert on his campus when planning a new Colorado College building:

> How does one reach this enviable position of knowing that the architect's fixture is wrong and proceeding to pick a good one as substitute? We had on our faculty, by remarkable coincidence, John O. Kraehenbuehl, who had taken early retire-ment from the University of Illinois College of Engineering and was known throughout the land (as I later discovered) as the preeminent expert on achiev-ing quality in illumination.[1]

In an intra-university coordination program the principal objective is to improve library service at reduced cost through cooperation with other campus departments. Secondary objectives are to increase library and university communication and to use personnel and service for mutual university and library benefit. This program assumes that most institu-tions have central business, purchasing, personnel, physical plant, de-velopment, photocopy, and bookstore offices and that the library can take advantage of centralized processing economies. Another assump-tion is that the library administration contacts campus officials in these areas regularly. Such contacts are an essential coordination program ingredient.

A well-planned coordination program should insure cost reduction or financial gain. In certain cases, financial gains will be small, and in others, the university rather than the library will gain immediate advan-tage. In the latter situation, however, the library benefits by working with the university to achieve savings that are potentially available for return. Funds do come to the library from the campus community as well. Recently, the University of South Carolina and University of Pittsburgh athletic departments transferred funds to their libraries.

Another coordination benefit is better public relations within the university. Those in close contact with university officials can make known not only library needs but also services and accomplishments. Previously, libraries have not adequately publicized their service to the campus. One means of doing such marketing is through intra-campus coordination. Such coordination can result in both budget additions and expense reductions. It is important to consider how campus departments can aid the library.

Purchasing Office

On every campus a unit is responsible for purchasing supplies and equipment. An objective of the Brown University Purchasing Department is to "make recommendations for consolidation and standardization of purchases in an attempt to reduce costs." In addition to "batching" orders, the Department maintains a vendor product source book library; keeps transaction records; has a vendor evaluation program; assists other departments in planning purchases; and provides a university stockroom for supplies commonly used.

The Library takes advantage of these services by sending its equipment and supply purchase requests via this Department. The Department is a member of several national organizations which aid in securing supplies and equipment on time, at the lowest cost, and of the highest quality. One is the National Association of Educational Buyers (NAEB), and its affiliate group, the Educational and Institutional Cooperative Service.[2] These groups work "to obtain the maximum ultimate value of each dollar of expenditure."

The Brown University Director of Purchasing says that major savings do not come from consolidating orders but rather from consolidating and bidding. As Rogers and Weber note, one of the three principal advantages in using university purchasing agents is their experience in negotiating and bidding. A second benefit is their knowledge which can be helpful in dealing with salespersons. Finally, their information and files can be valuable.[3]

Although university purchasing agents may not be familiar with library equipment and supply houses, they can be helpful in finding the highest quality furnishings at competitive prices. A reciprocal relationship should exist between the library and the purchasing agent. The agent can aid the library in finding general supplies and equipment, and the library administration can acquaint the agent with specialized supply and equipment items. The librarian should keep the agent up-to-date with library equipment developments. For example, the ALA's Library Administration and Management Association has sponsored institutes on equipment and furniture procurement and has published the proceedings.

Many purchasing offices assist in used equipment purchase and sale. At Brown, the Purchasing Department carries out the paperwork for departments, and the Plant Operations Department picks up and delivers. When the Library purchased a used microfiche reader from the Development Office, that office and the Purchasing Department carried out the fund transfer. The Library saved half the machine cost. An item no longer useable is either scrapped or the Purchasing Department authorizes sale to an individual.

Many purchasing departments also assist in specification preparation for new equipment and service purchases. Although the Brown *Purchasing and Property Control Manual* notes that "product specification rests solely with the originator," when the John Hay Library was being renovated, the Purchasing Department advised the librarians on specifications. Purchases of special equipment, such as computers, copiers, and word processors, must be approved by the Directors of the Computing Center and Graphic Services.

Business Office

The library can effect staff savings and increase revenue by working closely with university financial officers. Many contact points exist between the two units, including budgets, fund transfers, financial reports, and vendor payments. An example of both staff savings and financial gain is fines collection coordination. At Duke University, if fines are not paid when overdue books are returned or lost books are reported, the student's name and the amount and type of fine are sent to the Bursar's Office. The Library is thus relieved of the burden of billing and collecting yet receives the funds when fines are paid.

Intra-campus coordination can also save funds when compiling periodic budget reports. Many bookkeeping combination possibilities exist between the library and the business office. A basic assumption is that centralized accounting is automated. The library may have online access to the automated accounting system or may have its own independent automated acquisitions/bookkeeping system.

The Duke Library has its own automated acquisitions/accounts payable system that automatically encumbers funds, liquidates encumbrances, and writes checks. The University Business Office is spared the expense of posting individual accounts within the budget line for library material. The Library achieves budgeting accuracy by directly linking bookkeeping with ordering, cancelling, and receiving. The broader fund accounting is fed to the central accounting system via tape where it is entered into the total budget so the library can obtain an accurate monthly statement. The weekly internal reports and the official monthly report are reconciled to ensure that funds are neither over nor underspent.

The Stanford University Libraries do not maintain a separate internal acquisitions accounting system but rely on computerized Controller's Office monthly expenditure reports. Central system dependence allows the Libraries to avoid having a costly manual encumbrance system. The Controller's Office provides prompt and detailed monthly statements showing charges on each of the more than 100 book and journal funds. The Library circulates a summary expenditure report to selectors and concerned technical service staff members.

The Stanford Libraries also work closely with the Office of Management and Financial Planning and the Controller's Office to provide data for long range acquisition cost forecasts. The Libraries prepare detailed data on book, journal, government document and other scholarly material prices, information on what was acquired from abroad and data on growth in world scholarly material production. These data are used in the annual budget request and in cost models to project future University expenditures. One by-product of these contributions to the cost model has been a better University understanding of the Library's economic problems. Thanks to Library participation in this type of exercise, the proposed material budget can carry no surprises. The University is given time to prepare for an acquisition increase, and the Library can increase the University's confidence in its planning skill. A result of the joint participation has been strong acquisition budgets.

Other university offices are experimenting with planning models, also. A recent "Economics and Financial Management of Research Libraries" conference proposed a study of the "feasibility of creating a broad financial planning model for research libraries. . . ."[4] Brown is using the EDUCOM financial planning model with a component for acquisition budget growth. The Harvard College Library was used as a test of the planning model, and two preliminary conclusions were reached: "Growth in salaries for both . . . librarians and support staff is an important determinant of budgetary balance" and "Since a greater share of the acquisitions budget is allocated to monograph (and other non-serial) material than to serials, the budget balance was more sensitive to the rate of growth in monograph acquisitions than to the rate of serial growth."[5] It is significant and encouraging that university financial administrators are now analyzing library costs.

The Brown University Bursar's Office sends bills to students for overdue fines and serves as collector, also. This relieves the Circulation Department of considerable paperwork. Collection enforcement is coordinated through the Registrar's Office which will withhold diplomas if necessary. When the University is unable to collect, the Library Business Officer receives a bad debtor list. Having good Business Office relations insures smooth fines collection and additional library income.

When Brown had to make a large automated circulation system payment, the Office of Administration and Finance arranged an internal loan to be repaid from salary savings. For the first year, in order to commit proper resources to the system, loan payment was forgiven. An agreement was made for a seven-year payback, including commercial rate interest (later modified to a fixed rate). This assistance enabled the Library to make staff savings and increase overdue book income through more accurate records. It also provided better user service because of a more accurate circulating book inventory and a more effective recall system.

In summary, good business office relations can aid the library through 1) direct accounting savings; 2) improved cost data for budgets; 3) better long-range cost forecasts leading to university administrators' better understanding of library economics; 4) improved fines collection and 5) capital improvement assistance.

Personnel Office

Close personnel office relationships can save, also. The most obvious example is support staff recruitment and hiring. Support-staff candidates are sent to the library personally or on civil service manifests. When a manifest, listing job seekers and their civil service scores, is involved, the library has little leeway. It is still important, however, to be on good terms with the personnel office so all rules are clearly understood and every proper right and option can be exercised to ensure hiring the best available candidate and not necessarily just the candidate with the highest score.

More crucial to library welfare are clear understandings and good relations in a system that depends on campus personnel office referrals. Two signs can indicate need for closer cooperation: 1) when a vacancy occurs and weeks pass before even one candidate is sent for an interview while the library loses production; or, 2) when referrals are numerous but the appointees do not last long on the job. In such instances, because of training time and the paperwork involved, the library is doing poorly.

The first step toward establishing a good personnel office relationship is to have one library staff member responsible for personnel policy and practice. The next step is for that person to establish his/her credentials with the personnel office. The library personnel officer must become familiar with the problems and rules under which the personnel office functions. Within that context, the personnel officer must educate the campus office about library needs.

When job families were introduced at Duke, the Library was able to make a case for its own job family while still benefitting from non-library personnel use in areas like accounting, secretarial work, and data processing. Not to make a case for library specialization means functioning in a system that says all support staff members are inter-changeable. This can mean having to consider all campus support-staff assistants when the library is planning a promotion to senior assistant of a person on the library staff. It can also mean losing a skilled library worker to another department when layoffs are dealt with based on seniority. The job family concept recognizes the inherent differences in types of work. Libraries without a separate worker classification should prepare a justification and enlist campus personnel office support for it.

Even good knowledge of needs may not insure that the right kinds of applicants are sent to the library. At Duke such a diversity of skill and talent was needed at one job family level that the University funded a study to see if the ideal characteristics of such a worker could be dis-covered through testing and interviewing. Results are not yet available. Without a close personnel office relationship and University funding, such a study would have been impossible.

Development Office

A direct approach to solving austerity problems can be made by solicit-ing a higher level of outside funding support. An important part of such a program is close relations with the development office, responsi-ble for capital campaigns, alumni fund-raising, and donor relations. A library component should be included in fund-raising drives. Many capital campaigns include endowment funds for purchasing material, funds for library construction or maintenance, endowment of the uni-versity librarian's position, endowment for library equipment, particu-larly computers, and for special collections. Many other innovative and creative possibilities for gift and endowment funds exist. Harvard, for example, has recently received an endowment for preservation; Boston University received special funding for a microform center.

Development offices distribute gift solicitation notices regularly, often with a place to check off the contribution use preferred. The library should be listed. A recent Brown University solicitation in the form of an "L. L. Bean" type of catalog included library needs. Devel-opment office skill in brochure design can be useful with potential Friends groups. The development office can not only notify the library of grant possibilities but advise about responses to proposal requests and suggest an appropriate contact person.

If the library's special collection needs are explained to the develop-ment office, then development staff members can be alert to potential donors and their collections. The Brown Development Office corre-sponds with book fund donors and saves the Library's time. They pre-fer to maintain contact with these donors, and a library purchase report is an entrée. The Brown Library has also aided the Development Office by plating books in memory of deceased alumni. The Development Office then reports on the memorial to surviving family members. The memorial book plate program puts the Development Office in early touch with the family members of recently deceased alumni. The campus development office can be very helpful in establishing and sustaining a library Friends organization as well.

A number of universities, Stanford, Chicago, Northwestern, and Harvard among them, have established library development officer positions. This position relates closely to the development office. At Stanford, the Library produces a special annual report for donors which contains bibliographic citations and illustrations of certain recently acquired rare books and includes a selected list of the year's donors, funds, books and other material.

The *University of Chicago Library Society Newsletter*, a development publication, includes "shopping lists" of books needed and advertises the Fund of Books honoring individuals with a special bookplate and notification letter. Other libraries use a variety of mementoes to stay in touch with donors: book marks, greeting cards, keepsakes, facsimile maps, teas, exhibits, etc. Most library development offices work closely with the Friends group and assist with their administration or publication program. The University of Oregon Library shares a development officer with the School of Journalism. Such arrangements depend on institutional priorities and can vary periodically.

Academic Vice-President and Deans

One of the key relationships in any intra-campus coordination program is that between the library and the university administration. Without excellent relations, there is little chance that the library will reach its goals. The library must participate actively in university administration through the councils, committees, and other groups that set educational policies and programs. It must be aware of the changes which the university makes to cope with fluctuating societal needs. The university administration must be made aware of collection needs and proper support levels. The library must have a strong voice within the university administration.

The Brown University Library is involved in university administration in several ways. First, the Provost meets weekly with the Academic Council which includes the President, Dean of the Faculty, Vice-President (Biology and Medicine), Graduate School Dean, College Dean, Associate Provost, and University Librarian. This group considers proposals for new programs, for departmental staffing plan changes, for new cooperative or joint efforts with other institutions, for existing program renewals, and other matters. When a new master's degree in

Business Economics was under review, the Library component was considered, and the final proposal included Library expenses for collection build-up and steady state periods. Second, the University Librarian, who is an ex-officio Faculty Library Committee member, has customarily asked Assistant University Librarians to attend this group's sessions. Third, the University Librarian serves as an ex-officio member of the University (Board of Trustees) Library Committee. Since the President is its chair, the Library gets excellent exposure.

A representative working with the Provost and the Deans can have desirable effects on program expansion. At Brown, a Library Impact Statement insures that a Library representative will serve on the Graduate Council and the Educational Policy Committee. These groups review all graduate and undergraduate course proposals and the Library contributes an impact assessment of changes. By attending such meetings, the Library learns of departmental efforts to build their own "libraries." Recently, the Provost asked the Faculty Library Committee to survey departmental "collections" in order to monitor, and, where necessary, eliminate non-library book and journal collection growth.

It is also valuable to encourage university officials to join library organizations. The Research Libraries Group (RLG) has a Special Committee of University Presidents which is heavily involved in monitoring its finances. There is an RLG group for university treasurers. As another example, the Center for Research Libraries includes non-librarians on its board. This type of activity enables university officials to become familiar with library issues, develop fiscal problem awareness, learn about resource sharing, and increase austerity understanding.

Any deans' council must deal with the issue of financing new program development and old program expansion. As grant proposals are discussed, the representative should remind the deans of library needs. In an example of university officials' awareness of these needs, Brown allowed the Library rather than another department to compete for an NEH Challenge Grant to renovate the John Hay Library. Occasionally, a Special Committee is asked to investigate university library problems. In 1977, the Princeton President appointed a Special Committee on Library Acquisitions and Losses.[6] The report made several useful recommendations. The University of Missouri-Columbia Chancellor asked a consulting firm to undertake a Library Evaluation and Program Planning Study. A twenty-year plan for major physical renovation was the result.[7]

In summary, benefits will occur when the university administration is fully informed of library needs: 1) when courses or programs are added, 2) incipient departmental "libraries" can be canceled; 3) departments can add special funds to the library collection budget; 4) university officials can be alerted to resource sharing opportunities; and 5) special studies result which facilitate major capital improvements.

Faculty Library Committee

The Faculty Library Committee can be an important advocate for budget improvement and for other programs. At Brown the Faculty Library Committee has sent letters to the Advisory Committee on University Planning to support library statements of current service and collection adequacy for curriculum and course changes.[8] All graduate program evaluations must incorporate such an assessment, also. These stipulations assure support for adequate library resources and can be used in budgetary defense.

The Faculty Library Committee can investigate such problems as book theft and mutilation and encourage the faculty senate to advocate funds for security measures. The Committee can aid in enforcing fines collection from recalcitrant faculty. The Committee can also encourage studies of recurring problems. In 1977, the Carnegie-Mellon University Library Committee supported with a small grant a study "to evaluate whether the university's current policies in allocating resources to the library [were] . . . appropriate."[9] In 1981–82 the Brown Faculty Library Committee investigated acquisition budget endowment support and reported needs to the Corporation (Board of Trustees) Library Committee. Through these and other activities, the Committee can aid by advising the university on library policies.

Students form a valuable part of faculty library committees. Their awareness of problems can result in support. At Brown, students were told of Brown's history of poor acquisitions budgets and for three years the Senior class made acquisitions gifts to the Library. Concern has carried over to budget presentation meetings where students have supported acquisition fund requests.

In summary, the faculty library committee can 1) support budget requests; 2) explain unpopular operational changes due to austerity; 3) encourage studies of recurring problems; 4) require impact statements for new courses and programs; and 5) enlist student and faculty support.

Bookstore Coordination

Vendor discounts are never high enough and books never come in fast enough so acquisitions librarians seek ways to improve this situation. At the University of North Carolina, Chapel Hill, the Library and the Bookstore found a way to meet their separate needs and still benefit each other. The library agreed to order a certain number of sci-tech books and the Bookstore agreed to share the discount. Because the material ordered was current and from well-known publishers, turnaround time was good. The discount was mutually beneficial, too, because of the high library business volume and the resulting high discount rate.

Variations exist elsewhere. At Duke, for example, a plan is being explored by which predictable current literature, fiction and non-fiction, could be ordered on the basis of prepublication announcements judged against a Library profile. The Bookstore would increase its regular order of such titles by one or two copies each, depending on the profile, thus making it easier to qualify for higher discounts by higher volume orders. A librarian would pick the books off the Bookstore shelves, the Bookstore would enjoy increased sales, and the Library would achieve a better turnaround time and a higher discount. The Library would have eliminated the paperwork involved with regular orders. This arrangement covers only a select category of material and is not a substitute for traditional acquisitions through publishers and jobbers.

Duplicate material consignment can be another way to cooperate. Many libraries do not have the space or staff to conduct book sales. Even if adequate facilities exist, faculty public relations problems are associated with such disposal. By consigning its duplicates and unwanted material to the campus bookstore, the library serves the campus community by providing low-priced used books which bring in bookstore business, and it can share profits without staff or space investment. Certain institutions have found that libraries are the most efficient offices for ordering departmental and staff books and periodicals and actually assign staff members there to handle these orders. The persons may work half-time for the library and half-time for the department.

Reducing Telephone and Photocopy Costs

Few academic libraries can reduce telephone and photocopy costs without intra-campus cooperation. Both areas depend on extra-library technology and use patterns. Installing custom made communications systems should be done through university approval, cooperation and funding. The library should be prepared to explain why such changes are necessary, what can be gained from the change, and how the university itself can be better served by the new system. Basically, libraries should be interested in replacing rotary telephones having numerous extensions, lights, and buttons with touch-tone instruments having greater electronic and computerized flexibility at less cost per person served. Probably the institution has a communication coordinator who is aware of total communication activities and costs. The library should be prepared with information about its communication use and plans.

Most libraries do not participate in campus cost recovery programs, except for lost and mutilated material. Database searching and interlibrary loan seldom have realistic service charges. After meeting ongoing cost commitments, suppliers, services, equipment, travel, and other administrative expenses must often be budgeted on projected salary savings, duplicate material sale and photocopy revenue. Coin-operated copiers can pay for themselves and for administrative copying, too. But to increase revenue further, broaden campus service, and compete with cut-rate off-campus operaters, libraries must work with the campus administration. Many institutions have an office overseeing photocopier purchase, leasing, and installation, and it can advise on service economies.

When discussing a central library copying center, two arguments are in its favor: the library's central location and the fact that people copy a lot in a library and expect to find copiers available. It needs to take advantage of natural traffic patterns while considering access, ventilation, noise, relative locations of current periodicals, and security systems. The library should be able to justify staff and fund use to establish a copy center with high speed, versatile copiers until it is self-supporting. Without competing with campus print shop quick-copying, the library should be able to improve underfunded service areas from copy center profits.

Branch Library Management

Branch library management should be an integral part of any intra-campus cost control plan. Concern about branch proliferation is well placed. As Raffel pointed out, "The cost of decentralized departmental reading study libraries depends primarily on personnel requirements."[10] Departmental libraries also result in greater material, processing, equipment, energy, and building maintenance costs.

It is important to insure that departmental libraries are not added without careful consideration: "The director of university libraries, with the assistance of the faculty library committee, should have some control over the establishment of new campus libraries."[11] Many libraries have policy statements on the establishment of such libraries. Union lists, fiche catalogs, and online catalogs accessible by terminal can now be placed in offices, and with expedited delivery the departmental library is no longer the only alternative to geographic isolation.

If a branch is established, costs can be reduced through resource reallocation. A common means of controlling branch costs is through merging small branches into the central library. Many small branches have disadvantages of short hours, small staff, lack of space, and inadequate collections. At the University of Pennsylvania, two branches were moved into the central library, a total of over 130,000 volumes. These transfers also brought staff and aided in covering vacant positions in the central library. Other biology and medicine collections were merged into a unified bio-medical library. As De Gennaro noted, there was resistance: "The Music Department faculty, after opposing the move for several years, finally voted almost unanimously for it when it became clear that the Department's severe space problems could only be solved by moving the library into Van Pelt [the main library]."[12]

In 1971, Brown University merged its physical and biological science libraries into a centralized 14-storey tower library. The University of Chicago is in the process of merging its separate science collections into a central science facility. This has been accomplished through affiliation with the John Crerar Library which will join the central science library. As the Board of the Library reported: ". . . a move which would enable us to achieve consolidation of collections and services, not only eliminating duplication between Crerar and our present collections but also affording an opportunity to consolidate with considerable savings operations within our existing system."[13]

Other means of branch library management cost reduction include reducing staff and collections, operating branches with lower level staff, or providing centralized service to branches. A common example of the latter is centralized technical services. A variation of this is centralized processing for independent campus collections. At the University of Pennsylvania, a proposal was made to centralize technical processing for the Business School collection which had its own separate processing unit. Many institutions have totally independent professional school libraries and centralized processing is one means of coordinating service.

Another centralized assistance example is automated circulation. To save staff, the branch can tie into the central computer and use the central library's staff for file maintenance, recalls, overdues, and fine notices. Another aspect of centralized branch service is collection development coordination. At Cornell, a report recommended that a position be established to ". . . exercise full expenditure authority and review all physical science, engineering and other technical material being selected for the Physical Science and Mathematics Library, the Engineering Library and the Mann Library (Agriculture)" and to eliminate duplication.[14]

Branch library absorption into the central facility can lead to crowding there. A solution to this space problem is an on-campus storage facility. Cornell and M.I.T. have such facilities, containing lesser-used material, using compact shelving and paging for delivery. These factors reduce costs and may make consolidation of branch services into the central facility feasible. The principal saving from branch facility elimination is personnel cost reduction.

To summarize, an active branch management cost control program can incorporate 1) a policy statement to limit new branch establishment; 2) merging small departmental libraries into larger ones, frequently based on subject compatibility; 3) eliminating certain branches and integrating them into the central facility; 4) reducing staffing level, e.g., using support staff instead of librarians; 5) reducing hours; 6) reducing collections or services; 7) centralizing certain types of service, e.g., processing or circulation and 8) establishing a campus storage facility.

Market Surveys

An American Library Association program indicated that marketing "is the best relief for poverty."[15] Marketing can enable a library to become "an indispensable source of information for the community" and avoid budget cutbacks.[16] An early M.I.T. survey tested community response to library service. This cost-benefit study to aid in resource allocation used a survey of students, faculty members, and researchers to rank alternative ways to improve service or save money.[17] A recent Cornell user survey is being used for the Library's Project for Collection Development and Management. These are forms of market analysis. Marketing's aim is knowing and understanding "the customer so well that the product or service fits him and sells itself."[18]

Academic librarians have seldom surveyed user habits and attitudes but marketing focuses on user service. The M.I.T. Libraries 1969 Cost Benefit Analysis originated in an effort by the Center for International Studies to improve the collection in its field. The Center sponsored the study and both Library and Center provided financial support. Results pointed out areas needing more study, such as reserve services, copying, storage, study space, cataloging, and budgeting. Among recommendations were "computerized catalogs," doubling acquisition funds, and cutting photocopy prices. Also suggested were further research areas and recommended survey research as an appropriate means of "aiding decision-makers to solve problems of benefit measurement."[19]

Another example of campus resource use for analyzing needs is the University of Lancaster surveys. Buckland worked closely with Anthony Hindle, Department of Operational Research and Ian Woodburn, Department of Systems Engineering.[20] They concluded that the library could improve book availability through optimal combinations of acquisitions, weeding, binding, circulation, and duplication policies, and a variable loan and duplication policy increased library use. The study showed the advantage of utilizing campus resources to look at problems in a different manner. The circulation studies employed user surveys to determine loan policy success or failure. Work was done in a precise fashion relying on the disciplines of engineering and operations research. A number of British campuses have formed Library Research Units and employed cross disciplinary approaches to management problems.

In a recent campus personnel assistance example, Cornell professor

David Gautschi designed a survey of Users of the Research Collections of the University Libraries. It will aid collection planners in establishing "what faculty, graduate students and others are really doing with the library material at hand when they are engaged in research in the library."[21] It will also give information on how the collections are viewed "in relation to their research and teaching requirements."[22] One of the most serious problems facing collection development planners has been the lack of critical information on how to allocate resources to satisfy the user. One of the Kent study problems was its emphasis on circulation figures.[23] Most librarians now agree that circulation figures show primarily undergraduate rather than research use. A questionnaire may be used to study graduate and research use.

Another aspect of marketing is promotion which can be a fundraising device or budget justification. Two examples are the Brown University *Trustees Manual* and the Carnegie-Mellon University study. The former was produced by the Office of Institutional Research. It described the University to the trustees and contained a library section. That section contained information on material costs including Brown's expenditures with comparison from other libraries, automated systems, resource sharing, the collection, and grants received. The library must indicate not only its strengths but also its weaknesses, since the trustees can be an important force in finance, particularly fund-raising.

The Carnegie-Mellon report used a research assistant/programmer and measured the Library with comparable institution libraries to determine whether the fund allocation was appropriate. Based on a statistical analysis, the report concluded that "there is good evidence that a higher level of investment in the library would be repaid by a significant increase in the quality of the University's educational and research programs."[24]

Campus market analysis can bring important dividends in any austerity program. First, market analysis can help to focus collection development, thus reducing costs. Second, a user survey can suggest where the library should concentrate staff resources. Third, a market analysis can provide documentation supporting budget increases. Fourth, promotion can bring in grants. Finally, market analysis can lead to further user study and result in more efficient operation. In all of these situations, professional campus assistance can be immensely valuable.

Building Maintenance

Campus building maintenance departments are concerned with preventive maintenance, temperature control, lighting, heating, ventilating, air-conditioning, cleaning, water and other building systems. Several institutions now charge maintenance costs to the library and others are considering it. The librarian interested in making building maintenance savings must be in close contact with this department. Deferred maintenance can drain an institution's budget significantly when the deferred repairs cause problems. Indirect maintenance costs can be high. Major building repairs may interfere with service programs or lead to reduced allocation. Therefore, the librarian must consider maintenance costs in the austerity program.

Deferred maintenance is a common problem. It is the "larger and more expensive maintenance work that can be delayed and is not performed when needed or reported, usually because its cost is beyond the annual maintenance and operating budget of the physical plant department."[25] This more expensive maintenance will occur if one does not attend to regular, on-going preventive maintenance. "A building which is not maintained will rapidly deteriorate physically. Fire hazards, insects, and locks should receive special attention."[26] "Whenever possible in endowed institutions an additional sum of money beyond the cost of the building and amounting to 20% of it should be set aside as endowment to be invested and the income to be used to maintain and repair the structure."[27]

Metcalf also mentioned building features leading to low maintenance costs, e.g., furniture and fixtures which are easily cleaned or turned around, floors that can be easily maintained without constant care, janitor's closets available on every level, durable shades not requiring regular opening or closing.[28] Costs can be slowed down by regular maintenance covered by endowment income, or avoided through proper equipment selection and adequate maintenance planning. The library should also tell the administration its major maintenance needs and how long they can be delayed. The library can then be included in the university maintenance program priority list.

A computerized facility control system can be used for energy management. At Brown, where the university is now hard-wired with computer cables extending throughout the campus, such a system will be installed in 1982–83. The computer can automatically sense temperature variations and compensate for them. A master computer exists in the Plant Operations area and a microcomputer sends signals from each building. A facility control system, common in Europe, can reduce energy costs significantly. Plant Operations central office can monitor all campus buildings. Iona College has such a system.

Another system at the Schaumburg (Illinois) Township Public Library rents a Honeywell BOSS (Building Operations Services System) which paid for itself in the first eight months. "The system realizes its savings by sensitively allocating power and turning equipment on and off in the most energy-efficient manner."[29] The library could take maximum advantage of the system because its building was constructed with minimum window exposure and maximum insulation.

Three other Brown University measures aid in cutting energy cost. First, the University installed co-generation equipment. The main heating plant was converted to produce both heat and electricity by using steam twice, initially to drive a turbine and then in the heating system. This conversion process, called co-generation, will save the University an estimated 30 per cent of the overall annual million-dollar electrical bill.[30] Second, 3M reflector panels were installed on every library window to keep out summer heat and hold in winter heat. Third, the University hired an energy manager whose responsibilities are the Heating Plant (and co-generation), Heating, Ventilating and Air Conditioning (HVAC), and computerized control. This person can do energy audits and aid departments in energy management.

Smaller cost-cutting measures can be initiated, also. At Brown, for example, stack lights with timed switches automatically go off when time runs out (a maximum of fifteen minutes). According to a recent energy conservation workshop, dollars can be saved "by more efficient use of conventional energy sources."[31] Examples are "timers on a library's present conventional heating system which can save 33 per cent of fuel; a 1980 furnace burner can save 14 per cent over a 1970 model; every degree a furnace thermostat is dropped will save on costs; adapting to new ventilation standards can save a substantial part of fuel costs; installing new energy-saving electric bulbs is so cost-efficient that it will pay to throw out conventional bulbs, even if one installed them yesterday!"[32] Brown Library summer month operating schedules are modified to reduce electricity consumption.

At Brown, Plant Operation has now established a preventive maintenance division, and a staff member has been assigned to check library equipment daily, e.g., filters, fan belts, and bearings. When a simple job must be done, forms can be completed to permit the work to be done on site. If the job is more complicated, the preventive maintenance person notifies Physical Plant with the regular form and the job is placed in the queue. By establishing this service, the University hopes to avoid major repair expenses.

Regular building maintenance communication can provide benefits. Certain universities have installed computerized facility control systems and co-generation equipment. Others have assigned energy managers and preventive maintenance persons to monitor the HVAC systems. Finally, libraries can take special steps to improve current facility efficiency. Ideally, original building planning should include few windows, heavy insulation, wind and temperature entrance baffles, natural earth or tree shields against prevailing winter winds, extensive below ground area use, shaded windows, and natural ventilation techniques.

Other Ideas

At Duke, a committee identified certain University areas that would benefit from automation. The three campus libraries were selected as one group, and administrative support helped a library task force study and design an automated system with a cost benefit analysis.[33] The task force and a consultant, supplied free by an outside company, conducted interviews and drew on campus automation studies and files to find ways to share university resources while designing a system to serve libraries and users. This kind of planning emphasizes the need to extend staff resources, stretch dollars and make each campus system as interdependent as possible.

At the University of Oregon, the Library benefited from a Department of Computer Science graduate student's work. The student was hired to train staff in microcomputer use of standard software packages in order to produce a periodical list. For special projects and for those libraries that cannot afford a computer staff member, students are often available for part-time automation jobs. Certain departments will allow students to work on projects for credit instead of money.

The University of North Carolina at Chapel Hill School of Library Science offers carefully planned field work allowing students to participate in just such projects. Neighboring libraries must design the project and provide a librarian supervisor. Academic credit projects must be carefully planned to give the library control over work done while allowing the student freedom to learn. The student can seek advice from his/her faculty supervisor, also.

Conclusion

Probably intra-campus coordination exists on most campuses. And yet, library literature contains nothing under that term. Many conference programs have dealt with austere times. Catchwords include "managing under austerity," "doing more with less," and "where is all the money going (acquisitions emphasis)." The traditional approaches are interlibrary cooperation and intra-library study of ways to improve or maintain service. There is certainly glamour in interlibrary cooperation. The quest for self-knowledge is strong in our society, and adversity turns us inward. Introspection becomes necessary for survival. Intra-campus coordination is a combination of cooperation with outside organizations and an inward look at resource use. Why then is there no readily available body of literature on which to draw? Private industry practices the equivalent, especially when profit can be improved or cutbacks demand it.

We have seen that certain librarians are coordinating their efforts to conserve and stretch resources with those of business offices, bookstores, and personnel offices. If such coordination is widespread, why does so little documentation appear in library literature? Several answers come to mind. This type of activity takes much time and work and by the time an agreement is worked out, another must be begun. There is little time for writing papers about what one does to survive. Another possibility is that such coordination is so mundane that it does not occur to the principals that anyone outside of the campus would be interested in it. Another possibility is that such coordination is not widespread. Campus competition for dollars is so fierce that many departments do not want to surrender anything, even when everyone gains. It may be too that a library may not want to publicize its gains for fear that word may return to the campus and be misunderstood.

Higher institutions should encourage intra-campus coordination reports, short reports for the *Chronicle of Higher Education,* and more detailed journal reports. We believe that intra-campus coordination is more widespread than this paper reflects. Perhaps this paper will encourage project sharing and lead professional organizations to sponsor intra-campus coordination programs. Finally, this paper may lead *Library Literature* and other indexes to establish an entry for "Intra-campus Coordination."

References

1. Ellsworth Mason, *Mason on Library Buildings* (Metuchen, N.J.: Scarecrow Press, 1980), p. 30.
2. NAEB is located at 180 Froehlich Farm Boulevard, Woodbury, N.Y. 11797.
3. Rutherford D. Rogers and David C. Weber, *University Library Administration* (N.Y.: H.W. Wilson, 1971), p. 349.
4. "Economics of Research Libraries Meeting," *ARL Newsletter* 109 (December 4, 1981), p. 8.
5. Joe B. Wyatt, James C. Emery & Carolyn P. Landis, *Financial Planning Models: Concepts and Case Studies in Colleges & Universities* (Princeton, N.J.: Interuniversity Communications Council, 1979), p. 108. Obviously, the serial situation has changed since 1978.
6. Richard W. Boss, *Report of the Special Committee on Library Acquisitions and Losses* (Princeton, N.J.: Princeton University Libraries, May 27, 1977), pp. 1–2.
7. Thomas R. Mason & others, *Libraries of the University of Missouri–Columbia: Library Evaluation and Facilities Program Plan* (n.p., the Sasaki, Mackey, MIRA, Martin Team, December 1981), p. 5.
8. Brown University Faculty Library Committee, *Library Impact Statement* (Providence: May 19, 1980).
9. Judith R. Lave and David W. Miller, *Library Resources at Carnegie–Mellon and Other Universities: a Comparative Investigation* (Pittsburgh: Carnegie Mellon Library Committee, October 1977), p. 2.
10. Jeffrey A. Raffel and Robert Shishko, *Systematic Analysis of University Libraries: An Application of Cost-Benefit Analysis to the M.I.T. Libraries* (Cambridge: MIT Press. 1969), p. 29.
11. Rogers, *op. cit.,* pp. 75–76.
12. Richard De Gennaro, *The Challenge of Retrenchment, Report of the Director of Libraries University of Pennsylvania, 1976–1977 and 1977–78* (Philadelphia: October 17, 1978), p. vi.

13. The Board of the Library, *The University of Chicago Libraries, 1977* (Chicago: University of Chicago Libraries, 1977), p. 6.

14. J. Gormly Miller, *Collection Development and Management at Cornell* (Ithaca, N.Y.: Cornell University Libraries, April 1981), p. 40.

15. "Live from Denver," *American Libraries* 14 (March 1982), p. 178.

16. Joyce A. Edinger, "Marketing Library Services: Strategy for Survival," *College and Research Libraries* 41 (July 1980), p. 329.

17. Raffel, *passim.*

18. Peter F. Drucker, *Management: Tasks, Responsibilities, Practices* (N.Y.: Harper & Row Publishers, 1973), p. 64.

19. Raffel, *op. cit.,* p. 71.

20. Michael K. Buckland, *Book Availability and the Library User* (N.Y.: Pergamon Press, 1975), p. 143.

21. J. Gormly Miller, *op. cit.,* p. 80.

22. Ibid., p. 80.

23. Allen Kent, *Use of Library Materials, The University of Pittsburgh Study* (N.Y.: Marcel Dekker, 1979).

24. Lave, *op. cit.,* p. 22.

25. L. Terry Suber, "Coping with Deferred Maintenance," *Business Officer* 15 (May 1982), p. 22.

26. Rogers, *op. cit.,* p. 353.

27. Keyes Metcalf, *Planning Academic and Research Library Buildings* (N.Y.: McGraw-Hill, 1965), p. 48.

28. Ibid., p. 47.

29. "Computer Building System Saved Schaumburg, Ill. Big $$," *Library Journal* 104 (December 1, 1979), p. 2509.

30. "Co-generation Ready to Start Producing Electricity in December," *George Street Bulletin* 7 (October 16, 1981), p. 1.

31. "How to Save Money With Better Energy Use," *Library Journal* 107 (March 15, 1980), p. 667.

32. Ibid.

33. Carolyn Cox, et. al., *A Study of the Duke University Libraries Information System* (DULIS) (Durham, N.C.: August 1981), 246 p.

6. Negotiation Skills Improvement

Robert J. Merikangas and John F. Harvey

A NUMBER OF NEGOTIATION METHODS are gaining wide acceptance in labor, industry and international relations, and academic librarians should consider them. Negotiation is one of several roles that a librarian may play in austere times and this role may be helpful in improving program support. Negotiation skills are useful in a wide variety of management situations. The chapter will focus on the personal behavior of librarians and library managers and how that behavior can aid in reducing the problems aggravated by austerity. A number of the situations in which negotiation is commonly applied are dealt with in other chapters of this volume, also.

No doubt certain readers are ready for a more subtle and mature interface level with campus adversaries. Negotiation is an old and frequently used process which has won many victories. It is often a matter of cents and inches and even a slight improvement in the face of austere conditions is helpful. A person who can negotiate the library into an improved situation of any kind has made a major contribution. Many staff members evaluate managers now by their negotiation ability.

Many librarians' negotiation skills seem to need improvement. Often their lack of budget bargaining table success indicates that. Recent austerity provides another reason for negotiation instruction. In an austere era, intra-campus competition to obtain every possible advantage intensifies in all operation areas. The library can no longer afford to lose arguments. To some small extent austerity is negotiable, and close bargaining is the new order of the day.

Negotiation means arranging something by agreement rather than by authority or coercion. It has been called bargaining, wheeling and dealing, making deals and exchanging, and is omnipresent in everyday life.[1] Negotiating is the art of winning arguments, the art of surrendering a little less. It relates closely to military strategy and game theory and can be presented in mathematical models and matrixes. Negotiation theory has been called the logic of indeterminate situations.[2]

Negotiation is a basic means of getting what you want from others. It is back-and-forth communication designed to reach an agreement when you and the other side have some interests that are shared and others that are opposed.[3]

Negotiation is either explicit or tacit. Explicit requires face-to-face confrontation while tacit requires watching the adversary covertly and interpreting her/his actions. Negotiation is guided by the expectation of what the adversary will accept, and one side concedes only because it believes the other side will not. Usually, bargaining occurs in a situation in which it is either desirable or else mandatory to reach an agreement of some kind rather than let the matter drift.

In tacit bargaining, every aspect of the librarian's life, work, and play style is under scrutiny and evaluation. He/she should be aware of campus opinion about the make of car driven, church preference, quality of her/his residential suburb, tipping policy, television set availability, choice of sports, clothing selection and social life, for instance.

An increased awareness of negotiation as a process has developed recently among sociologists and managers.[4-6] This interest is related to that in conflict resolution, assertiveness training, and stress management. In negotiating, a person uses her/his own *self* as an instrument and brings to bear skills of observing, communicating, and judging. Negotiation involves mobilizing power, information, and people. This paper assumes that each librarian is responsible for her/his own development, needs a *theory* to guide action, a repertory of specific behaviors for various situations, and the ability to apply them selectively.

The Double Problem

Negotiation is one of the most subtle managerial skills and is heavily dependent on experience. Mintzberg identified ten managerial roles:

> *Interpersonal:* figurehead, leader, liaison;
> *Informational:* monitor, disseminator, spokesman;
> *Decisional:* entrepreneur, disturbance handler, resource allocator, negotiator.[7]

Leadership "permeates all activities."[8] As Mintzberg observed, ". . . formal authority vests the manager with great potential power; leadership activity determines how much of it will be realized."[9] Leadership in connection with outside relationships is based on the liaison role which "deals with the significant web of relationships that the manager maintains with numerous individuals and groups outside the organization headed."[10]

This linkage with the environment enables the manager to promote the flow of information out (as spokesperson) and inside (as dissemina-tor). The linkage is the basis for creative negotiation. Mintzberg gave an image: "The manager may be likened to the neck of an hour-glass, standing between his own organization and a network of outside con-tacts, linking them in a variety of ways."[11] Another student has con-cluded: "Typically, the negotiating function builds on several other managerial functions. In representing the unit, the manager serves as *symbolic figurehead* and *spokesman*, summarizing the organization's views. The negotiation will result in *resource allocation*, as something is given up or obtained from outside."[12]

Improving management negotiation skills is not merely a personal matter, however, for the other problem is the complexity of the campus political situation and the necessity to gain some control over it. One way of seeing the importance of campus negotiation is by an analysis of "job-related dependence" in academic libraries: an uncertain environ-ment, environmental dependencies, scarce resources, complex technol-ogy, and diffused authority—all meaning that a leader must give time to behavior which concentrates on the acquisition and use of power in order to cope with dependence.[13]

Negotiation is an effort to gain power by influencing others. In the manager's complex life, he/she should focus attention on negotiation leading to enhanced control over daily relationships. Agreement is sought and this involves "power dynamics." Library dependence is due in part to specialization—a director is dependent on many persons for information and cooperation—and to limited resources, exacerbated in austerity. Figure 1 attempts to survey a typical library environment in terms of high and low dependence.[14] Each library must assess its own position in this fashion and identify its chief dependency areas. Being dependent is a fact of life; what counts is what is made of it. Mintzberg makes the same point:

All managers appear to be puppets. Some decide who will pull the strings and how, and they then take advantage of each move that they are forced to make. Others, unable to exploit this high-tension environment, are swallowed up by this most demanding of jobs.[15]

The ideas in this chapter are designed for use in many kinds of internal and external negotiation sessions, in any discussion involving a staff member and leading to a decision affecting the library. Some sessions involve protracted discussion, others not. Staff members should be able to negotiate from a strong position if they have confi-dence in library service. Many of this paper's ideas are intended for thought, not for public expression. The successful negotiator uses shrewd and penetrating analyses and adroit yet covert manipulation of the situation but usually reveals no indication of her/his scheming to the adversary.

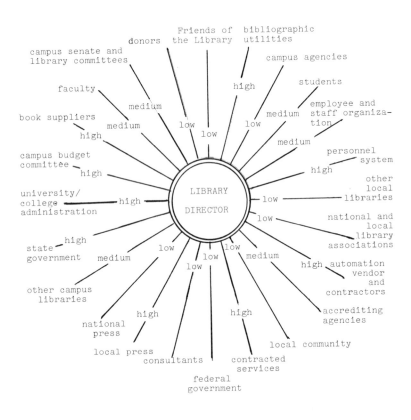

Figure 1. Dependence in Relationships: High, Medium, Low

A Team Approach

The object of negotiation is to obtain more power by getting control over resources, getting information and control over information channels, and establishing favorable interpersonal relationships.[16] In using these means, the negotiator's skill is the key. Decisions often depend on the climate of trust and willingness to cooperate. Permanent alliances and contacts must be maintained with various administrators, faculty, staff, and student leaders. Building an effective negotiation program is cyclic. One must negotiate in order to create relationships and create relationships in order to negotiate. One must obtain information in order to negotiate and negotiate in order to obtain information.

An integrated approach may be more effective than separate approaches. A *good* negotiating style goes beyond variations in management style depending on personality and work circumstances, in that common principles should inform it. An integrated approach requires effort to use a consistent negotiating method in interpersonal and intergroup dealings within and without the library. In this way, staff members can learn in their frequent interactions with each other the methods of negotiating useful agreements outside the library.

A program to improve negotiation skills must involve more than top management. Because of the vast campus scope and the numerous communication channels that must be used, no single person can gather all relevant data and carry out the communication needed to reach agreements supporting library programs. Staff members can be useful in gathering information on negotiable problems and in negotiating themselves. The Association of Research Libraries (ARL) Office of Management Studies offers a survey analysis service in support of major decisions and has developed a particular decision-making program for the preservation sub-field.[17] Such programs can serve as models of the preparation needed for negotiating a major agreement.

Negotiation is part of most job relationships. Middle managers who report to different supervisors must either negotiate agreements or take matters to a higher level, but negotiation is the preferred mode.[18] Also, each person can act as an internal entrepreneur and seek to get her/his best ideas adopted by the system. Negotiation is a central part of this influence-enhancing process.[19] Further, any librarian may act as a leader in campus environments or professional activities. In these contexts also a premium is placed on the ability to work out agreements when no authority exists. Often middle level managers can work out more beneficial arrangements that those at the top.[20]

Preparation for Negotiation

Success is more likely to occur if the negotiator, normally the library manager or director, is well prepared. Both her/his negotiation skill learning program and background information preparation must be well organized. A skills learning method must be chosen: a short experiential program, team training program, or individual study. What are the problems involved in changing one's negotiation behavior? Managers may take intensive workshops to improve skills. They are found by using lists of professional associations and commercial agencies and by scanning local adult education program advertising. A key point:

While these approaches seemed effective in leading to individual learning, they had several drawbacks when measured against specific participant and organizational requirements.[21]

Berger and Harrison developed an individualized structured training program. It spent 1.5 days on self-assessment activities, then 2.5 days in developing participant skills which they had identified as being needed. The last day was spent in working out strategies for applying newly learned skills on the job. Another desirable workshop feature is a follow-up program with a refresher session and an incentive to implement precepts.[22]

Some directories of courses and programs:

- *Bricker's International Directory: University Executive Development Programs* (Woodside, CA: S. A. Pond, latest)
- *Course Catalog*, American Management Association, 155 West 50th St., N.Y., N.Y. 10020
- Wasserman, Paul (ed.), *Training and Development Organizations Directory* (Detroit: Gale Research, latest)

Because learning requires practice, negotiation skills training might be part of a campus or library management development program.[23] Training requires checklist use and practice through role playing in case studies.[24] The possibility of team training should be investigated. For instance, the director may designate an automation team, composed of all those negotiating procedures with the campus computer center. The steps involved in team formation are not mysterious.[25] Dyer has stated, ". . . in ten years, most managers will take team building, unit development, organizational integration, or whatever it will be called then, as one of the prerequisites of doing the manager's job."[26]

Another training dimension involves reducing interteam conflict.[27] A librarian who can work successfully in an intralibrary group program will be better prepared for the intergroup conflicts characteristic of outside negotiation settings. A problem-solving approach may be recommended in which the problem is not defined prior to contact. It is developed *by and through intergroup contact*.[28] By using this method, managers can simultaneously deal with intramural intergroup conflicts and dysfunctional relationships and also be prepared to represent the library in extramural problem-solving negotiation sessions.[29]

In further preparation, staff discussion and assistance must be sought. Usually a discussion is needed to develop useful ideas and a defensible position on each controversial issue and to secure backing for them. In this preparation stage, the staff must identify and explore counterarguments, learn who is likely to present them and to lose something if the idea succeeds, and learn to counter them. Staff members can be organized to attack problem aspects and contact campus committees. The accountability problem must be faced and defenses developed.

The negotiator must get library priorities well in hand. To win the fifth-level item and lose the top four is an expensive victory. The negotiator must know what to push hardest for—either due to its intrinsic value or because it will facilitate other victories in domino fashion—and he/she must know what can most easily be surrendered. Similarly, in other circumstances, a fallback position must be agreed upon before the negotiation session, one beyond which the negotiator will not retreat. A strategic retreat must be based on logical principles. Without a convincing rationale the adversary will assume that you have caved in and that he/she can drive you to the wall.

The library file on the issue at hand must be studied, past history, successes and failures. Relevant journal and book literature must be read and applicable ideas noted. Material may be solicited from the nearest consortium office, the Association of College and Research Libraries, and ARL to show logical and useful arguments and how and why other libraries deal successfully with the problem. Precedent should be sought for the positions to be taken. Without backup information the negotiator is only partly prepared. While he/she will not win arguments with data only, fact examination is usually essential. "Seat of the pants" presentations are sometimes necessary but are increasingly outdated.

The manager must recognize personal negotiating strong and weak points. They can be critiqued by colleagues and by herself/himself through experience. He/she must try to steer negotiations away from points on which one personally or one's position is weak and into channels in which both are strong. Taking along a staff department head to explain a new project may or may not be productive. The person's project knowledge may exceed that of the manager, but leaning on such a person may suggest that the manager does not understand the project fully and thereby undermine her/his prestige.

Building outside support for projects is a very useful activity. Nothing should please the library more than to have students and faculty members, perhaps even alumni and trustees, visiting the vice president (or whoever the library director reports to) to argue the library's case. Campus committee support should be sought, especially with the faculty library committee. Deans profiting from the idea may be asked to support it. Student council support may be useful or counterproductive but must be considered. A comprehensive background information report should be prepared for the vice president. These activities may require considerable preparation time before faculty meeting discussion and vote.

An Introduction to Principled Negotiation

This paper cannot present a comprehensive explanation of negotiation principles and techniques since they are complex and lengthy. It summarizes, however, certain useful principles and refers the reader to more extensive treatments of them. Most of the guidance provided is based on common sense and represents simplified and practical ideas.

Through simple honesty and frankness, many managers attempt to develop a climate of trust which they think will lead to their supervisor's candor and support for recommendations. However, the extent to which that individual responds favorably is often hard to evaluate and may easily be overestimated. The agreeable manager is just what the domineering vice president may seek, at the expense of library service. In a situation in which the vice president does not reciprocate, library strategy needs revision.

Cohen stressed the idea that

to maximize your impact as a negotiator you must *personalize* both yourself and the situation. How do you personalize yourself? You make the other party see you as a unique, flesh-and-blood, three-dimensional individual, someone who has feelings and needs, someone the other person likes, cares about, and somehow feels obliged to—at least someone the other person wants to do something for. How do you personalize the situation? Try not to negotiate on behalf of an institution or organization, no matter how large or small. Negotiate on behalf of *yourself, representing* the institution.[30]

Prevention works best: "This means building a personal and organizational relationship with the other side that can cushion the people on each side against the knocks of negotiation."[31] It is hard to negotiate (or do regular business) with a stranger, so getting to know others informally is highly desirable. It is easier then to build a foundation of trust.

Fisher and Ury say their high level method is both hard and soft:

The method of *principled negotiation* developed at the Harvard Negotiation Project is to decide issues on their merits rather than through a haggling process focused on what each side says it will and won't do. It suggests that you look for mutual gains whenever possible, and that where your interests conflict, you should insist that the result be based on some fair standards independent of the will of either side. The method of principled negotiation is hard on the merits, soft on the people. It employs no tricks and no posturing. Principled negotiation shows you how to obtain what you are entitled to and still be decent. [It] . . . is an all-purpose strategy.[32]

Principled negotiation has four main points, which define the ethical method:

1. *People:* Separate the people from the problem.
2. *Interests:* Focus on interests, not positions.
3. *Options:* Generate a variety of possibilities before deciding what to do.
4. *Criteria:* Insist that the result be based on objective standards.[33]

After introducing the topic by urging the negotiator not to bargain over positions, the first negotiation point implies the need to build a working relationship with people as a basis for all other attention to perceptions, emotions, and communication modes. It is also the last point in that attention should be given to the people problem at every stage. The most important single factor here: "give them a stake in the outcome by making sure they participate in the process."[34] Be perceptive and communicate skillfully.

One of the central needs in negotiating is to "deal directly with the people problem."[35] You want to understand the other persons and help them to save face. Different people will have different styles, also, and writers on negotiation often try to categorize these styles. Johnson and Johnson offer five styles:

- the *turtles* (withdrawing)—give up personal goals and relationship both, to avoid conflicts;
- the *sharks* (forcing)—seek to achieve their goals at any cost, not concerned with the needs of others;
- the *teddy bears* (smoothing)—give up their goals to preserve a relationship, try to smooth over conflict;
- the *foxes* (compromising)—"moderately concerned with their own goals and their relationship with others"; they seek compromise, each giving up something
- the *owls* (confronting)—value both goals and relationships; "they view conflicts as problems to be solved and seek a solution that achieves both their own goals and the goals of the other person."[36]

Fisher and Ury's second point urges that negotiators work to reconcile *interests* not positions. Each side should go behind opposed positions to find interests: needs and concerns. Ask each other: why do you want that? List the interests. Express yourself strongly. Focus on the problem, not on the other people. Be firm on your interests and open to learn of the other side's interests.

The third point involves more complex activities—using creative methods to find varied alternatives. Don't assume a fixed pie. Each side should brainstorm as a group, and brainstorming by a joint group is also possible. Specific behavior techniques for a brainstorming session are given. The key step is to invent a number of options and then evaluate them. In the options, the idea is to look for mutual gain and ways to dovetail differing interests. Draft a possible agreement as an aid to clear thinking. The options could deal with ways to get resources, new organizational arrangements, alternatives for compensation, different procedures, varying deadlines.

Fisher and Ury devised a Circle Chart to guide four types of thinking: a) identifying the problem, b) analyzing the problem, c) variety of approaches to solutions and d) action ideas. The Circle Chart helps a discussion group to see where they are and work in a consecutive fashion.

The fourth point is to insist on objective criteria. At each stage, one frames the issue as a joint search for objective criteria. This approach is common in universities. The criteria might be national standards for library collections or comparative rankings with peer institutions. Unless there is agreement to apply the criteria, however, their proposal by one side is not necessarily effective. In the negotiation process, one should be like a judge, not a lawyer, and be open to reasons for applying other standards. If there is no agreement on the best criteria to use for fairness, the two sides might invite a neutral third party to decide.

After presenting these four points, Fisher and Ury deal with three "what if" questions that seem to present obstacles. First, what if the other side is more powerful? Power might go to the side with a stronger position, larger staff, more authority or resources. The library will not be the more powerful in all cases. In deciding whether to negotiate an agreement at all, one should have already determined one's BATNA— Best Alternative to a Negotiated Agreement.[37] This alternative avoids taking a poor agreement and should help your side to make the most of its assets—what does your side have of value to the other side?

Second, what if they won't play?[38] If the other side engages in positional bargaining, one can refuse to play that game. Continually focus on interests and criteria. Use questions, not attacks. Use pauses. Take their position as one option, and try to develop others, asking in each case how it meets fairness criteria. If this approach does not work well, and positions are hardened, a third party can be brought in. The one-text procedure can be used, in which the third party drafts texts which attempt to satisfy the expressed needs of both parties. This method was used by the United States at Camp David in 1978.[39]

Third, what if the other side uses dirty tricks?[40] Do not merely put up with them, do not respond in kind, but "engage in principled negotiation about the negotiating process."[41] Walk out if necessary. Be firm, for "it is easier to defend principle than an illegitimate tactic."[42]

This method as a whole is oriented toward *justice*, not a win-lose result. It provides a way for win-win strategies to be more effective by giving them a framework and a clear legitimacy. Because the theme is mutuality and joint control rather than competitiveness, it may be difficult for some persons to change behaviors to be congruent with it.[43] Carrying this out is similar to living the Golden Rule: the spirit may be willing, but the flesh weak. It is significant, however, that many books on negotiation advocate the win-win over other strategies.[44] Still others, however, retain freedom of action for managers and allow them to move into the unethical area when necessary.[45]

Practical Strategy and Tactics in an Imperfect World

Negotiation is an aspect of war. With limited resources available, library gains must normally be won at the expense of another campus unit, and every other unit needs those dollars desperately, also. On the surface, negotiation is a friendly exchange of views, but more deeply studied it is a much more serious and competitive situation. During negotiation the good old boy/girl librarian should have a heart of steel.

The negotiator must be conscious of the time frame in which he/she operates. In some situations, it is useful to stall, in others to press for a quick decision. Stall when the discussion is going badly or crises interfere with it but press for a quick decision when the discussion is going well. The negotiator should be imaginative, resourceful, voluble, and refer frequently to faculty and student opinion and demand. It is also wise occasionally to provide something for the vice president to brag about to the president. The vice president's pet library project may be supported but not without some logrolling of your own.

The library manager's "honeymoon" period in the first year on the job is the time to take advantage of initial good will (if any) and to tap the vice president's discretionary fund. In austerity, however, the honeymoon period's concessions are likely to involve only such things as a new secretary or unscheduled office redecoration. "Testing the water" in the early job years by overt acts designed primarily to see how far the university administration can be pushed or ignored has value. It should be carried out in a planned series of varied moves in several areas and directions.

Likewise, early negotiation sessions constitute the "feeling out" period when each side tries to discover the other's bottom line. Management is the art of the possible, with an occasional miracle thrown in. Identifying the possible's parameters—priorities, strong and weak points, power and flexibility—is what much of the negotiator's information-seeking behavior seeks. Time is wasted on arguments leading beyond them. This is similar to estimating an opponent's bridge-playing hand. It is not so important what each negotiator thinks of the other one but what each negotiator thinks the other one thinks of her/him. Being able to delay the final reckoning may be an advantage since it allows the adversary time to realize the hardness of the manager's position. Patience and endurance are two important negotiator characteristics.

Normally, bargaining should procede from small maters on which practice can be obtained to larger matters of greater complexity and importance. Dealing with several matters simultaneously may be advantageous since a concession on one may put the adversary in a weakened position on others. The restricted agenda has merit, also. It can be useful when the manager is not yet prepared to discuss other matters and is especially recommended to avoid harmful side effects when the present discussion on another topic is sure to lead to defeat. On the other hand, if the discussion finds the adversary in a very positive mode, then additional matters may be added with some hope of success. It is also true that package deals are sometimes easier to arrange than simple deals.

Usually fear of change must be fought. On many campuses, the imaginative manager will have difficulty with university administrators who have much to lose from change, or so they think. Therefore, negotiation to introduce change may need special care and reassurance for both university administrators and library staff members. Breaking precedent presents the same kind of problem. If the manager's argument can be couched in terms which suggest no disturbance of or even a return to the status quo, then it may be easier to win.

Keep the adversary guessing, especially when you are the more mentally adept. A surprise attack can be useful in disorienting her/him. A defensive posture should make her/him less self-assured. If the manager can demonstrate that certain of the adversary's key argument terms have varied definitions, their value may be lowered. But these generalizations, like many others in negotiation, apply in certain instances and not in others.

Bargaining power is the power to fool and bluff. To fool means to lie about facts and use tactical means to mislead the adversary. To bluff means to act boldly without the full means to support the action, to deceive, intimidate, or frighten. Deans and vice presidents use intimidation daily. A threat is designed to intimidate, not to penalize if carried out. Its usefulness depends on the opponent's credulity and must hurt the adversary more than the library. However, only modest threats are taken seriously, and few administrators would be alarmed by any modest library-based threat. Therefore, most libraries have no reasonable threat mechanism.

Talk is cheap but overt moves are not. Strategic moves should reduce the adversary's freedom of choice, like an opening chess move which immediately throws the opponent on the defensive. There may be some advantage in cultivating a hard-nosed image. After all, due to their indifference to dents and scratches, taxi drivers are given a wide berth.

Brinkmanship is a dangerous game in which the aggressor attempts to see how far he/she can go in bringing both sides near the precipice before the adversary adopts a more concilliatory attitude. For a few persons and situations, this may be a useful strategy. Non-compliance with an unfavorable ruling may be considered, also, when it is unlikely to be detected.

Should the manager try to become a buddy of the vice president or a foe? This relates to the strength of their relative positions and to their personalities. Becoming a foe has certain advantages if the bluff can be sustained. The strategy of campus unit heads who seem usually to fare well with the vice president should be studied closely. On certain campuses the most difficult-to-get-along-with department head has also gotten excellent decisions for her/his faculty. A middle position may enable the manager to command respect while avoiding the "difficult" label.

The manager must know when to be tactful and when abrasive, when docile and when aggressive. Certain persons respond better to one and others better to the other. The manager must know when to be firm and when to be flexible. Presumably he/she should be firm as much of the time as possible and flexible only when forced to be or when a long-range or trade-off library advantage is presented.

A person who cannot receive messages—because he/she is on vacation or ill, for instance—has the advantage that neither bad news nor bluffing can reach her/him. On the other hand, by absence, he/she may have forfeited the opportunity to rebut an argument. Another device is deliberately to reduce the scope of the manager's authority and confront the adversary with the strong feelings of a unanimous staff vote empowering her/him only to explain their views. He/she can retreat very little without antagonizing the staff and endangering her/his own viability in representing them.

When to obfuscate and when to jawbone. When the vice president pursues an idea that is inimical to the library's best interests, the manager may obfuscate, revealing little while talking much in order to elude inquiries. Diversionary tactics are similar, in which the manager leads the adversary away from her/his unpleasant topic. When the manager is explaining her/his own ideas, however, he/she may jawbone extensively in order to clarify all points. The fuller the explanation, the more likely is administrator acceptance, in most cases.

Promises (contracts) are of four kinds: bilateral (binding on both sides); openly unilateral (one side makes a promise and expects no immediate recompense); covertly unilateral (one side thinks it is bilateral and the other side thinks it is unilateral); and nonlateral (both sides think it is binding on the other side but not on her/his side). Openly unilateal library promises may be useful in prying loose concessions. They may take the form of abandoning hope for an expensive project, for instance. No doubt contracts of the third and fourth kinds are more common than is generally supposed. Iranians often say that no bilateral contracts exist there.

Sometimes there is power in weakness. Bargaining power may be an advantage or may not be, depending on how resourceful the manager is. The strong adversary can afford to compromise whereas the manager may be in too weak a position to do that. The poorly informed bargainer may throw herself/himself on the adversary's mercy and win more than he/she otherwise would. The weak bargainer has nothing to lose, the strong bargainer much to lose, her/his reputation. Merit can be seen in being able to recognize high priority ancillary advantages in occasional low priority projects. Certain low priority projects can pave the way for others of much greater value. An example is the establishment of an automated acquisitions system which can lead to data processing use in other departments.

At the discussion's end, the negotiator should try to leave the adversary with the last clear chance to decide the outcome after having been gotten into a position where he/she must decide in the library's favor. And finally, in order to maintain good communication with the vice president's office, cultivate the secretary.

A method has to be more than a collection of attitudes, maxims, or rules based on common sense and imagination. As Interaction Associates defined and illustrated it, "a method is an ordered sequence of strategies."[46] Having a multitude of strategies and tactics to choose from is useful.[47,48] How do we go beyond a *collection* and gain an *ordered sequence* of strategies? One way is to make up one's own short guide, incorporating a theory of action and checklists for each negotiation stage. The ideas must be reduced to a form that can be applied to actual situations.

The Arts of Persuasion and Opportunism

One day in 1961, a perceptive friend of one of the authors was overheard praising the work of her library school dean at Case Western Reserve University, Cleveland. The man being praised was Jesse Shera. Upon being asked her opinion of Shera's particular strengths, she replied that he was a persuasive speaker and a good opportunist.

To be able to negotiate with sincerity, enthusiasm, and eloquence about one's projects normally requires a certain natural gift for persuasion as well as some cultivation of it. Negotiation is only partly intellectual; an important element is presentation skill, speaking effectiveness. Is the persuasive personality born or learned? Probably some of both. Certainly, speech skills can be improved by instruction. Establishing a climate of persuasion is essential. The negotiator must know how to motivate interest, agreement, and even enthusiasm and to popularize library projects. Widespread campus gain may be emphasized. The goal is to convince each adversary sufficiently that he/she can argue for the project convincingly with her/his own supervisor.

How to be convincing. It is easier to prove the truth of a true statement than a false one, if proof is required. An irrevocable commitment is often convincing, one which the speaker will hold to till death, but the speaker must make sure of her/his commitment despite future changes. A final offer must be final or all future offers will be considered temporary. A director may stake her/his position on a pet project's success, such as an automated charging system, but he/she must do this with full staff and administration knowledge and be prepared actually to resign if it fails. The negotiator must convince the adversary of her/his emotional commitment to the present argument also.

Most negotiators are more persuasive with certain adversaries and less so with others. Some can persuade a statistics-lover more successfully than a poet, a woman more easily than a man, an instructor more easily than a professor. In addition to eloquence, this calls for tacit bargaining, being able to read her/his personality, character, vulnerable and invulnerable points, likes and dislikes.

The opportunist knows when to sit back and tell amusing boyhood stories and when to push and shove aggressively. After lining up her/his needs, he/she must be very alert to recognize opportunities and move actively after them. For instance, when an outstanding employee is identified on someone else's staff, the opportunist knows how to wait patiently, cultivate from afar, fence out other managers, provide incentive, and then present an opportune and very persuasive offer. The opportunist must have a considerable variety of formal and informal news sources, even gossip. He/she should know more about the adversary's problems than the adversary does. Certain opportunists force opportunities to occur. They turn situations around by the force of their personalities. They will not be denied.

Campus Politics

The library must be recognized as a campus political entity. Probably it is a potent force on few campuses, but that situation may be changing as it becomes increasingly politicized. Due partly to staff size, the library is potentially a strong force on the questions on which the staff takes a united position. Skillful use of this potential is the manager's obligation. He/she must become the spokesperson for carefully chosen issues and lead the negotiation for their approval. But he/she must be wary of opportunities to choose sides on issues of low library, staff, or scholarly relevance.

Staff members who are active campus politicians can be helpful. The local situation must be studied: faculty vs. administration, department vs. department, science vs. humanities, student vs. faculty member, liberal vs. conservative, and person vs. person. Informants must report regularly on campus committee meetings, school and departmental developments, as they relate to the library.

Faculty political leaders—deans, department heads, committee heads, shop stewards and other opinion leaders—must be identified and studied, particularly for their library attitudes. Contacts must be developed with them and the library's viewpoint toward controversial matters explained. The faculty library committee can play a useful advisory role here. With proper briefing, the student council, student newpaper and magazine can influence opinion and facilitate negotiation. A reporter should be requested to cover library stories weekly, and full explanation of them should be provided.

In addition, certain community business and personal users, alumni, trustees, and state government higher education and library officials must be cultivated and their views discussed, if campus administrators permit such contacts. All of them have a vested interest in library progress. Ideas can be gotten into their heads which will ease future negotiations. Certain trustees may have a strong and useful interest in scholarship, building, or book collecting.

A key decision on each issue is that of chosing allies vs. remaining neutral—where do the library's interests lie? Neutrality avoids the chance of having picked the losing side, but may miss the opportunity to support a scholarly advance, a winning idea or candidate. Most ideas which clearly agree with the library's best interests should be supported. Every semester the library should list these ideas for staff discussion and use; of course, each library list will be different. Any choice of sides will offend someone so the manager should discuss issues with staff members before commitment. Timid managers may be reluctant to oppose the university administration, but this must be done where the staff position warrants it.

Library staff room politics is an intramural game in which no one wins, least of all the director. On certain campuses, this room demonstrates life in the raw, an island of the real world inside the ivory tower. The viciousness of personal critiques and self-centered games has led many staff members to avoid these rooms and to question their benefits, especially when not heavily used, over simple canteen service provision. If the manager can win arguments here, he/she can win them anywhere. At the least, however, the manager should endeavor to avoid the situation where the staff room denizens are fighting the very ideas which library department heads are trying to sell to the university administration.

Committeepersonship requires learning the art of successful committe service. Committees inside or outside the library provide a good setting in which to practice negotiation skills. The key offices are those of the chairperson who controls the agenda, work flow, voting, and meeting scheduling and the secretary who controls activity recording and meeting announcements. Sometimes the two offices are combined or else one succeeds the other in the following year. By regular attendance, by considering issues carefully, asking thoughtful questions, and making useful position statements contributions can be made. Support activity must be carried out for certain committee issues which are taken to the general faculty meeting, also.

The Power Approach

In developing negotiation skills, the manager must confront the temptation to use a power approach. Much literature exists on how to win control—by intimidation and by calculated manipulation of others. Advocates assume all of life to be a win-lose contest and that we either control or are controlled. Perhaps it is, especially in an austere and competitive situation, or perhaps only part of it is so desperate. To avoid being controlled, we must at least be assertive, and beyond that, advocates say, constantly play "the power game." Power game masters "play the game twenty-four hours a day . . . instinctively trying to control every life situation . . . and to place as much of an obligation as possible on the other person."[49] This "success" literature may seem to be extreme, but we may at least wish to be aware of the basket of tricks and clever ploys which can be used against us.

We are advised to note innumerable physical postures and movements, all designed to achieve or avoid domination. Such observations can be made in many social situations. For instance, a recent colleague of one of the authors would often entwine her legs tightly when in conversation with him (suppressing strong negative emotion?), a secretary usually looked at him from the corners of her eyes (shy and critical?), an earlier staff member always stood facing him squarely when talking business (to get and hold his attention?), while a male cataloger's pipe seemed always to be between us (for hiding behind?).

Feet, we learn ("foot power") are especially significant, and "power people are very sensitive about feet" and shoes.[50] For men, the well shined shoe may indicate the status seeker, the unshined shoe the nonconformist, the slipon the lazy librarian, the plain toe the simple (or clear-thinking?) mind, the ornate toe the ambitious nonsophisticate, the too tight shoe the idealist, the unrepaired shoe the poorly organized primitive, the much repaired shoe the conservative, the tennis-shoed dean the unstylish bumpkin, the sandal the relaxed conversationalist, the boot the dominator, and the loafer the loafer.

Because so many contacts are made by telephone, certain authors have summarized phone negotiation characteristics: a) being misunderstood is easier on the phone than in person, b) saying no is easier, c) the party with more power or the better argument usually wins, d) calls are quicker, e) calls are a greater risk, f) and the advantage is to the caller. The statement that the caller with the stronger case (position and facts) has an advantage has been corroborated in a recent report, as has the fact that lies are more difficult to conceal on the phone.[51,52] What to do, then? Select the time and situation for a phone call carefully, be the caller, be well prepared, and write a confirming call memo.

Library Applications

Budget

The manager must learn the budget request approval process, who will make final decisions and under what constraints. In negotiating a budget, the manager carries out a highly political task, but objective criteria application is especially relevant. Standards and cost accounting can contribute to the objective measures needed to establish priorities and justify requests.[53] Budget support flows from the library's service reputation and public relations image, but the actual approval process may be arbitary unless it permits creative negotiation. Often the president deliberately limits it to avoid negotiation sessions. In any case, bargaining with a supervisor is limited by her/his supervisory power. Perhaps the creation of a better budget process protocol should be given a high priority.

Generally, budgets advance or retreat annually by small percents, with each campus unit being treated in much the same way. Thus, most of the campus marches forward or backward in lock step. The crucial problem is to identify a rationale so persuasive as to convince the vice president to permit the library to break step and advance faster, or retreat more slowly than other units. Strategy must be developed to guide each request's size, also. Should the library request the whole project initially or only one part at a time, request what it can probably obtain, a little more, or much more? To obtain one quarter of a project is a small victory but also continues the problem.

Commitments should be qualitative rather than quantitative, based on a well developed rationale, rather than a number. Numbers are too continuous to provide good resting places. For instance, nothing magic exists about spending 5.0 per cent of the educational budget, and it is hard to defend the difference between 4.9 and 5.0 per cent. Providing a full-service library program in response to strong faculty and student demand can be defended eloquently, however. Budget bargaining often results in using standard approaches, such as "splitting the difference" and "round numbers."

Many libraries cannot project a clear picture showing when budget cuts begin to hurt deeply, and certain campus administrators do not understand very well the relation between library budget cuts and service. In an academic department, after maximum class size has been agreed upon, faculty member reduction reduces in a direct ratio the number of students the department can teach. Therefore, with a reduced budget, the academic department has a way of showing sharp and blatant deterioration of its campus contribution. In contrast, since it would remain open, check-in periodicals, select, order and catalog new material, charge out material, provide reading room and reference service, and supervise its staff members even after a sharp cut, the library is less able to show the cut's consequences in a blatant way. So a sharp library budget cut may concern a vice president less than a corresponding academic program cut.

Negotiation may occur between the manager and other campus unit heads, also. The skillful negotiator can sometimes persuade them to contribute funds to the library from their own budgets in the form of order searching, funds for material, special collection purchases, literature searches, library instruction to thesis students, exhibits, extra departmental library opening hours, or other services.

When fund-cutting negotiations are lost, the manager may yet have a final word. The cut may be made in a way sure to cause loud user protestations which can then be redirected to the administrator who won the negotiation session. An additional step can be taken, also. One of the authors has many times used the principle of coercive deficiency—deliberately exhausting certain accounts early in the fiscal year so supplementary funds must be provided.

Fund-Raising

Negotiating gifts depends on the clarity of institution purposes and extensive awareness of needs. Fund-raising ideas have been applied to libraries in many ways.[54] A systematic fund-raising program should be integrated into certain departmental activities. Normally, several other campus units will have well organized fund-raising programs, also—the alumni office, medical school, art and music schools, law school, business school, engineering school, and athletic program, for instance.

Of central importance is the question, who will negotiate? The library manager as leader should form teams to carry out parts of the program. Certain staff members may be given particular responsibilities such as the library development officer and the special collections head, but many staff members should be involved. A key relationship should exist, of course, with the campus development office.

The criteria for accepting and policies for handling gifts should be well known. Flexibility can be applied to negotiation for an important gift. The list of options on conditions and recognitions should be lengthy: tax information, naming, publicity, and access rules. Contacts with individuals must be informal and personal to build strong working relationships. The need to stress the people problem is particularly evident in dealing with Friends of the Library groups and individual benefactors. In the *Friends of Libraries Sourcebook,* the central role of negotiating activity stands out in two basic areas: the relationship between the library staff and the Friends, and the role of Friends as library funding lobbyists.[55] The Friends of the Library group provides both a potential donor group and a donation recognition group.

Negotiations start with full briefing on the potential donor. What are her/his motives, resources, ambitions, interests, potential for continued interest and for major contributions? Friends can learn about the potential donor's personal interests. Helping donors to realize their goals is a useful approach. The more useful the manager becomes, the more cooperation he/she should receive. Entertaining and rewarding donors is part of the art of negotiation and cultivation. The reward must fit donor expectations. Fund-raising can be competitive, also, not only with potential donors but with other institutions.

What is being sought, as in any negotiated agreement, is mutual gain, a match between library and donor needs. Donors have normal basic human needs, including security, a sense of belonging, personal gratification, and community recognition. Objective constraints should be known to all concerned—Bureau of Internal Revenue Service regulations and laws for wills and donations—and they should be used to advantage, with university attorney assistance.

Gifts may be accepted in funds or in material. Often the latter is much easier to negotiate than the former since the library can provide a home and user group for it, whereas an unrenewed fund will depreciate steadily in value. The collection development department should be well informed about development plans and the availability of collections for purchase on which the library needs assistance.

At some point a donor briefing must be held on the project which the library wishes to fund, such as a new building or a special book fund. This session must explain the project's functions and provisions, the donations needed, and possibilities for donor recognition. The project must be fully costed so the potential donor can see how a contribution will fit into overall financing. The crucial stage requires jawboning. Stressing the project's value to the entire university and to the community is important as well as stressing the lasting value of books and buildings. The excitement and benefits of scholarship may be described, also.

A continuing relationship should be fostered with the donor. Providing that person with a thorough and personalized introduction to the university and library can be recommended. The sense of belonging can be strengthened by Friends group, alumni association, and community advisory council membership activities. Getting the name on the university cultural event and library newsletter mailing lists is helpful, also.

Labor

Negotiation is used in formal bargaining with or without union representation.[56] Probably few librarians have had experience with this negotiation type but more will have that experience in the future. These are likely to be of longer duration than other library negotiations. They are also less likely to be preceded by staff discussion since a staff member group is the adversary. The campus personnel office may take a leading part in them. Much negotiation literature deals with management-labor relations, but little of it discusses the negotiation process details, as opposed to issues, positions and outcomes. A recent report on a negotiation series offered an interesting admonition: "It is important that management delegate the task of negotiating to staff (members) close to the work of the union."[57]

Lobbying

Lobbying at the local, state, and national level is another form of negotiation in which training and experience are desirable. It is an increasingly important part of the librarian's job in austere times. Certain states have established legislative networks to coordinate this function. The principles of knowing the political picture in detail, knowing one's own interest and having objective criteria apply here.

The function of lobbying is to explain persuasively to legislators and government officials the measures which the library wants passed and why they are important for citizens. The lobbying program must be carefully organized, funded, and staffed. Extensive discussion should precede its start. A team will be needed which contains persons with persuasive ability, good appearance, and winning personalities. Being able to spend large chunks of time on lobbying is important. Volunteers may save personnel funds, but printed literature will be needed for distribution, also. Endorsements are needed from persons whose names will influence legislators and voters. Friends, heavy users, and trustees can be helpful here. Opponents of the legislation should be identified, jawboned and their questions answered thoroughly. A way to counteract the influence of continuing opponents should be found.

On-campus lobbying is equally important. Not only can Friends be used in off-campus lobbying, but faculty library committee members can be used in on-campus lobbying. Their influence is often strongest within their own schools and departments. They can be used to testify before faculty committees and contact administrators to argue the library's case. As prime users, their arguments are often more persuasive than those of librarians whose interest is self-serving. Other heavy faculty users may be persuasive, also. Librarians and faculty library committee members must lobby Senate leaders when the agenda includes a library-supported project. The Council of Deans provides an opportunity for quiet persuasion by the library dean or director to support high priority projects. Similar lobbying may be needed when the Student Council discusses library matters.

Literature Use

If the manager chooses not to use the workshop approach, a great deal can be gained from negotiation literature.[58–63] This material may be studied to learn successful bargaining instances, but it is difficult to learn the methods used since they are seldom reported. The literature will suggest:

a. Almost anything is negotiable;
b. Many tricks and strategems can be tried in order to get a good deal;
c. Pay close attention to the forms of power, including precedent, persistence, persuasion, and expertise, in order to use them;
d. Time is important—don't reveal your real deadline to the adversary;
e. "Information is the heart of the matter." How do we obtain valuable information? Seek it from anyone likely to have it. Reveal information (selectively) to get information. Listen effectively and be sensitive to nonverbal factors.
f. Be aware of the tricks of "Soviet style" negotiating: use of limited authority and emotional ploys.
g. Try for agreements based on making the pie larger, rather than just dividing it: use the collaborative Win-Win approach.[64]

Can social science research certify certain negotiation methods as effective? Rubin and Brown compiled a review of the "findings of social psychological laboratory studies," but there has been little field study of real-life bargaining transactions.[65] After scanning this review, the reader is likely to conclude that the negotiation process is complex and, as they admit, "how little is really known about it."[66] The primary use of this work is in raising questions and stimulating observations.[67] Experience can be turned into effective learning if theoretical questions are applied to it and a personal philosophy and method are put together. For example, Rubin and Brown suggest that a

theory of bargaining will almost certainly have to include a clear conceptualization of the process of information-seeking and disclosure. This process, after all, is what we believe bargaining is largely about. It is through the selective, strategic exchange of information that bargainers attempt to discover the other's true preferences, expectations, and intentions, while at the same time revealing as little as possible about their own. And it is the quality and content of this information exchange, as well as the influence attempts to which it leads, that is ultimately responsible for the effectiveness with which bargaining proceeds.[68]

At an even more complex level, several books have been designed to make the core of management science available to librarians.[69] In Rizzo's chapter on "Group Problem Solving and Conflict Resolution" we find extensive guidelines for discussion group leadership and Filley's Integrative Decision Method for joint problem-solving.

Methods of bringing to bear the appropriate existing strategy on a given library situation are needed. In order to do this we need

> a. A clearinghouse or method of identifying, describing, and indexing collaborative problem-solving and other negotiation methods;
> b. Ways of learning how to use these methods in an experiential way;
> c. Library managers' willingness to put these learned methods and strategies into practice.

Who can provide the clearinghouse, planned in relation to academic library problems? Perhaps ARL or a library school. How could the methods be learned? From courses, such as the experiental ones described above. Will managers be willing to learn new skills? "People do not necessarily learn from experience; only from reviewing the meanings which they attribute to it."[70] Managers must be willing to go over the meanings they find in their negotiating and problem-solving activities. Those who do so may find a great interest in learning new and more effective methods.

Data are needed on the negotiation activities already being used in academic libraries. Full description of the principles and techniques used and reactions obtained would be useful. A detailed individual diary is needed to show what happened to one negotiator in the course of many negotiations. An approach which featured the diaries of several negotiators with one particular adversary could be useful. With several diaries or case studies, the researcher could begin to speculate about common features. Such information should be helpful to those of us who seek to negotiate our way out of austerity's hole.

References

1. See Anselm Strauss, *Negotiations: Varieties, Contexts, Processes, and Social Order* (San Francisco: Jossey-Bass, 1978), p. 1.
2. Thomas C. Schelling, *The Strategy of Conflict* (N.Y.: Oxford University Press, 1960), p. 25.

3. Roger Fisher and William Ury, *Getting to YES: Negotiating Agreement Without Giving In* (Boston: Houghton Mifflin, 1981), p. xi.
4. Strauss represents this strong interest by researchers: "Negotiation is not merely one specific human activity or process, of importance primarily because it appears in particular relationships (diplomacy, labor relations, business transactions, and so on), but is of such major importance in human affairs that its study brings us to the heart of studying social orders." Strauss, *op. cit.,* pp. 234–35.
5. Herbert Cohen, *You Can Negotiate Anything* (N.Y.: Bantam Books, 1982).
6. Schelling, *op. cit.,* p. 27.
7. Henry Mintzberg, *The Nature of Managerial Work* (N.Y.: Harper and Row, 1973), p. 59. A chapter is given to the definition of the roles.
8. Ibid., p. 61.
9. Ibid., p. 62.
10. Ibid., p. 63.
11. Ibid., p. 52.
12. Allan R. Cohen, et al., *Effective Behavior in Organizations: Learning from the Interplay of Cases, Concepts and Student Experiences* (Homewood, Ill.: Richard D. Irwin, 1976), p. 202.
13. John P. Kotter, *Power in Management* (New York: AMACOM, 1979). See especially Chapter 5, "Situational Differences in Acquiring and Using Power."
14. Ibid., p. 55.
15. Mintzberg, *op. cit.,* p. 51.
16. See Kotter, *op. cit.,* Chapter 3.
17. Pamela W. Darling with Duane E. Webster, *Preservation Planning Program: An Assisted Self-Study Manual for Libraries* (Washington, D.C.: Association of Research Libraries, Office of Management Studies, 1982).
18. The common sense position that it is best to have "problem-solving at the level closest to the problem with the simplest means available" is well defended by Donald E. Walker, *The Effective Administrator: A Practical Approach to Problem Solving, Decision Making and Campus Leadership* (San Francisco: Jossey-Bass, 1979), in his chapter "Teamwork, Coalition and Negotiation," with quote on page 136.
19. For a broader view, see Robert J. Merikangas, "Leadership by Non-Administrators in Academic Libraries," *Journal of Library Administration* 4 (Winter 1980), pp. 21–39. A good collection of articles on this topic is Herman Resnick and Rino J. Patti, *Change From Within: Humanizing Social Welfare Organizations* (Philadelphia: Temple University Press, 1980).
20. Seymour B. Sarason and Elizabeth Lorentz, *The Challenge of the Resource Exchange Network* (San Francisco: Jossey-Bass, 1979).
21. Mel Berger and Kenneth Harrison, "A New Approach to Interpersonal Skills Development," in Cary L. Cooper (ed.), *Developing Social Skills in Managers: Advances in Group Training* (N.Y.: Wiley, 1976), p. 128.
22. Valerie and Andrew Steward, *Managing the Manager's Growth* (N.Y.: Wiley, 1978).
23. See such handbooks as Robert L. Craig (ed.), *Training and Development Handbook: A Guide to Human Resources Development* (N.Y.: McGraw-Hill, 1976), and the issues of *Training and Development Journal.* For a bibliography, see Theodore T. Herbert and Edward B. Yost, *Management Education and Development, an Annotated Resource Book* (Westport, Conn: Greenwood Press, 1978).

24. Arthur Marsh, "Training Managers in Industrial Relations Negotiations," in Bernard Taylor and Gordon L. Lippitt, *Management Development and Training Handbook* (London: McGraw-Hill, 1975).
25. Mike Woodcock, *Team Development Manual* (N.Y.: Wiley, 1979).
26. William G. Dyer, *Team Building: Issues and Alternatives* (Reading, Mass.: Addison-Wesley, 1977), p. 138.
27. Ibid., pp. 117–22.
28. Robert R. Blake, Herbert A. Shepard and Jane S. Mouton, *Managing Intergroup Conflict in Industry* (Houston: Gulf Publishing Company, 1964), p. 90.
29. Norman R. F. Maier, Allen R. Solem and Ayesha T. Maier, *The Role-Play Technique: A Handbook for Management and Leadership Practice* (La Jolla, CA: University Associates, 1975).
30. Herbert Cohen, *op. cit.*, p. 241.
31. Fisher and Ury, *op. cit.*, p. 38.
32. Ibid., p. xii–xii.
33. Ibid., p. 11.
34. Ibid., p. 27.
35. Ibid., p. 21.
36. David and Frank Johnson, *Joining Together: Group Theory and Group Skills* (Englewood Cliffs, N.J.: Prentice-Hall, 1982), pp. 283–85.
37. Fisher and Ury, *op. cit.*, Chapter 6.
38. Ibid., Chapter 7.
39. Fisher and Ury see this as a success of a method: the one-text procedure. Herbert Cohen sees it as "attributable to the patience and persistence of Jimmy Carter" (Cohen, p. 84), a matter of a person, style and effort. A method can be replicated, not a personal style, or mere persistence.
40. Fisher and Ury, *op. cit.*, Chapter 8.
41. Ibid., p. 135.
42. Ibid., p. 149.
43. Compare models I and II in Chris Argyris and Donald A. Schoen, *Theory in Practice: Increasing Professional Effectiveness* (San Francisco: Jossey-Bass, 1974).
44. See Herbert Cohen, *op. cit.*, and Tessa A. Warschaw, *Winning by Negotiation* (N.Y.: McGraw-Hill, 1980). Also Thomas Gordon, *Leader Effectiveness Training, L.E.T.: The No-lose Way to Release the Productivity Potential of People* (N.Y.: Wyden Books, 1977).
45. For example, see the contingency view expressed by John E. Beck, "Changing a Manager's Construction of Reality: The Perspective of Personal Construct Theory on the Process of Management Education," in *Advances in Management Education,* ed. by John Beck and Charles Cox (N.Y.: Wiley, 1980).
46. *Tools for Change: Basic Concepts in a Sequential Diagrammatic Form* (San Francisco: Interaction Associates, n.d.), item 5.
47. Royce A. Coffin, *The Negotiator: A Manual for Winners* (N.Y.: AMACOM, 1973).
48. Chester L. Karrass, *Give and Take: The Complete Guide to Negotiating Strategies and Tactics* (N.Y.: Thomas Y. Crowell, 1974).
49. Michael Korda, *Power: How To Get It, How to Use It* (N.Y.: Ballantine Books, 1976), p. 6.
50. Ibid., p. 208.

51. Howard Muson, "Getting the Phone's Number," *Psychology Today* 16 (April 1982), pp. 42–49.
52. Cohen, *op. cit.*, pp. 210–15.
53. See Betty Jo Mitchell, Norman E. Tanis, and Jack Jaffee, *Cost Analysis of Library Functions: A Total System Approach* (Greenwich, Conn.: JAI Press, 1978).
54. Patricia Sean Breivik and E. Burr Gibson, *Funding Alternatives for Libraries* (Chicago: American Library Association, 1979).
55. Sandy Dolnick (ed.), *Friends of Libraries Sourcebook* (Chicago: American Library Association, 1980), pp. 83–98.
56. For a recent survey, see Robert C. O'Reilly and Marjorie I. O'Reilly, *Librarians and Labor Relations: Employment Under Union Contracts* (Westport, Conn.: Greenwood Press, 1981).
57. Frederick C. Lynden and Ronald Falk, "Management Lessons from Negotiations With Support Staff," Association of College and Research Libraries, Second National Conference, October 1–4, 1981, Minneapolis, Minnesota (Microfiche).
58. See Donald I. Dewar, *The Quality Circle Guide to Participation Management* (Englewood Cliffs, N.J.: Prentice-Hall, 1982).
59. Ian Mangham, "Team Development in Industry," in Cooper, *op. cit.*, p. 126.
60. Josiah Dilley, "Self-Help Literature: Don't Knock It Till You Try It," *Personnel and Guidance Journal* 56 (January 1978), pp. 293–95.
61. John Ilich and Barbara Schildler Jones, *Successful Negotiating Skills for Women* (Reading, Mass: Addison-Wesley, 1981).
62. Natasha Josefowitz, *Paths to Power* (Reading, Mass.: Addison-Wesley, 1980).
63. Johnson and Johnson, *op. cit.*
64. Herbert Cohen, *op. cit.*, p. 101.
65. Jeffrey Z. Rubin and Bert R. Brown, *The Social Psychology of Bargaining and Negotiation* (N.Y.: Academic Press, 1975), p. viii.
66. Ibid., p. 289.
67. Otomar J. Bartos, *Process and Outcome of Negotiations* (N.Y.: Columbia University Press, 1974)
68. Rubin and Brown, *op. cit.*, p. 299.
69. John R. Rizzo, *Management for Librarians: Fundamentals and Issues* (Westport, Conn.: Greenwood Press, 1980).
70. L. F. Harris and E. S. Harri-Aubstein, "Learning to Learn: The Personal Construction and Exchange of Meaning," in M. J. A. Howe (ed.), *Adult Learning: Psychological Research and Applications* (London: Wiley, 1977), p. 85.

7. A Realistic Objectives Management Program

Edward R. Johnson

PLANNING IS A BASIC MANAGEMENT FUNCTION for library administrators. During retrenchment periods its importance increases. The first step in a formal planning process is to identify and describe organizational objectives. Such objectives, according to Drucker, "are needed in every area where performance and results directly and vitally affect the survival and prosperity of the business."[1] The survival of certain library services may be decided by the end of this decade.

As the "new depression," to use Mayhew's phrase, became increasingly severe, many academic institutions implemented management controls.[2] As a result, formal planning has become common. "Explicit in virtually all utterances about planning," Mayhew said, "is the primacy accorded the development of a clear statement of institutional mission and purpose."[3] The depression has forced colleges and universities to review their goals and objectives and to reconsider many of their assumptions.

A detailed planning process, however, is time-consuming and may not be feasible in an immediate crisis. Institutional mission and purpose and academic and administrative unit strategic objectives must be established as prerequisites to planning. If they are lacking, hasty decisions may be made in a financial emergency. These decisions may be based on insufficient information or communication, made without sufficient regard for their organizational impact and by only a few individuals. Because it is affected by so many varied campus activities, the library is particularly vulnerable to damage under such conditions.

Wishful thinking, on the other hand, even if written down, does not represent usable objective formulation. We must concentrate on a planning process that develops *realistic* objectives. Too many staff members are ". . . dismayed with the amount of energy devoted to committees charged to review the existing goals, objectives, or missions of organizations."[4] Furthermore, successful plan implementation and commitment depend on "how honestly and candidly" we have evaluated internal assumptions.[5] Therefore, this chapter will emphasize the assistance to be gained from a realistic objectives management program in austerity.

Definition of Objectives

"There are many words used synonymously for goals. . . . ."[6] Pings listed *objectives, missions, purposes, directed behavior, motivation, desired results, ends, targets,* and *intentions.* Definition becomes even more complicated in planning language when terms such as *strategic, operational, long-range,* and *short-range* are used as qualifiers. Usually, the writer is thinking of a hierarchy which leads from broadly-worded statements of general aims and purposes to highly specific, closely defined operational intentions about implementing those aims. Because realistic objectives are emphasized, the term *goals* will be used to mean broad statements of intent directing library programs to achieve university purposes. *Objectives,* means specific operational statements at all levels that specify the steps by which the broader goals will be achieved.[7]

Those definitions imply that the librarian can discern the university's purposes. Although these purposes may seem obvious, they are not. For example, Blyn and Zoerner stated their concern over the confusion of purpose apparent in much of academia. Elegantly-written mission statements that discuss the values of Western civilization may not be translatable into ". . . precise day-to-day operational terms. . . ."

Institutional objectives, in the case of the academy, are much more vaguely defined than in business or even in government. Though many colleges and universities have prepared impressive "mission and goals" statements, they are usually general, offering little in the way of guidance as to what the institutions should or should not be doing. Nor have many institutions seen fit to provide a quantitative dimension to their objectives, apart from the setting of enrollment targets.[8]

An academic institution needs general goals to satisfy public expectations, the state education department, or the board of regents. In fact, so much effort has been devoted to this activity recently that it has been described as "mission madness."[9] Another reason for writing goals may be to overcome misunderstandings between administrators and staff.[10] Most goals cannot be implemented as stated since they represent a philosophy or an ideal vision of the future. Nor can such ideas be measured quantitatively.

Traditionally, the next step is to translate these broad goals into workable, operational and "realistic" objectives. A *realistic objective* is defined as a statement of intent that is clearly written and sufficiently specific to be measured with an end result that is achievable, given existing constraints and resources. Each institutional unit must determine how to translate goals into action. The library must respond to goals not set by itself. Also, because the library is a grouping of administrative, support, and service subunits, its overall objectives affect, and in turn are affected by, those subunits' own objectives. On any campus many documents illustrate the relation of academic support objectives to institutional goals. They should be consulted in the process of specifying the library's objectives. Such documents include trustee charters and bylaws, personnel manuals, policy and procedure manuals, minutes of administrative and academic councils, state or federal mandates and legislation, accreditation reviews, self-studies, consultants' reports, and other purpose and intent statements. While these documents probably do not state goals, they may provide valuable information regarding constraints, priorities, and decisions. They suggest where objectives are needed.

If, for example, the university seeks new ways to attract students (as many do), the library needs to know what plans are under consideration. Many schools are increasing night and weekend course offerings for the non-traditional student and, of course, the library's hours and services will be affected. For another example, curriculum planners are notorious for forgetting library resources when approving new courses and academic programs. It is important to have access to the written decisions of university committees. Campus communication is often poor. Decisions on finances, personnel policies, building priorities, instructional support, computers, etc., may be made at the cabinet or regents level without notifying the library. In order to develop objectives that respond to institutional plans, much search for information may be required. Just getting and staying on various mailing lists can be a challenging job.

Writing Objectives

One way to design library objectives is to regard them as questions about the institutional goals that must be answered before proceeding further. Realistic objectives writers should put themselves in the place of an outside evaluator. Would such a person be able to assess the objective as it is written? A number of criteria should be considered. Realistic objectives should be:

1. *Understandable.* Objectives should be written in clear, simple language. Their purpose is to communicate to others what the library plans to do in concrete terms. Rambling, ambiguous, or jargon-filled statements will only confuse.
2. *Measurable.* Objectives should be specific enough that the staff can determine whether or not they have been achieved. "To

disseminate knowledge" may sound impressive but is difficult
to measure.

3. *Achievable.* Objectives should be achievable, "Doable" in terms
of desired ends, resources available, and hurdles to overcome.

4. *Aimed at improvement.* While objectives need to be realistically
attainable they should not be so narrow as to lack imagination.
A worthy objective may be one that requires the organization
to stretch itself to achieve it.

5. *Accountable.* Idealism should be tempered by the realization
that objectives must stand the assessment of the state government, auditors, university administration, alumni, faculty, and
even students. Objectives should be agreed upon by program
planners and those to whom these objectives are accountable.

6. Feasible. Criticism of the Delphi technique, for example,
shows that even experts are poor at prediction. Short-range
objectives are verifiable while long-range objectives are vague
beyond a certain point. Planning over a long period may not
be feasible.

7. *Specific.* Objectives should be written by the unit managers who
will implement them. They should understand the problems
and constraints of that particular objective (and the people
who must achieve it). The director should establish objectives
for the library as a whole while delegating that task for the
subunits to the most appropriate level of operational
specificity.[11]

8. *Understood.* Planning is designed to implement change con-
structively. Obtaining commitment to plans and overcoming
resistance requires that staff members at all levels participate
in the process so they can understand reasons for change.

9. *Reviewed, evaluated, and updated.* Objectives should be reviewed
regularly, at least quarterly, or perhaps as often as the budget
is reviewed, to reflect changing university and library requirements. They should also be evaluated occasionally in order to
measure progress toward desired outcomes. If circumstances
have changed drastically, then the objectives may need to be
dropped, re-written, or modified.

How to set realistic objectives:

1. The director should write down her/his own library goals for
the next five years. These goals should be based on an understanding of university priorities and be imaginative and for-
ward-looking. They should, however, also be practical in order
to set the stage for developing objectives aimed at achieving
those goals. It would be preferable, for example, not to set as a
goal "to automate x department." A more achievable and mea-

surable goal would be "to install an x size Circulation Department mini-computer by 1984." This goal then sets the stage for realistic objectives such as how many records to convert into machine-readable form, new staff required, personnel changes, further automation plans, additional equipment needed, and so forth.

2. All levels should be asked to develop objectives to achieve the goals outlined by the director and, if appropriate, to suggest further goals. Extensive staff involvement is time-consuming and expensive, but it is ". . . an investment in the future of the organization by improving decision-making."[12] Further, it was previously noted that the lower the level of operational specificity, the greater the probability of an objective being realistic. Each department and unit should have its own set of goals and objectives. Such involvement is also necessary to obtain staff interest and support. To recommend representative committees or a self-study is obvious, and the administrator should avoid the temptation to do it herself or himself in order to save time. An outside consultant or facilitator is worth considering at this stage.

3. The objectives should be revised, reviewed, discussed, and agreed upon. The director may need to exercise authority to resolve disagreements or vagueness in thinking. Re-writing may be necessary to clarify objectives and, perhaps, to compromise on resource allocation or priorities. The quantifiable measures are determined at this point, i.e., "to acquire 40,000 volumes," "to buy three disk packs," etc. Finally, timetables are set and agreed upon ("in six months," "by January 1985," etc.).

At this point, most groups will find some disagreement about when objectives can be reached. Probably administrators are more optimistic about timetables than staff members. Open and frank communication is crucial if objectives are to be realistic. An individual may hold back concerns or criticisms to prevent disharmony but this lack of support, commitment, or understanding may later return to haunt the library. As Schleh has concluded: ". . . objectives state the specific accomplishment expected of each individual in a specific time period so that the work of the whole managment group is soundly blended at a particular moment."[13] In other words, objectives are an important communication medium.

Advantages and Disadvantages of Realistic Objectives

If the criteria for writing realistic objectives have been followed, a number of advantages will result. Because the objectives have been written in clear language they will be meaningful to readers. The objectives also have staff understanding and acceptance with the result that purposeful actions leading to objective achievement will be encouraged. Also, realistic objectives have the advantage of facilitating interunit comparison.

Measurable objectives facilitate monitoring progress toward achievement of desired results. The staff can readily determine if the organization is moving in the right direction. As a result, each unit's daily activities can be closely related to its established objectives. Peripheral activities can be evaluated in terms of whether they inhibit or support objectives. Finally, because realistic objectives are aimed at improvement, they can be used to advance public relations.

There are certain inherent disadvantages in establishing realistic objectives, also. One is that the administrator has publicly committed the organization to achieving specific objectives. Management must monitor progress toward them. If not regularly evaluated, delays or problems will be obvious and much of the public relations value may be lost. Another disadvantage is that objective quantification is difficult. Lack of experience in writing objectives and the inherent difficulty of translating objectives into precisely measurable terms can make the formulation process traumatic.

Another disadvantage is that librarians are not well-prepared to write realistic objectives. Writing objectives becomes easier as experience increases. Perhaps the most obvious disadvantage is that conditions change, necessitating continual adaptation. It is a challenge to write objectives that can be adapted to environmental variations.

Clarifying Quantified Objectives

In order to clarify objectives a process is needed that focuses on specific needs and responses. This process is illustrated in a 1981 ACRL Conference paper. Newman related his experience in developing goals and objectives. His library began with the college's overall goal "to expand the services of the nonprint media center," but this goal required elaboration. The library developed these objectives toward the achievement of the college goal:

1. to improve physical facilities by building new storage cabinets;
2. to improve media equipment by replacing outdated, nonfunctioning items;
3. to increase faculty and student awareness of the media center by hiring a part-time media specialist and involving faculty and students in media through media classes, planning media programs, and otherwise demonstrating the possibilities of media use.[14]

These objectives are clear and concise but would have been more realistic if they had been quantifiable. O'Donnell believed that "it is of utmost importance that the selected objectives be quantified. . . . There is a need to know 'how much' in order to determine what resource commitment is necessary and whether the objective is achieved."[15] Things which can be stated in terms of dollars and cents (profit, sales, output) are easy to quantify, but, "there will be some objectives which are difficult or impossible to quantify directly. Examples would include morale, developing and training managers, social responsibility, creativity, quality and public image."[16]

Many library services could be added to that list. Technical service objectives, such as number of volumes to be cataloged, tend to be easy to quantify, but many public service objectives, especially those associated with values, are more difficult. The Association of Research Libraries' Office of Management Studies (ARL/LOMS) has compiled examples of public service goals and objectives in its *SPEC Kit,* number 84. If the objective itself cannot be quantified then sometimes elements of it can be so stated (such as absenteeism as a factor of morale).[17] Realistic objectives relate generalizations to specific targets for action such as budget.

In addition to specificity and quantifiability, realistic objectives should have a date established for their accomplishment. Target dates should be feasible but objectives should be both short-term and long-term in scope. Short-range objectives will be based on the organization's sense of its priorities in regard to its long-range objectives. "Some things simply need to be done first."[18] Short-range objectives tend to be more specific; they describe those things that should be done in the first year and should lead to the accomplishment of long-range objectives: ". . . it may be concluded that maintaining balanced progress toward all objectives is almost insuperable." But,

This need not be true. A sophisticated manager counters his own weaknesses and understands that all objectives are important, not only for their own sakes but especially because their proper accomplishment is a prerequisite to the success of the long-range plan.[19]

Objectives Management and Austerity Management

Austerity conditions require difficult choices. Insufficient resources dictate that libraries cannot do everything that is desirable. Most librarians would argue persuasively that the resources available have seldom, if ever, been sufficient for all programs. Austerity makes decisions based on priorities even more difficult because the options are fewer and the constraints are more difficult. Many librarians have been forced to retrench.

At a few institutions retrenchment has been carried out through a planned and logical process. In the late 1970's, for example, the Pennsylvania State University administration began a five-year planning cycle to cut back many units. The University Libraries were given financial reduction target figures and were instructed to produce a five-year plan which specified the steps needed to achieve these reductions. The resulting plan, updated annually, stated in specific operational terms the units or programs to be modified or eliminated, the positions identified for collapse by attrition, and when these events would occur. Penn State involved staff extensively in this process. The establishment of measurable, quantifiable, and realistic objectives was made less traumatic by extensive consultation.

The challenge of austerity management is to match financial conditions to library objectives realistically. A number of systems may be used to establish realistic objectives. Goal formulation systems "can be particularly useful as diagnostic tools. . . ." These systems allow administrators to "become pro-active, rather than reactive, molding forces to meet needs, rather than responding only to problems as they occur."[20] Three of the most common systems are: Management By Objectives (MBO), Zero-Base Budgeting (ZBB), and Planning-Programming-Budgeting System (PPBS).

Management by Objectives

Despite its widespread use, the diversity of MBO applications makes it difficult to define. "MBO, like ice cream, comes in twenty-nine flavors."[21] McConkle defined MBO as

a managerial process whereby organizational purposes are diagnosed and met by joining superiors and subordinates in the pursuit of mutually agreed upon goals and objectives, which are specific, measurable, time bounded, and joined to an action plan; progress and goal attainment are measured and monitored in appraisal sessions which center on mutually determined objective standards of performance.[22]

MBO is based on two assumptions: it focuses on objectives to be achieved, and the setting of those objectives should be a participation process between superior and subordinate.[23] Research has found cautious support that MBO improved managerial goal setting and overall planning.[24] McConkle found widespread support for "the need to have [performance] appraisals conducted on the basis of objective performance standards which are mutually agreed upon by both superiors and subordinates."[25] MBO has had many critics, also, often relating to the goal-setting process. Too many goals are said to be rigid, inappropriate, and unimaginative. Olivas, however, concluded that MBO's problem is that it is difficult to learn and its participants frequently fail to teach "its nature and philosophy."[26]

Several libraries experimented with MBO in the 1970's, but the literature on academic library application is sparse. Lewis found academic librarians to perceive MBO's use to be limited by the large number of highly structured library jobs and the difficulty of quantifying public service activities. But, Lewis concluded, it can be applied successfully to libraries.[27] Apparently, its academic library use is not extensive.

Martin, while recognizing MBO problems, believed that it offered "the possibility of improving both product and process because it requires close scrutiny of every activity in a library."[28] This scrutiny is necessary because MBO requires measurable and clear objectives. Carefully developed objectives are expected to be the MBO process' useful end products, but Martin warned of too much goal emphasis. Overemphasis on method may lead to rigidity in thinking or confusing technique with results. MBO cannot be applied in just a few areas of an organization. It is a philosophy of management in addition to being a method and requires "total commitment" to achieve its ends.[29]

Recently, the University of Lowell introduced Management by Objectives. Goodwin and Ford stated that the quality of decision-making was difficult to evaluate but "the process of resource allocation . . . has improved dramatically." Among the other benefits cited were better communication, clearer budgeting priorities, and improved planning.[30]

Zero-Base Budgeting

ZBB is a planning technique that requires all new or established programs to be evaluated and justified regularly, usually annually. It has been defined as "a comprehensive, analytically structured process that enables management to make allocation decisions regarding limited resources."[31] ZBB is different from traditional line item or incremental budgeting in being a planning process aimed at developing an institutional budget without regard to the previous year's budget. ZBB also differs somewhat from usual budget techniques because of its emphasis on defining objectives and analyzing them in terms of cost and benefit. Each program must justify its continued existence every year or be reduced to zero.

Zero-base budgeting is not a new concept. It was developed in industry but has been widely used in government. President Carter brought attention to ZBB by his efforts to use it to control government programs. While ZBB did not transform government it is still being used widely at local, state, and federal levels. While acknowledging many criticisms (especially its complexity), Chen concluded that ZBB has many benefits such as a fairly well-documented belief that it helps to clarify institutional goals and objectives.[32] Denman developed a case for ZBB in "service-oriented" organizations. He, too, placed strong emphasis on its value in establishing goals and objectives.[33]

The State University of New York at Buffalo's Lockwood Library began a zero-base budgeting process in 1977. Budget requests were developed from a "zero-base" rather than on "historical justifications." Using a variety of standardized forms developed for the purpose, library departments were required to state their purposes, consider alternatives, assign detailed costs to their functions, and to describe as accurately as possible their "quantitative package measures" (such as reference questions answered, number of service hours, number of data bases searched, secretarial support, etc.). The reference and collection development staff members were quoted as finding "their ZBB experience successful in that it gave them complete and precise data immediately useful for their staff justification."[34]

Planning-Programming-Budgeting System

PPBS too has been widely used, especially in government. PPBS is an outgrowth of program budgeting which emphasizes justifying and defining programmatic goals and objectives. PPBS is based on: identifying goals and objectives, identifying future implications, considering associated costs, and systematic analysis of alternatives.[35]

PPBS has its critics and its proponents, too. One critic believes PPBS "has now mercifully retired into obscurity."[36] It is complex and time-consuming, as are MBO and ZBB. A Michigan administrator declared that one of PPBS's major benefits was that its "structure and its application do not permit the luxury of casual assumptions that certain effects will occur (impacts) if certain activities (outputs) are carried out."[37] Summers agreed that the "crux" of PPBS was its identification of explicit objectives and a cost-benefit analysis of those objectives.[38]

"Few institutions employ a total PPBS approach, and those which do follow the usual pattern of politics in allowing for exceptions."[39] It appears that few institutions use MBO, ZBB or PPBS in their "purest" forms but use hybrids with techniques from one or more systems adapted to local conditions. Texas, for example, requires its public academic institutions to submit biennial budget requests in a program format that seems to include elements of ZBB, PPBS, and perhaps MBO as well.

Other Goals and Objectives Programs

In addition to these systems, many institutions have developed their own long- and short-range planning programs. Identifying goals and objectives are important elements in them, also. Elements common to MBO, ZBB, and PPBS can be found in most of them. As the academic depression has made itself felt more strongly, higher education institutions have been forced to re-examine their priorities. This trend can be observed in the goals and objectives statements produced by their libraries. ARL/OMS has published several *SPEC Kits* dealing with goals and objectives.[40] These documents are similar in style and format but varying in content. A few contain specific and quantitative objectives written at the unit level. Many list broad, sweeping generalities on overall library purpose and mission. In 1975 OMS found that

> For many libraries the task of formulating or revamping a comprehensive goals and objectives system has been a complex task. Unclear or ambiguous perspectives of library purpose, unranked priorities, and skepticism among staff members as to the utility of goals and objectives statements have proven to be some of the obstacles in establishing goals and objectives statements.[41]

A more recent ARL/OMS *SPEC Kit* gives interesting new examples of written goals and objectives.[42] In 1981, for example, the University of California/Riverside, Library published "The UCR Library Plan for the Eighties." This document is used as an overall planning program and as a mechanism for annually updated goals and objectives from the library's units. It is a comprehensive document that considers the Library's role in the University, the University of California system, the region, and the nation. The plan makes several assumptions about technology, academic development, publishing trends, institutional cooperation, and funding prospects. The Library's mission, goals, and objectives are then spelled out in extensive detail.

Of particular interest is the UCR Library Plan's extensive set of public service objectives. The Reference Services Department, for instance, has several goals and objectives. One goal is "to provide effective and knowledgeable reference assistance to users by hiring and training well-qualified librarians with appropriate subject training. . . ." One short-term objective is to "offer reference desk service 60–65 hours per week, with 80 hours of staff." A long-term objective is to "produce a written reference services policy statement. . . ."[43]

Public service goals and objectives statements are included in this *SPEC Kit* from ten ARL libraries. All appear to be parts of broader mission and goal statements. It is obvious that many librarians are still developing written goals and objectives in the 1980's just as they were in the 1970's. Lack of precision still seems to characterize many statements.

Obstacles to Realistic Objectives

A massive North Texas State University goals and objectives program was completed a few years ago just as the president resigned. In the intervening three years, the University had four presidents. Consequently, it has been nearly impossible to develop formal University

Libraries goals or realistic objectives. A newly-appointed president has just initiated a long-range planning process with goals and objectives to be developed in the next few months. This example is cited only to demonstrate that the greatest obstacle to writing realistic objectives may be the institutional environment. Most libraries are constrained by governmental or institutional priorities, policies, procedures and personnel.

One further problem, noted by the ARL/OMS, especially in relation to public service objectives, is the general lack of "precise performance measures." *SPEC Kit* number 84 lists only two libraries that have attempted to develop such performance standards and evaluation measures. The University of California/San Diego's "performance standards" for interlibrary loan specify procedures and deadlines for that unit. The Arizona State University's performance evaluation relates librarians' job goals to documented or observed performance. It does not, however, specify detailed measures of performance for reference librarians.

OMS concludes that "goals and objectives projects are most likely to be successful in a climate of perceived need for the product, organizational readiness and willingness to be open to new directions."[44] Of course, OMS is referring primarily to participants' attitudinal concerns. In addition to their support, to be successful, library goals and objectives must be realistic and in tune with the overall institutional environment. They must also overcome the numerous hurdles in their path, such as lack of quantitative standards.

Conclusion

Despite problems, many institutions have found, as did Spyers-Duran, that a goals and objectives statement

helped us to define library techniques of participatory management, to articulate more clearly our programs' and services' purposes, to focus our attention to actions, to measure our achievement, to present our needs to the University community, and to plan for the future.[45]

Economic realities have required most institutions to develop planning and budgeting systems that allocate resources in some fashion other than through the personal influence, or "clout," of each administrator. Austerity has further revealed that many administrators "often have responsibility without authority."[46] And, some feel, "the academy is surely the most difficult of organizations to manage well."[47] Logical, more rational planning systems based on goals and objectives have been developed to address these difficulties.

If the planning process is to be successful, realistic objectives must be formulated. The test of realistic objectives is whether they can withstand sincere and objective appraisal. Pings found that "the mark of a healthy organization does *not* rest on goal statements or on studies to get goal statements, but it does rest on the fervor with which it tests goals."[48]

ARL's OMS found in the late 1970's that certain libraries had indeed encountered discouraging problems in formulating goals and objectives. OMS cited staff skepticism, excessive time requirements, and uncertain administrative support as major negative factors. In 1979, in another *SPEC Kit* on goals and objectives, OMS found that administrative commitment, flexibility, and widespread staff involvement were major positive factors working against the problems reported earlier.[49]

Administrators today can develop meaningful plans, even under austere conditions, through realistic objective formulation. These objectives, developed through widespread staff participation and occasionally tested with "vigor," have proven to be of major benefit at the departmental and unit level. "For," concluded OMS, "it is at this level that the specifics of the library's work are defined and carried out."[50]

Administrators should not forget, however, that politics is still an important factor in determining resource allocation. As Benveniste observed:

Goal specification requires a high level of political consensus. When such consensus exists, goal specificity does not create political costs. When many divergent views exist, however, the possibility of establishing well-defined goals that satisfy everyone becomes much more difficult. Even the process of spelling out goals may result in considerable conflict as each contending faction struggles to place its own preferences high on the list of objectives. Vague and ill-defined goals are an equivalent to having secret goals. As long as goals are secret, it is possible for competing groups to pursue their own ends without necessarily appearing to encroach on each other.[51]

Librarians are accustomed to competing for scarce resources. Often they are given priority for public relations' reasons but are poorly supported because of more pressing needs elsewhere. Consequently, during the current austere period library administrators' political skills may prove to be as important as their management abilities.

References

1. Peter F. Drucker, *The Practice of Management* (N.Y.: Harper and Row, 1954), p. 63.
2. Lewis B. Mayhew, *Surviving the Eighties* (San Francisco: Jossey-bass, 1979), p. 112.
3. Ibid., p. 116.
4. Vern M. Pings, "Use or Value of Goals and Objectives Statements," *Journal of Library Administration* 1 (Fall 1980), p. 56.

 5. Mayhew, *op. cit.*, p. 116.
 6. Pings, *op. cit.*, p. 56.
 7. Jeffrey J. Gardner and Duane E. Webster, "The Formulation and Use of Goals and Objectives Statements in Academic and Research Libraries," *Office of University Libraries Management Studies, Occasional Papers, no. 3* (Washington: Association of Research Libraries, 1974), pp. 6–16.
 8. Martin R. Blyn and Cyril E. Zoerner, "The Academic String Pushers: the Origins of the Upcoming Crisis in the Management of Academia," *Change* 14 (March 1982), p. 22.
 9. Richard Chait, "Mission Madness Strikes Our Colleges," *Chronicle of Higher Education* 18 (July 19, 1979), p. 36.
10. Pings, *op. cit.*, p. 56.
11. Mayhew, *op. cit.*, p. 120.
12. Edward R. Johnson, "Academic Library Planning, Self Study and Management Review," *Journal of Library Administration* 2 (Summer 1981), p. 75.
13. Edward C. Schleh, "The Basic Management Design: Management Objectives," in: Harold Kountz and Cyril O'Donnell, eds. *Management: A Book of Readings* (N.Y.: McGraw-Hill, 1972), p. 121.
14. George Charles Newman, "Planning for Small College Libraries; the Use of Goals and Objectives," presented to the ACRL Conference, Minneapolis, 1981 (microfiche), pp. 3–4.
15. Cyril O'Donnell, "Planning Objectives," in: Harold Kountz and Cyril O'Donnell, eds. *Management: A Book of Readings* (N.Y.: MacGraw-Hill, 1972), p. 129.
16. Ibid., p. 129.
17. Ibid., p. 129.
18. Ibid., p. 132.
19. Ibid., pp. 132–133.
20. Paul F. DuMont and Rosemary Ruhig DuMont, "A Goals Typology and Systems Model of Library Effectiveness," *Journal of Library Administration* 2 (Spring 1981), pp. 22–23.
21. J. S. Hodgson, "Management by Objectives: the Experience of a Federal Government Department," *Canadian Public Administration* 16 (Fall 1973), p. 423.
22. Mark L. McConkle, "A Clarification of the Goal Setting and Appraisal Processes in MBO," *Journal of Library Administration* 2 (Spring 1981), p. 81.
23. George S. Odiorne. *Management by Objectives* (N.Y.: Pitman, 1965), p. 55.
24. McConkle, *op. cit.*, p. 73.
25. Ibid., p. 81.
26. Louis Olivas, "Adding a Different Dimension to Goal-Setting Processes," *Personnel Administrator* 26 (October 1981), pp. 25–26.
27. Martha Lewis, "Management by Objectives: Review, Application and Relationships with Job Satisfaction and Performance," *Journal of Academic Librarianship* 5 (January, 1980), pp. 329–334.
28. Murray S. Martin. *Issues in Personnel Management in Academic Libraries* (Greenwich, Conn.: JAI Press, 1981), p. 191.
29. Ibid.
30. Susan A. Goodwin and Oliver Ford, "The University of Lowell," *Educational Record* 63 (Spring 1982), pp. 45–49.
31. Ching-chih Chen. *Zero-Base Budgeting in Library Management: A Manual for Librarians* (Phoenix: Oryx Press, 1980), p. 12.

32. Ibid., p. 59.
33. Richard W. Denman, "Zero-Base Budgeting for Academic Libraries," in: Sul H. Lee, ed. *Library Budgeting: Critical Challenges for the Future* (Ann Arbor: Pierian Press, 1977), pp. 20–21.
34. Chen, *op. cit.*, p. 162.
35. William Summers, "A Change in Budgetary Thinking," in Gerald R. Shields and J. Gordon Burke, ed. *Budgeting for Accountability in Libraries: a Selection of Readings* (Metuchen, N.J.: Scarecrow Press, 1974), p. 22.
36. Martin, *op. cit.*, p. 191.
37. Philip Jager, "The State of Michigan Program Budget Evaluation System as Applied to Higher Education," in: Sul H. Lee, ed. *Planning-Programming-Budgeting System (PPBS); Implications for Library Management* (Ann Arbor: Pierian Press, 1973), p. 64.
38. Summers, *op. cit.*, p. 22.
39. Murray S. Martin. *Budgetary Control in Academic Libraries* (Greenwich, Conn.: JAI Press, 1978), p. 50.
40. Association of Research Libraries, Office of Management Studies, *SPEC Kit,* no. 1, September, 1973; no. 15, January, 1975; no. 58, October, 1979; no. 84, May, 1982 (Washington, D.C.: Association of Research Libraries)
41. *SPEC Kit,* no. 15, January, 1975, p. 2.
42. *SPEC Kit,* no. 84, May, 1982
43. Ibid., pp. 21–28.
44. Ibid., p. 1.
45. California State University, Long Beach. *Goals and Objectives of the University Library* (Long Beach: California State University, Long Beach, University Library, March, 1978), p. iii.
46. Blyn and Zoerner, *op. cit.*, p. 22.
47. Ibid., p. 21.
48. Pings, *op. cit.*, p. 61.
49. *SPEC Kit,* no. 58, October, 1979, pp. 1–2.
50. *SPEC Kit,* no. 15, January, 1975, p. 1.
51. Guy Benveniste. *The Politics of Expertise* (San Francisco: Boyd and Fraser, 1977), p. 85.

8. The Library Standards Program

Donald E. Oehlerts

A STANDARD IS ANY MEASURE or code by which one judges a service or product as authentic, acceptable, or adequate: an authoritative rule or principle. Standards have existed for many years in manufacturing, product testing and other areas where their use is recognized as helpful. They are accepted by product or service users as indicating consistent quality. At the very least, they provide some assurance of minimum quality.[1]

Another term is frequently used in library standards writing: a guideline. Guidelines are policy statements issued by persons, occupational fields, or associations which have authority in the particular discipline.[2] As used in librarianship, guidelines are most frequently qualitative statements. Library standards have been primarily practice models, guidelines, not enforceable codes. Guidelines, such as used in accreditation, have a professional and moral basis, but are not legally binding. Library standards have been stated primarily as criteria by which services are evaluated, but they exclude bibliographic description standards, cataloging practice codes, and products.

College and university library standards have been described as "unenforceable guidelines" and "ambiguous generalities." They have been termed "descriptive," thus making any evaluation difficult.[3] Qualitative standards have had their advocates, but other persons have declared them to be too general to be useful. At other times standards have been criticized as arbitrary value judgments with no research foundation. Many commentators have cautioned that "meeting the standards" may not be viewed by college administrators as the minimum effort required but as fully satisfactory support.

One of the most persistent library standards criticisms is that they are not objectives or performance measures which can be precisely stated, quantified, and measured.[4] Almost all readily available library data relate to input measures: collection size, volumes added, staff size, and expenditures. The trend in library investigation, accreditation agency evaluation, and academic program self-study is toward examining results, outputs. Does the library assist in meeting institutional goals, how does library service support academic programs, and how does it meet user population information needs? Although librarians have supported both quantitative and qualitative standards, regional accreditation associations have resisted quantitative measures.[5]

Early twentieth-century efforts to develop college library standards occurred within regional accreditation associations. Later standards were developed in various American Library Association (ALA), Association of College and Research Libraries (ACRL), and Association of Research Libraries (ARL) committees and councils and in professional accrediting associations.[6] The basis of these standards has been primarily the judgments of academic library leaders and the data published by the National Center for Education Statistics, ARL, and ACRL. Standards have been expressed in terms of minimum or adequate levels or even as averages of particular library groups.

Standards are written as qualitative or quantitative measures, or combinations of the two. Separate institutional types are now covered by separate standards: universities, four-year, and two-year colleges. Criteria have been developed for personnel, collections, services, facilities, administrative organization, and financial support. Standards are meant to provide self-assessment encouragement and assistance. Through a process of measuring services and comparing them with those of similar libraries, an increase in resources and services may be obtained from the institutional administration.

College Library Standards

ACRL college library standards were first published in 1930 and last revised in 1975. They are designed for use in institutions with four-year programs or with limited master's programs. They contain qualitative statements about objectives, material organization, service delivery, administrative organization, and financial support. Specific quantitative formulas are given for collection size, staffing, and space. The 1975 standards were sufficiently flexible to accommodate varied college purposes, contained both qualitative and quantitative measures, and were sufficiently broad to accommodate future development.[7,8] They accounted not only for enrollment, but also faculty size and academic program quantity and levels.[9] They expect a clear objectives statement in accord with college goals, that the collection will comprise all college-owned material, that the material will satisfy most user needs, that collection size will be determined by a specific formula, that the collection will be organized to provide physical and bibliographic access, that the staff will be adequate to meet program demands (also determined by formula), that appropriate information service will be provided, that the space and facilities will be adequate (a formula included), that an effective administrative structure will exist, and that the college will provide an adequate budget.

Recent studies have attempted to determine the number of libraries actually meeting ACRL standards. Hardesty and Bentley found that while 70 per cent of the libraries had collections of 100,000 volumes or more, only 20 per cent or less were able to sustain a collection growth rate of 5 per cent and a college budget share of 6 per cent.[10] These researchers expressed concern that the standards did not include measures of library effectiveness (results of services), productivity, recognition of nonprint resources, and provision for academic program evaluation.

Using 1977/78 data, Carpenter analyzed reports from 1,100 college libraries.[11] He included 95 per cent of the institutions classified as colleges by the Carnegie Commission on Higher Education. Half of the libraries had collections which met the holdings standard. However, only 20 per cent of them had staff in sufficient numbers to meet standards. Only 16 per cent of them received the 6 per cent budget share and only 25 per cent had a collection growth rate of 5 per cent or more. Carpenter concluded that these libraries were underdeveloped, understaffed, and underused.

University Library Standards

Standards specifically designed for university libraries were not published until 1979. They were formulated by several ACRL and ARL committees and are used to evaluate libraries serving extensive undergraduate, professional, and graduate programs. These standards are completely qualitative.[12] The 1979 standards place special emphasis on services supporting institutional programs, providing bibliographic and physical collection access, making this material available to all users, providing sufficient staff to support the necessary service, providing facilities which care for present and future collection and service needs, and providing adequate funding for operation.[13]

A recent study attempted to determine university library directors' attitudes toward the 1979 standards. Half of them responded. While there was general satisfaction with those standards which could not be quantified, there was widespread concern about the lack of specific minimums or medians for those standards which could be quantified. A number of respondents supported the idea of standards revision.[14]

Stubbs attempted to answer questions about the relationships of library and university data.[15] ARL and ACRL 1978/79 statistics were used in the study. Some general conclusions were that university libraries have staffs containing one-third librarians and two-thirds support staff, they spend about one-third of their operating budgets for material and half of those material budgets for subscriptions and standing orders.

According to Stubbs, library size can usually be understood by examining university data. The strongest relationship was between library size and graduate enrollment. Stubbs devised a formula by which the data for 196 libraries were examined and an overall score determined. He concluded that a library must have at least 600,000 volumes to have the essential characteristics of a university library. Libraries must identify and measure those services which provide user access to information and specific material when needed, Stubbs said.

Two-Year College Library Standards

The history of two-year college library standards was reviewed by Wallace.[16] First issued in 1932, these standards were revised in 1960, 1972, 1979, and 1982. The 1972 standards were reviewed and approved by ACRL, American Association of Community and Junior Colleges, and the Association for Educational Communications and Technology (AECT). Beginning with 1972, they used the term "Guideline" instead of the traditional "Standard."[17] They have also included all learning resource centers in the guidelines: the library, media center, and computer center. The guidelines are to serve as a document for "self-evaluation and projective planning," not as minimal standards. The 1979 document attempted to establish "minimal" and "good" levels for staff, collection, space, and equipment for colleges in different enrollment categories.[18] The 1982 Guidelines cover all units that support academic programs. Thus, they go well beyond being merely a set of library standards.[19]

An additional set of guidelines has been used to cover extension service.[20] The major concern expressed in this document is that credit and degree programs offered to non-traditional students at remote locations do not receive adequate service.

Carpenter used the "Statement on Quantitative Standards" in his study of 1,100 two year colleges that reported 1977/78 data to the National Center for Education Statistics (NCES).[21] Two-thirds of these colleges had enrollments of 3,000 or less. Carpenter's study concluded that nearly 80 per cent of these libraries lacked sufficient staff to meet the standards. Collection size was below standard in most institutions. Public colleges did far better than private at meeting the collection growth standard. According to the study, most libraries would need to double their operating budgets to meet the recommended 7 per cent institutional budget share. Wallace stated one caution about the Carpenter study.[22] There is a strong possibility that the NCES reports did not include data on college learning resources departments which were separate organizationally from libraries. As a result, total learning resources may have been underreported.

Standards and Austerity

In spite of decades of effort, the development of satisfactory qualitative and quantitative standards has been only partially successful. Standards have been accepted in some form by several accreditation associations, but actual implementation has not limited the trend to evaluate each institution independently, based primarily on local goals. The comparison of one institution with another is not part of the 1980s regional accreditation process.[23]

Even after a quarter-century of growth many libraries fall far short of meeting selective quantitative standards. During the eighties enrollment and public support are expected to show very modest growth or even reduction. It is unlikely that libraries will obtain the budget increases necessary to support higher collection growth. It seems unrealistic to expect staffing level improvement in the next decade.

While half or more of the libraries may have collections of adequate size, the quantity of new material added annually can be expected to remain below the standard. Purchasing value of material expenditures has declined for a decade. Although the book and periodical price inflation rate may decline, continued erosion of real value can be expected. In addition, libraries are required to select from an ever growing book and periodical output. While smaller quantities of new material are added to collections, these collections are being used and misused to the point that substantial purchases may be required just to replace disintegrating, mutilated, and heavily-used material.

A majority of academic libraries are understaffed, according to the above comparisons. Personnel costs often represent between 50 and 60 per cent of the library's operating budget. During the present austere period it is unrealistic to expect that many libraries can increase staff size. Actually many libraries have lost positions, and this trend may continue. Necessary salary and benefit increases will continue to work to the detriment of collection budgets. At the same time libraries may experience a productivity decline as support staff, student, equipment, and supply expenditures are reduced in order to sustain subscriptions and retain librarians.

For decades libraries have voluntarily participated in an interlibrary loan and photocopy network. However, the increasing costs of providing delivery of these resources is having an impact on lending library personnel. The number of requests received is now beyond the ability of many lending libraries to handle adequately without reducing local user service. Borrowing libraries must absorb some of these service costs.

Participation in systems and consortia has allowed libraries to provide additional service but at some additional cost. No library should expect to satisfy another's user needs except for an unusual item or for advanced research. Libraries must be self-sufficient in supporting most of their institution's programs. The best course during a prolonged austerity period may be to develop procedures for relating service more closely to academic programs, for formulating budgets, and for establishing collection development policies.[24]

Library Standards and Accreditation

The development of non-governmental and voluntary higher education evaluation is related to the historical evolution of post-secondary education. The lack of national government direction and control created the situation in which colleges and universities eventually agreed to develop an accreditation procedure by which the public could be assured of consistency and quality. Postsecondary education accreditation is the responsibility of six regional associations: New England, Middle States, North Central, Northwest, Southern, and Western. Staffs and voluntary evaluators comment on self-studies and provide general evaluation. Accreditation is a method of self-improvement, not an act of regulation. Each college is evaluated on the basis of its educational objectives.[25]

The relationship between academic libraries and accreditation was explored recently.[26] Each regional association provides its evaluators with criteria and guidelines. They include sections on library objectives, collection, organization, personnel, facilities, budget, and inter-institutional cooperation. The library must prepare a self-study of objectives, structure, staff, collection quality, and services supporting the academic program.[27]

In addition, nearly fifty professional organizations have jurisdiction over specific degree programs and their accreditation reviews occur outside the regional visitation framework. Each one of these organizations attempts to incorporate library support evaluation for its specific program into the accreditation process.[28]

Evaluation criteria have increasingly emphasized the review of results rather than focusing only on input measures.[29] More visiting teams are examining support for various academic programs, the collection use inside and outside the facilities, library use assignments by faculty, and various measures of user satisfaction with collection and service.[30]

Library review is thought to be enhanced if librarians are team members.[31] A similar statement could be made for academic programs and support services, such as computer and media service. Other observers have been critical of librarians who overemphasize library review.[32] Library self-study quality improvement may be a better evaluation improvement method.

Through its Office of Management Studies, ARL has gained considerable experience in assisting with self-studies.[33] The self-study should focus on those service aspects that will be most important for regional and professional accreditation association review. The self-study should state library objectives, the methods used to determine and review objectives, the methods used to evaluate collection and service, special library characteristics, strengths, and weaknesses, and the library's place in institutional organization. The self-study must show how academic programs are supported by collection and service.

Conclusion

For a decade or more, a widening gap has been evident between academic program and user information needs and library ability to meet these demands. Financial conditions preclude substantial funding increases. The choices appear to be: increase the institutional budget share devoted to library operation, reduce the academic programs supported, reduce faculty and student library expectations, or drastically modify library operation to fit anticipated funding level.[34] Libraries must adopt the evaluation philosophy which guides regional institutional accreditation; what are the educational objectives and results of programs? Libraries must devise methods to determine objectives and to monitor on a continuing basis, not just periodically.[35]

The number and level of academic programs which must be supported by library collections and services is the most crucial user demand determinant. As the Clapp-Jordan formula recognized, one of the most important parts of a library collection formula is the number of undergraduate, graduate, and professional programs served.[36] Library operations must relate closely to these programs if successful service output is to occur. Services must be examined to determine costs and benefits. Measurement must be established because information needs will always exceed the resources available to satisfy them. User population composition changes must be examined annually. New courses, research interests, and degree programs can potentially increase demands on collection and service.

O'Neil has identified several major 1980s library issues.[37] These include creation of new academic programs to meet changing student needs, careful review of existing programs to determine those that can no longer be justified, the relationship between library policies and academic departments, library status relative to other instructional support services (computer, media), preservation of disintegrating research collections, and new technology use. These issues can only be addressed on the local level. Further revising traditional library standards will not assist in solving them.

References

1. Felix E. Hirsch, "Introduction: Why Do We Need Standards?" *Library Trends* 21 (October 1972), p. 159.
2. Ibid. p. 259.

3. Frederick W. Lancaster, *The Measurement and Evaluation of Library Services* (Washington: Information Resources Press, 1977), p. 288.

4. Ibid., pp. 296–97.

5. Jasper G. Schad, "The Evolution of College and University Library Standards," in *Libraries and Accreditation in Institutions of Higher Education*, eds.: Julie C. Virgo and David A. Yuro (Chicago: American Library Association, 1981), pp. 9–17.

6. David Kaser, "Standards for College Libraries," *Library Trends* 31 (Summer 1982), pp. 7–19.

7. Helen M. Brown, "College Libary Standards," *Library Trends* 21 (October 1972), pp. 204–17.

8. Kaser, *op. cit.*, pp. 10–13.

9. "Standards for College Libraries," *College and Research Libraries News* 36 (October 1975), pp. 277–83, 290–301.

10. Larry Hardesty and Stella Bentley, "The Use and Effectiveness of the 1975 Standards for College Libraries," paper presented at the Association of College and Research Libraries Conference, 1 October 1981.

11. Raymond L. Carpenter, "College Libraries: A Comparative Analysis in Terms of the ACRL Standards," *College and Research Libraries* 42 (January 1981), pp. 7–18.

12. Beverly P. Lynch, "University Library Standards," *Library Trends* 31 (Summer 1982), pp. 39–44; David R. Watkins, "Standards for University Libraries," *Library Trends* 21 (October 1972), pp. 190–203.

13. "Standards for University Libraries," *College and Research Libraries News* 40 (April 1979), pp. 101–10.

14. Lynch, *op. cit.*, pp. 44–46.

15. Kendon Stubbs, "University Libraries: Standards and Statistics," *College and Research Libraries* 42 (November 1981), pp. 527–38.

16. Four papers by James O. Wallace: "The History and Philosophy of Library Standards," in *Quantitative Measures in Librarianship*, eds.: Irene Braden Hoadley and Alice Clark (Westport, Conn.: Greenwood Press, 1972), pp. 39–56; "Two Year College Library Standards," *Library Trends* 21 (October 1972), pp. 219–32; "An Overview of the Guidelines for Two-Year College Learning Resources Programs," in Virgo and Yuro, *op. cit.*, pp. 19–23; "Two-Year College Learning Resources Standards," *Library Trends* 31 (Summer 1982), pp. 21–31.

17. "Guidelines for Two-Year College Learning Resources Programs," *College and Research Libraries News* 43 (January, February 1982), pp. 5–10, 45–49.

18. "Statement on Quantitative Standards for Two-Year Learning Resources Programs," *College and Research Libraries News* 40 (March 1979), pp. 69–73.

19. "Guidelines," *op. cit.*, pp. 5–10, 45–49.

20. "Guidelines for Library Services to Extension/Noncampus Students: Draft of Proposed Revisions," *College and Research Libraries News* 41 (October 1980), pp. 265–72.

21. Ray Carpenter, "Two-Year College Libraries: A Comparative Analysis in Terms of the ACRL Standards," *College and Research Libraries* 42 (September 1981), pp. 407–15.

22. Wallace, "Two-Year College Learning Resources Standards," *op. cit.*, p. 29.

23. Patricia A. Sacks, "Standards for College Libraries: Trends and Issues," in Virgo and Yuro, *op. cit.*, pp. 25–31.

24. Beverly P. Lynch, *op. cit.*, p. 45.

25. Kenneth E. Young, "Overview of the Accrediting Process," in Virgo and Yuro, *op. cit.*, pp. 3–8.

26. Virgo and Yuro, *passim.*

27. Ibid., pp. 89–99.

28. Dorthy G. Peterson, *Accrediting Standards and Guidelines* (Washington: Council on Postsecondary Accreditation, 1979), p. 42–43, 93–94, 139.

29. George M. Bailey, "Evaluation of Libraries in the Accreditation Process—From the Standpoint of the Library," in Virgo and Yuro, *op. cit.*, pp. 57–63.

30. Patricia Thrash, "Evaluation of Libraries in the Accrediting Process from the Standpoint of the Accrediting Association," in Virgo and Yuro, *op. cit.*, pp. 47–56.

31. Harold E. Wade, "How Can the Evaluation of Libraries Be Made Effective," in Virgo and Yuro, *op. cit.*, pp. 65–70.

32. Ronald G. Leach, "Identification and Modification of Criteria and Procedures for Evaluating College and University Libraries by North Central Association Accrediting Teams," (Ph.D. dissertation, Michigan State University, 1980), p. 78–81.

33. Duane E. Webster, "The Assisted Self-Study Approach to Improving Academic Libraries," in Virgo and Yuro, *op. cit.*, pp. 41–46.

34. Herman H. Fussler, "University Libraries and Change," in *Louis Round Wilson Centennial Day* (Chapel Hill: University of North Carolina, School of Library Science, 1977), pp. 43–53.

35. Thomas J. Waldhart, "Implementing Results-Oriented Management in Academic Libraries," *Journal of Academic Librarianship* 4 (September 1978), pp. 209–13.

36. V. W. Clapp and R. T. Jordan, "Quantitative Criteria for Adequacy of Academic Library Collections," *College and Research Libraries* 26 (September 1965), pp. 371–80.

37. Robert M. O'Neil, "The University Administrator's View of the University Library," in *Priorities for Academic Libraries*, eds.: Thomas J. Galvin and Beverly P. Lynch (San Francisco: Jossey-Bass, 1982), pp. 5–12.

Recommended Reading

"An Evaluative Checklist for Reviewing a College Library Program," *College and Research Library News* 40 (November 1979), pp. 305–16.

Downs, Robert B., and John W. Heussman, "Standards for University Libraries," *College and Research Libraries* 31 (January 1970), pp. 28–35.

Jones, F. Taylor. "The Regional Accrediting Associations and the Standards for College Libraries," *College and Research Libraries* 22 (July 1961), pp. 271–74.

MacVean, Donald S. *An NCATE Evaluation of a University Library: A Case History* (ERIC Document, ED 171240, 1979).

Webb, Mary Alice. "A Study of the Perceptions of the Presidents, Academic Deans and Learning Resources Administrators in the Public Community Colleges in Florida Regarding the 1972 Library Standards; Guidelines for Two-Year College Learning Resources Programs," (Ph.D. dissertation, Florida State University, 1980).

Yates, Dudley V., *The Impact of Regional Accrediting Agencies Upon Libraries in Postsecondary Education* (ERIC Document, ED 135337, 1976).

9. Building Planning Austerity

Gloria J. Novak

BUILDING PLANNING AUSTERITY—the first thoughts that come to mind are bleak, cold, uncomfortable, ugly, shoddy, inferior, cheap. However, other, more invigorating thoughts also come to mind: rigorous, disciplined, simple. The concept of quality is partially described by these adjectives. As contrary as it may appear at the outset, the appropriate response to austerity is good quality. The chapter will explain this statement, describe an approach to planning for economy and quality, and discuss building design, construction and equipment examples which can be considered in order to achieve economy.

Austerity and Quality

Periods of economic austerity emphasize the benefits realized from minimizing waste and optimizing investment, both of which are aspects of quality. Waste is an anathema when trying to meet austerity's demands. Often planners fail to recognize that they plan waste, in the name of austerity. Reducing the initial construction cost by specifying inferior quality material which will in turn require excessive maintenance is planning for waste. These false savings produce especially serious consequences in an austere economy in which maintenance funds are not available. Deferred maintenance compounds the problem because further deterioration increases the damage and repair cost. Although quality has the connotation of being expensive, it is essential to overcome the minimum-initial-cost syndrome that rises from austerity's intimidation and recognize the economy in good quality and the waste in poor quality.

Another type of library waste is created by a building that requires an excessive number of staff members to operate. Quality can be achieved here only by careful library planning and responsive and talented architects. This kind of waste seldom receives attention because it is not an obvious component of the initial construction cost. Cost-cutting for items that affect appearance and comfort is a kind of waste that receives initial cost attention but is not recognized as waste. Often the result of this economy measure is a library that repels rather than attracts users, a priceless waste. How can one measure the extent to which a poor environment reduces education quality by turning students away from the library and information?

Energy waste can be measured. The United States has a long building design history that promotes energy waste. Glass curtain walls, inefficient heating, ventilating, and cooling systems are examples of waste and poor quality. Librarians have been sensitive to these design shortcomings for a long time. However, their concern was not for energy waste but for collection damage and building occupant discomfort. For many years librarians fought a tough battle to disuade designers from imposing such problems on them. Ironically, the energy shortage has now turned out to be the librarians' ally.

Europeans, long ago confronted with energy and inflation problems, recognized the necessity to optimize investment and turn to quality: "European imports stand for the best of everything—the best autos, wines and textiles."[1] A quality trend has more recently begun in the United States and has been revealed by the extensive research of two New York advertising agencies. They found that Americans, confronted with ever-increasing prices, were becoming more discriminating. They wanted more "bang for the buck," so they bought products that lasted longer and provided more satisfaction.[2] In other words, they bought quality products. It's the economical thing to do, a first-rate austerity measure, and applies to buildings as well as to automobiles, wines, and textiles. To obtain more "bang for the buck" from a building implies more than reducing construction cost. A building is useful and economical only in relation to the activities that it contains. To deny quality and elevate the importance of cheapness beyond the requirements to support those activities is to create waste and defeat austerity's purpose.

Planning for Economy and Quality
An Approach to Gathering and Analyzing Information

Having given examples of quality's role in austerity, the next step is to offer an approach to planning for economy and quality. This is not intended to be a guide to writing a library building program. Rather, it is intended to aid in formulating elements appropriate for a building program conceived in an austere climate. It is also intended to aid in producing the information necessary to convince funding authorities that the building program's merits warrant investment even during hard times.

A number of planning process aspects will be examined to identify the barriers to quality and the techniques helpful in achieving reasonably priced quality. These aspects include problem identification, objective identification, and cost and benefit analysis. The critical thread running through this examination is information. The quality of the information gathered and of its analysis will determine the quality of the final product. To obtain maximum benefit from information, one must understand its nature and purposes. Information "describes, explains, predicts, evaluates and produces discoveries."[3] The better a library gathers, organizes, and analyzes information appropriate for each planning process step, the greater the potential for constructing a high quality building.

Problem Identification

Identifying the problem is the first step. Often this planning aspect is subverted by persons who decide on a solution before the planning process has begun. They think that common sense alone is sufficient to make complex decisions, but it is not. A building which misses the point and fails to solve the library space problem is intolerable in austerity.

Common-sense solutions are based on obvious and easily recognized problems. However, the problem may not be as obvious as common sense suggests, but may be a case of mistaken identity instead. A symptom may be mistaken for a problem. A common example is the space shortage complaint. It may include overcrowded working conditions, tight traffic corridors, or inadequate material processing storage. The real problem could be poor housekeeping, poor spatial organization or poor work-flow design, all more easily resolved than an actual space shortage problem would be.

To avoid mistakes and lost opportunities, gather full and accurate information on the existing situation. A valuable information source is the staff, all levels from clerk to manager. Determining operation steps is usually difficult without full discussion with the individuals who perform them. Supervisors are not always fully aware of all details or problems. Analysis of this information, however, must be done carefully because staff members do not always identify problems correctly. The perception problem affects all of us because so many environmental factors color our impressions. We are too close to problems and too entrenched in traditional thought processes containing both valuable and outmoded approaches. The situation must be stripped of its nonessentials before the real problem can be revealed. "Do not be conditioned by tradition."[4] This does not mean to ignore tradition but to be aware of its power to blind. Many material-handling and work-flow problems, for example, were created by tradition and generate excessive operating costs. A useful tool for analyzing work process information is the flow chart. This operation map can reveal a host of problems not readily apparent, such as complicated work-flow traffic patterns, unnecessary material double-handling and split functions. A flow chart is only one example of a model constructed to detect operation problems.[5] A model represents an imaginative and abstract idea that aids thinking. Its purpose is to picture something that cannot be directly observed in order to aid understanding and solve problems. A model can give form to the information gathered and help test concept value. Whatever form of model is used, good building planning requires adequate information. Gathering and analyzing this information is essential in order to separate unproductive from productive activities, thus enabling planners to identify the problems to be resolved.

Library Objectives Identification

Having correctly identified the problems causing the need for physical facility expansion or change, the next planning process step is to determine the library objectives which the physical space must support. Again, tradition can hold the library hostage. Space is such a strong dictator of how something should be done that it may be difficult to imagine an improvement. Therefore, it is important to think abstractly of, for example, an ideal organization for technical processing functions. The act of consideration partially frees staff members from tradition and opens the way to improvement.

The ideal spatial relationship between departments can be visualized without undue influence of tradition through using another model, a matrix. Figure 1 shows an example of a departmental relationships matrix. Such a model is useful in communicating to the architect an important aspect of the library's operational objectives. The architect can then translate these abstract spatial relationships into a design.

However, before establishing matrix elements, one must consider that austerity sets its own objectives—efficient and economical operation achieved by the lowest possible construction investment. Austerity objectives, thoughtfully approached, can benefit other library objectives as well. For example, staffed public service areas may have proliferated over the years in response to varied needs. Now, however, with the increasing number of interdisciplinary teaching and research programs, these areas have become both costly to operate and counterproductive academically. A physical change making consolidation possible would serve both the objectives of austerity and of teaching and research. In this instance, austerity objectives provide the impetus for positive change.

Another objective is to plan for economic service delivery and staff operation since these are on-going costs. During austere periods, one must work diligently to prevent planning that will lead to uneconomic operation. Frequently the threat emanates from the funding source. To

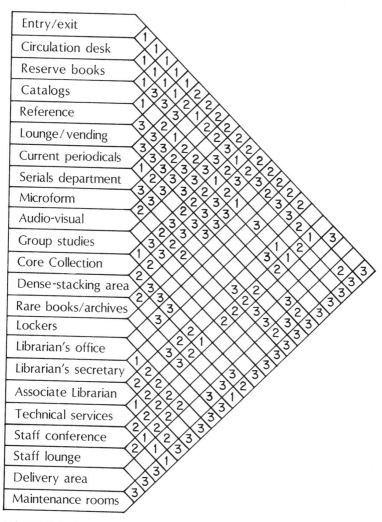

Entry/exit
Circulation desk
Reserve books
Catalogs
Reference
Lounge/vending
Current periodicals
Serials department
Microform
Audio-visual
Group studies
Core Collection
Dense-stacking area
Rare books/archives
Lockers
Librarian's office
Librarian's secretary
Associate Librarian
Technical services
Staff conference
Staff lounge
Delivery area
Maintenance rooms

RELATIVE DEGREE OF IMPORTANCE

equal importance	1 pt. to each criterion
minor difference	1 pt. to more important criterion
medium difference	2 pts. to more important criterion
major difference	3 pts. to more important criterion

Figure 1. Matrix of Relationships

keep construction cost low, pressure may be exerted to re-use inappropriate existing space, construct a smaller addition than is needed, forgo a new building even though the old one will never fill the library's new technological needs, or compromise in a hundred other ways. The only way to meet this challenge to objectives is through strong and statistically sound justifications.

Cost-Benefit Analysis

Strong and convincing building program justification can be produced by comparing the costs and benefits of various potential solutions to fulfillment of the library's objectives and to its problems. Cost-benefit analysis carries the strong potential not only to convince others that a project is worth funding but also to make it possible to produce a high quality library. Cost-benefit analysis is very useful in liberating capital investment project decisions from the initial-cost bias. Its basic principle is that the "worth of any action, project, investment or strategy equals the excess of the benefits it yields over the costs (sacrifices) it entails."[6]

In developing the building program and its justification, one must consider the total building cost which consists of both its short-term and long-term costs, also described as life-cycle costs. These costs include the initial construction cost and the maintenance, repair, and operation costs during its lifetime. Quality in construction and optimization of investment occur when these costs balance and the building demands the least library objective sacrifice and produces the least budget strain. A quality building supports its service, processing, and preservation functions at minimum staffing, maintenance, energy, and change cost. When benefits exceed costs, quality is achieved and austerity's demands are met.

To achieve the most favorable cost-benefit ratio, think of the library as an ecological system. All parts must work together to achieve a healthy input-output balance. In man-made environments this balance can be accomplished only by thoroughly planning and carefully weighing costs against benefits.

Intangible costs and benefits increase the difficulty of applying this analytic process. Consider specific issues by singling out those operations that represent costs and those that represent benefits and by thinking of them not only in the sense of funds spent or saved but also as objectives lost or gained. Deal with the uncertainty of an action's effects by identifying its results explicitly and determining the amount of injury that would be done to the library or the academic institution by its absence. The injury projected may spread beyond the local scene and, when anticipated, can be incorporated into the analysis. An evaluation matrix may be used to analyze building solutions and incorporate both intangible and tangible costs and benefits. Two steps are used in this analysis and are represented by the charts in Figures 2 and 3, the

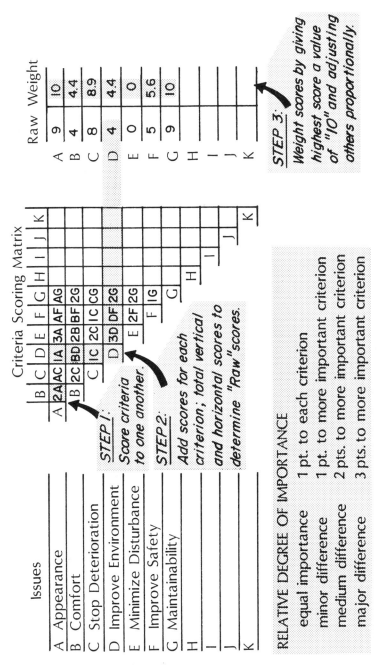

Figure 2. Criteria Valuation

ISSUES/CRITERIA	Value (1-10)	No. 1	No. 2	No. 3	No. 4	No. 5	No. 6	No. 7	No. 8	No. 9
Appearance	10	6 / 60	5 / 50	8 / 80	8 / 80	8 / 80				
Comfort	4.4	3 / 13.2	8 / 35.2	8 / 35.2	8 / 35.2	8 / 35.2				
Stop Deterioration	8.9	– / –	– / –	– / –	– / –	– / –				
Improve Environment	4.4	6 / 26.4	5 / 22	8 / 35.2	8 / 35.2	8 / 35.2				
Minimize Disturbance	0	8 / 0	9 / 0	8 / 0	7 / 0	5 / 0				
Improve Safety	5.6	– / –	– / –	– / –	– / –	– / –				
Maintainability	10	9 / 90	7 / 70	7 / 70	8 / 80	7 / 70				

Weighted Value from the Criteria Valuation Form ← | *STEP 1: Assign value to Option's response to each criterion.* | *STEP 2: Multiply score by value of criterion.*

STEP 3: Add Totals to derive Total Option Score. | *STEP 4: Ranks Options by Scores.*

| Score | | 189.6 | 197.2 | 220.4 | 230.4 | 220.4 | | | | |
| Rank | | 4 | 3 | 2 | 1 | 2 | | | | |

Figure 3. Option Evaluation

criteria valuation chart and the option evaluation chart.[7] The criteria valuation chart is a matrix which enables the reader to compare each criterion individually with every other criterion. This exercise gives a weighted value to each criterion. The evaluation comparisons are composed of numerical scores (see charts). The point total for each criterion is determined by adding both vertically and horizontally the number of times a letter is entered—all A's, B's, etc. In order to use the criteria scores more easily in evaluating options, the highest score is made equivalent to 10 and the other scores are changed proportionally.

The option evaluation chart is a matrix which allows the reader to score each option for its response to each criterion. The reader assigns a score from 1 to 10 for every option on each criterion, with 10 being the most satisfactory response. Each one of these scores is multiplied by the weighted value of the criterion as determined from the criteria valuation chart. The sum of this process is each option's satisfaction score.[8]

Evaluation models provide tools for comparing on an equal basis values which can be measured in dollars with those which cannot. While the foregoing evaluates both tangibles and intangibles, the following discussion will emphasize evaluation models for tangibles. Energy is a significant tangible cost and a major contributor to world austerity. Since buildings represent major energy-consuming units, initial cost alone is an inadequate measure of a particular building design's economy.

Cost analysis formulas can be used to combat the initial-cost myopia with which funding sources approach building projects. The National Bureau of Standards sponsored the research and publication of a handbook to help designers make energy decisions calculated to produce buildings with good energy cost-benefit ratios. Four cost models were developed: life-cycle costs, net benefits or savings, savings-to-investment ratio, and discounted payback.[9]

The life-cycle cost model, also described as cost-in-use, provides a technique for making comparative analyses.[10] Although developed primarily to compare building designs and planning alternatives, it can also be used to compare any alternative means to a given end. It can be used to determine a building project's investment magnitude. It can be used to select the design alternative with the best cost-benefit ratio, applicable equally to a complete building or a single interior system. It can compare savings with costs, evaluate efforts to achieve the maximum dollar value, and compare overall cost savings through use of various energy conservation measures. A sample formula follows:

$$LCC = P - S + M + R + E$$

LCC—Life-cycle costs   M—Maintenance and repair costs
P—Purchase and installation costs   R—Replacement costs
S—Salvage value   E—Energy costs[11]

The net benefit or saving model provides a technique for finding the difference between life-time savings and life-time costs and is used to compare alternate investments. It can also be used for the same purposes as the life-cycle cost model to determine investment size, maximized dollar benefit level, energy-conservation measure savings, and best solution. A sample formula follows:

$$(B - C) = E - (P - S + M + R)$$

B—Benefits   P—Differential purchase and installation costs
C—Costs   S—Differential salvage value
(B—C)—Net benefits or savings   M—Differential maintenance and repair costs
E—Reduction in energy costs   R—Differential replacement costs[12]

The savings-to-investment ratio model is different from the other cost models in that costs are expressed in ratios rather than dollars. "For positive net savings, the ratio must be greater than one. The higher the ratio the more dollar savings realized per dollar investment."[13] This model is used to determine which of competing options will produce the greatest benefits. It can also be used to compare savings to costs. A sample formula follows:

$$SIR = (E - M) \div (P - S + R)$$

SIR—Savings-to-investment ratio   P—Differential purchase and installation costs
E—Reduction in energy costs   S—Differential salvage value
M—Differential maintenance and   R—Differential replacement costs[14]
   repair costs

The discounted payback model "measures the elapsed time between the point of initial investment and the point at which accumulated savings, net of other accumulated costs, are sufficient to offset the initial investment cost."[15] A sample formula shows how to find the payback period, Y:

$$\text{Find Y such that } \sum_{j=1}^{Y} (E_j - M_j - R_j + S_j) = P$$

Y—Summation from years 1 to Y R_j—Differential replacement costs in year j
E_j—Reduction in energy costs in S_j—Differential salvage value in year j
   year j   P—Differential purchase and installation costs[16]
M_j—Differential maintenance and
   repair costs in year j

Applying these cost models to the architectural design should be the design consultant's responsibility. Results should be shared with the planning team members responsible for evaluating consultant design proposals. This requirement must be clarified during the architectural selection process and in the design contract to insure that this planning aspect will not be denied to the client.

The following are examples of building design features which may be considered for energy conservation and can be analyzed by using one or more of the preceding cost models. Their appropriateness for a particular library will depend on the site's macro- and micro-climate. "One of the most powerful determinants of building form, as we approach the end of this century, is the cost of energy and energy conservation."[17] The most cost-effective manner in which to attain energy-conservation objectives is to take maximum advantage of natural elements to reduce consumption. Once the demand has been reduced through passive measure use, then the various active measures using mechanical and electrical systems can be considered.

The first factor to consider is the site. A building's sun and wind orientation is important, a fact nearly forgotten by modern man. Site landscaping can reinforce proper orientation to reduce energy requirements further. A favorable arrangement of trees and shrubs can protect a building from the sun and provide passive air cleaning and humidifying. Fountains can also provide a passive means to humidify and cool hot dry air. The insulation properties of earth are superior to those of any man-made insulation. Therefore, landscaped earth berms can provide substantial protection from cold winter winds for buildings above grade. Underground buildings experience far less energy loss by air transmission and filtration through walls, ceilings, doors, floors, and windows than do those above ground.

Building shape, organization, and material can reduce heat gain and loss in summer and winter. More than most other shapes, a low, square building will provide a minimum of exterior surface from which to lose heat to cold and wind. Cold wind protection can also be achieved by locating unheated areas, such as parking and storage, on the building side subjected to this wind. Atriums and interior courtyards, long the bane of librarians, if properly designed, can provide a variety of energy-saving benefits. For example, an atrium oriented to the south can provide passive solar winter heating, summer shading, and interior daylighting all year long. In cold winter climates, the "winter garden" concept, utilizing atriums and interior courtyards, can provide a tempered and protected micro-climate beneficial for the building and its occupants and is especially appreciated for its ability to extend spring and autumn temperatures into winter months.[18]

Heavy construction has also proved successful in conserving energy. By providing building mass through use of material, such as concrete for the roof and structural masonry for the walls, energy can be stored and used more efficiently. The foregoing measures will reduce the building's mechanical and electrical system workloads substantially. Since heating, cooling, and lighting consume most energy, the greater the number of these measures that can be incorporated into the design the better the library will be able to withstand economic constraints.

Lighting can be imaginatively designed to control energy costs and create a pleasant ambiance. Carefully designed building envelope penetrations can control heat loss and take advantage of the sun and also provide natural light to supplement the artificial light required. An efficient balance between artificial and natural light can be achieved through photoelectric switching. Other ways to conserve lighting energy include use of task lights, high-intensity discharge fixtures, and fluorescent fixtures with special energy-saving ballasts. Lighting applications must be carefully considered to achieve appropriate and good quality light. A lighting consultant is highly recommended.

Electronic controls can produce energy savings in mechanical and electrical systems. Computer-based systems can analyze and control energy input, storage, and output. These controls can be installed on existing as well as new mechanical systems and they have become popular because increased energy costs have shortened their payback period. However, poor control design may create excessive long-term maintenance and replacement costs. New technology side effects are often inadequately understood so one must adopt new technologies with caution. When planning a new building, it may be wise to design for future solar and other renewable energy technology system installation. When these systems are deemed cost-effective and through long-time use the equipment is perfected, then it can be installed at minimum cost.

Other Economy and Quality Planning Considerations

The planning considerations selected for discussion here have become increasingly important during this austere period and contain the potential to change the nature of solutions to library space problems. They do not represent an exhaustive list of such issues. They do tend to fall into four categories: equipment, library standards, cultural mores, and design and construction. They share the potential for requiring substantial investment and providing substantial benefits. They also share attractive and obvious benefits but not so obvious costs.

Librarians often check the space shortage solutions of their colleagues, but they should beware of seeming panaceas. It is insufficient to accept another library's solution without analyzing its success and the likelihood that that solution would work well locally. To determine if a concept will work in a different setting, it is necessary to devise a model based on identifying all significant elements, assigning concrete magnitudes to them, and making explicit the assumptions and logic. The purpose of a model is to represent a simplification of reality. Through this simplicity, models can "indicate how things fit together and explain how they function so that we know better how to cope with them or forecast their behavior."[19]

Equipment

Equipment plays an increasingly important role in library building design and operation. Any technique that can assist in improving equipment selection also becomes important. In the following example, identifying the characteristics of a particular equipment type suggests the elements of a cost-benefit model. Recently, the University of Illinois at Urbana required more shelving space. In order to shelve the maximum number of volumes at least cost, compact shelving on rails was selected. The resulting bookstack addition will shelve two million volumes in half the space that conventional shelving would require. Because this concept will work well at Illinois, the hazard is that, without careful study, other libraries will automatically adopt it or be forced to do so by budget-conscious campus administrators or state finance advisors.

First, in studying this case, the access elements must be considered. Is the book-stack addition required for public access or will the books be paged by library staff members? Illinois bookstacks will be open to public access. Since the space saving in this compact shelving type is in aisle reduction, providing one aisle for every ten shelving ranges, will this equipment's use cause serious problems? Will it generate excessive user frustration and complaint because of wasting time while someone else is using another aisle in the block? Will it generate excessive staff costs because shelvers spend so much time waiting for aisles to be free for reshelving? At Illinois, a count of people concurrently using aisles in ten-range blocks at various times revealed that few would be inconvenienced by aisle reduction.

At what point does scale make this concept workable? Currently Illinois supports a library system with 30 branches and a three million volume bookstack. Would a campus without branches experience special difficulties in using this concept? Is the effectiveness break-even point for this concept two million volumes, one million, 500,000 or what? What role is played by the campus population size or the campus population size specifically served by the collections proposed for compaction?

Second, spatial relationships. Where is a planned addition to be located in relation to existing bookstacks, to public service areas, to library staff? Might the location create confusion not only for users seeking specific items but also for those not accustomed to this equipment and who can find no staff assistance?

Third, what is the purpose of the new space? For Illinois it is specifically for collection shelving. However, for another library additional reasons might exist for the new space: the need to create more reader stations or a better physical relationship between readers and collections. At Illinois the existing bookstack has few seats and provides an uninviting reader environment. No seating is planned in the addition.

If new or renovated space were intended to increase use or if the design caused this to happen, then calculations for compact shelving use should change.[20]

Fourth, the compact shelving equipment itself. What kinds are available in the marketplace? Are they reliable? Is any one manufacturer's product far superior to the others? Do state laws require competitive bidding or contain other limitations that may prevent a library from obtaining the highest quality product? Would a poorer quality product wipe out this concept's advantages? Will maintenance be a major problem either because no service representative is available locally or replacement parts are difficult to obtain?

All the essential elements of a model must be available to produce valid conclusions. One element inadequately accounted for can produce devastating results. For example, if the fact is overlooked that compact shelving requires a 250–300 pound per square foot floor-load capacity, compared with conventional shelving's 125 pounds, the construction budget will be underestimated substantially or the planned use of existing space must be cancelled.

The foregoing represents examples of elements that may be incorporated into a decision model. Emphasis must be placed on the nature of the library and the appropriateness of the solution for that particular setting. A space-saving concept must not be allowed to overwhelm a library operation, especially if costs outweigh benefits. In times of austerity one must be particularly alert to this possibility, because the added cost for space savings may need to be covered by service reductions.

Compact shelving on rails is just one example of space-saving equipment. New types of equipment and improvements provide constant sources of potential space savings. These changes are so rapid and equipment inadequacy identification so difficult that each alternative must be analyzed carefully for each application. Equipment that works well in one library may be a disaster in another. All variables in a library's operation and environment that are impacted by the new equipment must be studied before making a space-saving decision. No equipment piece represents a panacea for every facet of library operation. Each equipment piece has its own cost and benefit pattern in each location. The object is to select the equipment that will provide the greatest benefit for the cost, including intangible as well as tangible costs.

Another type of space-saving equipment deserves mention. Motorized microfiche equipment, not often used by libraries but heavily used by banks, can save 20 to 120 percent in space at a cost equal to or less than that for standard cabinets. Cost and space savings depend on collection size, the larger the collection the greater the savings possible. For this equipment type, the model selected determines the savings, some taller providing substantially greater capacity than shorter models with little floor space increase. This equipment also provides easier and more convenient access to the microfiche than does the standard cabinet. This feature promotes user acceptance of microfiche and substantially increases staff efficiency.

Over time, changes in library operation and no change in the extent of library space often results in too many functions and people jammed into too little space. As space becomes tighter and each individual's territory becomes more restricted and more frequently impinged upon by others, tempers get short, social conversations increase, concentration becomes more difficult, and work efficiency decreases. Furniture systems, often referred to as office landscape furniture, can reduce these problems and at the same time decrease the space required for a single work station by 30 to 40 percent.

Furniture systems consist of panels or screens, acoustical or non-acoustical, on which work surfaces, shelves, file bins and other work organization elements, lights, power, and telecommunications accessories can be hung. Successful planning for this type of system must include early recognition that the office will function differently and must be managed differently from that of a roomful of free-standing desks. Once management has come to terms with the operational changes required by this equipment, the library will benefit not only from space but also cost savings for renovation or the ability to avoid renovation when change is required.

The video disc promises significant space savings, especially for archival, photographic and map collections. A prototype system developed at the Public Archives of Canada (PAC) merits attention. As equipment improves, its usefulness will be extended. In 1981 the PAC system used optical recording by laser beam for all types of archival items on a video disc. The video disc was tied into a floppy-disc minicomputer and a small, intelligent terminal through which commands were given to access any frame. One standard filing-cabinet can house 19,000 discs with a 4,000,000 map capacity, while standard map cases covering 42,000 square feet would be needed to house the same collection.

The computer, which can enhance video disc storage by providing a remarkable access level for difficult-to-control archives, has already impacted standard library operation substantially. One result is to free the library's spatial organization from the rigid physical location dictated by card catalogs. Both the public and the staff can now use the catalog from more convenient locations such as a private office, academic department, or individual desk.

Library Standards

Standards have long been a primary consideration for persons making major capital improvement budget decisions. Collections and reader stations are the two most vociferous space consumers and have become major space control targets challenging library standards. Another challenge to these standards lies in the extraordinary development of electronic technologies. Observations on how the computer is increasing the complexity of predicting collection space needs can be extended to reader stations as well.[21] The paperless society's success and its implementation time frame will affect the library profoundly and depend on many elements outside library control. They include the state of the economy, the speed of new technology development, and the laws or lack of them which will impede or foster these developments and even dictate their direction. Will librarians in 20 or 30 years be disseminating information from their electronic cottages or the same old library building? The best that we can plan is adaptable space which can change gracefully. Successful planning must be based on models constructed from the best information available.

Models can be used to support library standards which austerity has called into question. The standard requiring seating for 25 percent of the student population is one of those questioned. If this standard were based on performance criteria rather than a specific number, it would be easier to understand and accept. In practice, seating is needed for many purposes in many locations, such as reference, periodicals, reserve books, and bookstacks. The seats needed in each area can be determined by organizing appropriate data into a feasible, predictive model. The effort to limit library building growth can be met positively through creatively using models to develop new solutions to space problems. Gathering a great deal of information for these models is not necessary. Collecting the appropriate information and interpreting it to develop reliable numbers is necessary. "With skill, effort and imagination, one can quantify almost anything *usefully*, if not precisely."[22]

Cultural Mores

Solutions to library problems are significantly impacted by the cultural mores of the times. The cultural value of providing access to buildings and collections for the disabled not only affects physical designs but also construction cost for renovation and new space. The following illustration is an excerpt from the current California building code:

> (c) Library general use areas such as those housing card files, book stacks, periodicals, reading and reference areas, information desks, circulation counters, etc., shall be made accessible to the physically handicapped. 1. Open book stacks (those available to customer use) may be of normal height, but shall have main aisles no less than 44 inches (111.7 mm) in width and side aisles no less than 36 inches (914.4 mm) in width.
>   EXCEPTIONS: 1. In existing buildings, shelving in the amount of not more than 15 percent of the total amount

of library shelving may be located on an inaccessible mezzanine area.

2. In existing buildings, multi-tiered, closed book stacks (those restricted to employee use) are exempt from these accessibility standards.

2. Unless an attendant is available to assist physically handicapped persons, all book shelving shall be located not more than 54 inches (1371.6 mm) above the floor.[23]

This code's impact is that new or renovated areas will require approximately 11 percent more floor space for public access bookstacks. Many other states have also similarly revised building codes to insure access for the disabled.

Austerity itself affects cultural values which in turn affect building costs. Due to austerity, library collections and other building contents have become increasingly attractive to thieves. Book detection and building security systems are becoming popular library building components. The decision to use a book detection system, however, must be made carefully. There is increasing evidence of damage to books in which detection devices have been placed. Emergency exit doors represent a serious security leak that has plagued librarians, also. Electrically-operated locks are not yet widely used but are slowly winning fire marshall acceptance. Again, librarians must approach these installation decisions cautiously. Cost, dependability, and local code authority acceptance are critical factors.

Design and Construction

A different approach to building design and construction is being developed in response to austerity and the desire for better buildings. This method will be referred to here as design/build, and the following is a simplified description of it.[24] An architect and the engineering consultants establish the design criteria for a building project. They produce bid documents, drawings, and specifications that establish the design criteria and performance standards required rather than the complete, detailed working drawings and specifications of the traditional design method. Architect-contractor partnerships, rather than contractors alone, submit bids.

The bids consist of a project schematic design as well as construction cost. Bidders are allowed two to four weeks to develop these bids and to determine the material to be used and total cost. The architect-contractor entity must develop a total building package, essentially a turnkey operation, for which it takes total responsibility for proper construction and building operation based on the design criteria and performance standards.

For example, the heating and ventilating system must be designed in accordance with the design criteria and must operate in accordance with performance specifications. If it does not, then it is the entity's responsibility to make the necessary modifications. The bid documents require a five-year guarantee and maintenance program for all building components. Another unique design/build feature is that construction is phased with design, a process known as fast-track construction, to reduce project completion time. Construction begins on certain building elements while others are still in the design phase.

Design/build has several advantages. The first is that the client knows the project cost early in the design phase. In the traditional design and bidding process, the client doesn't know the cost until the bids are received. Frequently the bids exceed the project budget, and the project, or parts of it, must be re-designed or cancelled. Often last minute re-design creates a chain of problems which seriously compromise building program and quality. Another advantage is the cost savings realized by the reduced time required to design and construct the building. Construction costs are currently escalating at a rate of one to two percent per month. A year's cost escalation of 12 to 24 percent can halt a project. Design/build could save it. The third advantage for the client is a clear knowledge of who is responsible for solving any problems that may develop. With usual procedures, when a building settles or develops leaks, assigning responsibility to the contractor, subcontractor, or architect is complicated and difficult and often results in costly litigation.

One of the major design/build disadvantages is the speed at which the final design must proceed. This gives librarians a short response time to the designs submitted. It can be disastrous if the architect lacks an understanding of basic library operation and if the firm and its consultants are particularly unresponsive to library requirements. This situation is difficult enough to deal with effectively even with an extended design time schedule.

Another disadvantage is that architects strongly dislike it. Architects object on the grounds that it will foster poor design, because it emphasizes profit. The tug-of-war of values represented by the profit-motivated contractor and the society-motivated architect seems to many architects impossible to reconcile without damaging design. However, safeguards can be built into the design/build process to prevent design deterioration. One might accept this optimism if academic institutions are not forced to take the lowest bid and if selection can be based on aesthetics as well as how well the design meets performance criteria.

For those of us who have worked with architects and engineers whose designs suffer from their profit motives, architects unsympathetic with the building program design criteria, architects and engineers who refuse to address the energy question and produce building systems which are operational nightmares, design/build may be an alternative worth investigation. If the design is well done an architect can make a greater profit than the current fee structure permits. However, under the normal design contract the architect's responsibility and liability for building design and performance is limited to the most gross failures. If he/she is willing to take the risk of greater responsibility and be motivated to produce a better quality building, the client will not object to greater profit. If this theory works in practice, design/build will represent another possibility for responding appropriately to austerity.

Conclusion

The appropriate response for planning austerity is not just to make buildings cheaper but to plan buildings to minimize waste and maximize investment. To accomplish this formidable feat, one must develop the knowledge and skill to gather the right information and to analyze it properly. The first step is to identify the library's objectives and problems correctly. The next step is to analyze the costs and benefits of the alternatives for meeting these objectives and solving these problems. An essential tool for performing this analysis is the visual technique called the model. An effective model facilitates organizing and simplifying the information gathered. The model and the information from which it is constructed can be designed to describe, explain, predict, evaluate, or produce a discovery. Throughout the planning process, several types of models may be developed for addressing various project aspects. Library buildings represent far too large an investment in funds, human emotions, academic goals, and posterity to sacrifice quality to austerity.

References

1. Bill Abrahms, "Research Suggests Consumers Will Increasingly Seek Quality," *Wall Street Journal* (15 October 1981), p. 25.
2. Ibid., p. 25.
3. Alfred R. Oxenfeldt, *Cost-Benefit Analysis for Executive Decision Making, the Danger of Plain Common Sense* (New York: AMACOM, American Management Association, 1979), p. 107.
4. Gordon L. Glegg, *The Design of Design* (London: Cambridge University Press, 1969), p. 26.
5. P. Matthew Murgio, *Communications Graphics* (N.Y.: Van Nostrand Reinhold, 1969). Models can take any form that will help the user reach a valid conclusion.
6. Oxenfeldt, *op. cit.*, p. 32.
7. Patrick Quinn and Francis Oda, *Graduate Theological Union Library Program* (Berkeley, CA: February 1971), p. 44.
8. Kaplan/McLaughlin/Diaz, Architects/Planners. "Facilities Plan for Doe Library, University of California, Berkeley." *Report* (San Francisco, 1982), pp. E-1—F-3.

9. Harold E. Marshall and Rosalie T. Ruegg, *Simplified Energy Design Economics, Principles of Economics Applied to Energy Conservation and Solar Energy Investments in Buildings*, edited by Forrest Wilson. National Bureau of Standards Special Publication 544 (Washington: U.S. Government Printing Office, 1980), p. 5.

10. P. A. Stone, *Building Design Evaluation, Costs-in-use* (London: E. & F. Spon, 1980), p. 169.

11. Marshall and Ruegg, *op. cit.*, p. 10.

12. Ibid., p. 11.

13. Ibid., p. 11.

14. Ibid., p. 17.

15. Ibid., p. 12.

16. Ibid., p. 12.

17. Ibid., p. iii.

18. Canada. Public Works, Energy, Mines and Resources. *Winning Low Energy Building Designs, Projets Architectureaux Economisant l' Energie* (Ottawa: Public Works Canada, 1980), p. 66.

19. Oxenfeldt, *op. cit.*, p. 59.

20. Telephone conversation with Hugh Atkinson, University of Illinois Library, March, 1982.

21. Ralph E. Ellsworth, "The ABCs of Remodeling/Enlarging an Academic Library Building: a Personal Statement," *Journal of Academic Librarianship* 7 (January 1982), pp. 335.

22. Oxenfeldt, *op. cit.*, p. 107.

23. California. *State Building Code, California Administrative Code*, Title 24, pt. 2, ch. 2–8 (1981): p. 38.

24. H. L. Sisson, "Fair Weather Reports from Three Small Firms," *AIA Journal* (ser. 2) 55 (February 1971), pp. 39–41.

Recommended Reading

Ahuja, Hira N. *Successful Construction Cost Control* (N.Y.: John Wiley, 1980)

Ellsworth, Ralph E., *Planning the College and University Library Building: a Book for Campus Planners and Architects* (Boulder, Colorado: Pruett Press, 1960)

Goldhaber, Stanley and Chandra K. Jha, *Construction Management, Principles and Practices* (N.Y.: John Wiley, 1977)

Handler, A. Benjamin. *Systems Approach to Architecture* (N.Y.: American Elsevier, 1970)

Institution of Electrical Engineers. *International Conference on Effective Use of Electricity in Buildings, 1980.* Conference Publication no. 186 (London: Institution of Electrical Engineers, 1980)

Langmead, Stephen and Margaret Beckman, *New Library Design: Guide Lines to Planning Academic Library Buildings* (Toronto: J. Wiley, 1970)

Metcalf, Keyes D. *Planning Academic and Research Library Buildings* (N.Y.: McGraw-Hill, 1965)

Thompson, Godfrey. *Planning and Design of Library Buildings* (London: Architectural Press, 1977)

10. A Statistical Data Collection And Analysis Program For Austerity

Theodore Samore

> When you can measure what you are talking about, and express it in
> numbers, you know something about it; but when you cannot measure
> it, when you cannot express it in numbers, your knowledge is of a
> meager and unsatisfactory kind. . . .
>
> —William Thomson, Lord Kelvin
> *Popular Lectures and Addresses*, 1891–94

ALTHOUGH IT IS POSSIBLE to measure something and still not know very
much about it, society could scarcely function without access to enormous amounts of statistical data. For many years, American academic
libraries have collaborated in reporting the extent of their collections,
staff and other items in order to provide a statistical portrait of a portion of existing information resources. Even more important is the fact
that individual libraries need data about their operation for planning,
scheduling, budgeting, and control. This chapter will discuss the problems, practices, and principles of collecting and reporting academic
library statistics during austere times.

Specifically, these topics will be covered:

    Overview of Past and Current National, State, and Institutional
       Statistical Reporting Programs
    Problems with Library Statistics
    Statistics and Austerity
    Basic Statistical Methods
    A Statistics Program
    Collection and Analysis Program Examples
    Data and Research Needed

Overview of Past and Current National, State, and Institutional Statistical Reporting Programs

Non-Government Agencies

Two major agency clusters have been involved in gathering and disseminating significant statistics: government and non-government, including individual libraries. The diverse non-government agencies involved in reporting statistics can be grouped into five categories: 1) private networks or consortia such as the Center for Research Libraries and the Online Computer Library Center (OCLC); 2) organizations such as the Medical Library Association, Association of American Library Schools, and American Association of Law Libraries; 3) accrediting bodies such as the Accreditation Association of Bible Colleges, Committee on Accreditation of the American Library Association, United Business Schools Association, National Council for Accreditation of Teacher Education, National Association of Trade and Technical Schools, North Central Association of Colleges and Secondary Schools; 4) private for-profit enterprises such as the R. R. Bowker Company, Gale Research Company, Association of American Publishers, Educational Media Producers Council; and 5) individual academic libraries.

The amount of statistical information collected and made available by these agencies ranges from the minute to the substantial. They collect statistics for the following reasons:

a. To serve the accrediting process;
b. To provide data so libraries can compare themselves with similar libraries;
c. To provide data enabling libraries to meet legal reporting requirements;
d. To provide statistical evidence for quantitative standards;
e. To provide data to vendors and others involved in the library market;
f. To measure library use, effectiveness, and needs;
g. To assist management in financial planning, budget justification, staffing, and accountability.

A description of the dozens of non-government bodies involved in reporting statistics can be found in the now somewhat obsolete *National Inventory of Library Statistics Practices*.[1] Although ALA's Library Administration and Management Association (LAMA) does not report statistics, its nine specialized statistics committees exert considerable influence throughout the field and have previously advised the National Center for Education Statistics. In addition, a supervisory body, the Statistics Coordinating Committee, integrates and harmonizes their work. These committees, representing a mixture of library function and type, and their responsibilities are shown below. Only their charges relevant to academic libraries are given.

1. *Statistics for Circulation Services.* To recommend standardized statistical gathering instruments pertinent to circulation services and collection management; to explore the uses of circulation data to measure the performance and utility of libraries; to study the feasibility of establishing a clearinghouse for standards and guidelines relating to circulation statistics; to foster research in the gathering, manipulating and interpreting of statistical data relating to circulation activities; to cooperate with the circulation services section in planning programs that will explore the methodology and application of research in the areas of circulation and collection management.

2. *Statistics for College and University Libraries.* To review the collection and publication of statistics of academic libraries, and to recommend inclusions, definitions, procedures and policies related to statistics.

3. *Statistics for Nonprint Media.* To review the collection and publication of statistics and data related to all types of nonprint media, and to recommend inclusions, definitions, procedures, and policies concerned with such forms of library materials.

4. *Statistics for Personnel.* (No charge available.)

5. *Statistics for Public Libraries.*

6. *Statistics for Reference Services.* To review the collection and publication of statistics and data related to library materials and services of a reference nature, and to recommend inclusions, definitions, procedures, and policies concerning reference service statistics.

7. *Statistics for School Library Media Centers.*

8. *Statistics for State Library Agencies.*

9. *Statistics for Technical Services.* To review the collection and publication of statistics and data related to the acquisition and organization of library materials, and to recommend inclusions, procedures, and policies concerning these library activities.[2]

Library folklore stoutly maintains that "more cooks improve the broth," therefore even more cooks will improve the "broth" even more. The various committees have labored long and hard in their respective spheres, but too often nitpicking and haggling have vitiated their effectiveness.

One other body produces significant information on library statistics, the American National Standards Institute (ANSI). Its Z39.8 Committee has toiled arduously to achieve agreement by all interested parties on term definition, standardized concepts, and statistical measures. Its efforts have resulted in the draft *American National Standard for Library Statistics*.[3] Prospects are good that LAMA's sundry statistics committees will soon bestow their approval upon the draft and that ANSI will publish the document soon after that.

Government Agencies

A host of federal, state, and local government agencies collect and disseminate statistical data valuable to academic libraries. This is done for three reasons:

  a. Statistical data are required by law, such as for fiscal accountability in federally funded projects, for certification, and for census purposes
  b. Statistical data are used as evidence before legislative bodies or by legislative bodies which require the information in considering proposed programs
  c. Statistical data are part of a government service to citizens who need the information to transact their business or service, e.g., as a measure of the market for publishers, media producers, and library suppliers; as guidelines to city and state administrators concerning library service quantity and quality.

The National Center for Education Statistics (NCES) is the most active agency in collecting and distributing library statistics. Its Learning Resources Branch is responsible for gathering, disseminating, and analyzing statistical data for libraries and museums. NCES and its predecessors have been compiling national academic library data since 1960; its reports provide the most extensive series in existence. They include national and institutional data on library expenditures, staff, collection and salaries for over 2500 libraries.

Parenthetically, the oldest continuous series of academic library statistics publications are those released annually by the Association of Research Libraries (ARL). In one form or another these statistics go back to 1919–20. The latest compilation includes 113 libraries' data for over

30 items including collection, personnel, expenditure, interlibrary loan, and enrollment.[4] Several researchers have identified deficiencies in the compilations, but ARL has not responded officially to these suggestions.[5–6]

For a variety of reasons, NCES statistics have not been exploited fully. However, Baumol used both NCES and ARL data to project cost and growth trends, and Beazley produced a succinct account of statistical trends, 1968–1977.[7–8] Yet because of uncertainties regarding the reliability and comparability of these data, researchers seem reluctant to examine and analyze the mass of accumulated NCES information. In the Fall 1982, NCES again conducted its annual Higher Education General Information Survey (HEGIS) which, as in the past, contained a library data section.

Problems with Library Statistics

Despite tons of data generated by various agencies, an appreciable number of reviewers has expressed dissatisfaction with it.[9–13] The basic problem lies in the lack of comparability among libraries. All record volumes, staff, and expenditures, for instance, but what each library means by these terms may be nebulous if not downright bizarre. Even when NCES supplies definitions in the HEGIS form, libraries may "interpret" them otherwise. Nor does it help when NCES modifies definitions over a time period. Lack of comparability is obviously based on the absence of consensus on definitions which has plagued the library world for decades.

Currently, two works aim to bring order out of lexical chaos: the NCES *Library Data Collection Handbook* and the draft *American National Standard for Library Statistics*.[14–15] Definitions in these works are usually identical but inconsistencies still exist for certain terms, e.g., book, physical unit, print material, and volume equivalency. Furthermore, certain terms in each work are not consonant with terms used in cataloging practice as represented by the *Anglo-American Cataloging Rules*, 2nd ed. (AACR2). For example, both statistical works use audiocartridge, audiocassette, audiodisc, etc., while AACR2 uses sound cartridge, sound cassette, sound disc, etc. Minor perhaps, but still irritating. And nowhere is the word "monograph" defined. Muddying the waters even more is the practice of several states which provide their own unique definitions for various library-related terms.

Another quandary is:

Part of the problem stems from the conflicting purposes, or even the lack of purposes, for which data are collected. Many data are collected in anticipation of demands by parent organizations or constituencies; for surveys conducted by government agencies or professional organizations to obtain historical trend data; as well as to measure and evaluate library services.[16]

A third perplexity is that of attempting to correlate statistics with quantitative standards. Presumably, everybody understands numbers, but what significant correlation, if any, is there between certain standards and the statistics which describe a particular library's resources, staff, and expenditures? Compounding the difficulty is the fact that a set of "standards" may refer to either quantitative minimum inputs of resources, staff, and expenditures, or desired objectives. Finally, the lack of sufficient financial and staff resources to record and report data is particularly trying in austere times. Fortunately, the increasing automation of routine library operations should provide both readily and inexpensively much data valuable for planning and budgeting.

Statistics and Austerity

Generally, libraries collect and report two types of measurements: input and output. The former provides data on a library's collection, expenditures, staff, and physical facilities—its total resources. Output measures provide data on services, the "products" which are made available to users. Typical output measures are circulation, reference queries, interlibrary loans, and turnstile counts. Managers collect those data that assist them in planning, staffing, budget justification, and fiscal accountability to central administration. Certain libraries maintain elaborate files on almost every aspect of their activities; others collect just those data needed for the HEGIS questionnaires.

Inflation has caused managers to reassess the utility of collecting and reporting the traditional kinds of data on resources, expenditures, and services. For example, the spread of bibliographic utilities, resource sharing, and automated integrated systems has rendered collection size data meaningless. Theoretically, through rapid interlibrary lending, every library can offer Universal Availability of Publications (UAP) to its clients. Hence, the focus has shifted from merely collecting unsystematically both input and output data to that of evaluating library service.

Lancaster identified three evaluation levels:

1. How well the system is satisfying its objectives, which will usually mean how well it is satisfying the demands placed upon it. Here we are evaluating the effectiveness of the system.
2. How efficiently (in terms of costs) it is satisfying its objectives. This is cost-effectiveness evaluation.
3. Whether the system justifies its existence (i.e., system worth). In evaluating system worth, we are concerned with cost-benefit relationships.[17]

In addition, three general incentives exist for assessing or evaluating library service, according to ARL's System and Procedures Exchange Center:

> First is the need to avoid the natural tendency of many service organizations toward bureaucratic behavior. Because there is no obvious, quantitative account-ability for most service organizations, such as a profit and loss statement, they frequently become insular. They design programs which respond to what they want to do, rather than what their clientele wants them to do. They can become defensive when criticized, concentrating on defending past practice and relying on existing policies to maintain the status quo. A second incentive lies in libraries' responsibilities to contribute to their parent institutions' missions and their rec-ognition that this cannot be done effectively without some formal approach to assessment. A third—and perhaps most important—incentive is the opportunity that assessment provides for improving library performance. An understanding of relative success of current programs helps libraries adapt to new user needs and demands, introduce new programs, and phase out existing programs. Per-formance improvement occurs most successfully when it builds on recognized strengths, and performance assessment helps to identify those strengths.[18]

In sum, then, during austere times academic libraries require a statis-tics program which will achieve three goals:

1. Identify opportunities for economies
2. Provide greater operation and service understanding and control
3. Identify operations and service which can be improved without increasing cost

It cannot be emphasized too strongly that a library must collect only those statistics which contribute to these three goals.

Basic Statistical Methods

There is no dearth of library statistics books.[19-25] Each one of them contains in more elaborate form what is summarized here. Statistical methods involve measuring which is the age-old process of ascertaining the amount, extent or value of something in numbers, that is, a quan-titative description of observed phenomena. As a singular noun, statis-tics refers to facts stated in quantitative terms or numbers; as a plural noun, statistics refers to a particular method or operation used to ana-lyze numerical data and to draw conclusions from them. A dramatic definition of statistics as a plural noun is this:

Statistics deals with methods for decision-making under uncertainty using in-complete information. Modern statistical inference handles the problems of uncertainty by means of probability theory. Sampling techniques provide a means for obtaining incomplete information (samples), and then drawing inferences about the broader groups (universes or populations) from which the incomplete information has been obtained.[26]

Traditionally, there are two major statistical methods: 1) descriptive statistics, which aims to provide a quantitative portrait of some phenomenon or problem such as the mean number of Wisconsin library volumes held, or the steadily rising periodical subscription costs, and 2) inferential statistics, which seeks to derive conclusions or make predictions from data by using mathematical techniques such as regression analysis, CHI square technique, and others. Forecasting, for example, assumes that the future will repeat the past, more or less. By using time series analyses a statistician can readily identify a growth or decline rate.

Related methodologies may also involve statistical techniques such as systems analysis, which seeks to optimize control and efficiency of an organization's functions by detailed procedural studies. Closely related is operations research, which aims to improve decision-making by using advanced statistics, probability theory and mathematical models.

Statistics abounds in both technical terms and jargon. The totality of a thing being studied is called a universe and each universe member has characteristics which when quantified are called parameters. Any entity being studied is called a variable; examples are age, number of periodical subscriptions, and binding expenditures. A quantitative study of all universe members or population is called a census while a study of any universe part is called a sample. Generally, the sample is drawn to represent the universe so generalizations can be made about that universe.

Statistical investigations require three essential steps:

1. Identifying the problem or the population to be studied. For example, the problem could be finding means to improve cataloger productivity or determining optimum reference service staffing.

2. Collecting appropriate data after determining in advance what statistical techniques will be employed to analyze them.

3. Applying certain statistical techniques to tabulate and analyze these data. At the risk of oversimplification, statistical techniques fall into two classes: 1) those which describe the phenomenon in generalized quantitative terms, a sort of statistical portrait which summarizes masses of raw data, such as frequency distribution tables or measures of central tendency (mean, median, mode) and 2) those techniques which allow inference and predictions based on probability;

probability refers to the relative likelihood of events occurring (inferential statistics).

The third step is the most challenging, although if the first two are not done properly the result is garbage. Descriptive statistics can provide a measure of central tendency—mean, median, mode—which can be manipulated to indicate the degree of a variable's dispersion or distribution. Also, derivable from descriptive statistics are ratios, proportions, percentages, and indexes; these measures compare variables of different sizes. An index is defined as a number which measures how much a variable changes over time. An example is the government Consumer Price Index. Moreover, ratios, proportions and percentages express comparisons by using different symbols. Suppose that all the reference transactions during one week in Library X totaled 4,000. Of these 4,000, 2,000 were directional, 1,000 informational, and 1,000 research. Table 1 shows how the comparison of different reference transactions could be expressed.

Inferential statistics' basic tool is the null hypothesis, a proposition which states that no relationship or correlation exists between two or more variables. Among the techniques that can be applied to determine the degree and strength of association are regression analysis, the chi-square test, and the contingency coefficient test. Other useful terms are:

> *validity,* which refers to the degree to which a particular characteristic being measured is actually measured;
> *reliability,* which refers to the degree to which the results of a study can be replicated if carried out by someone else;
> *forecasting,* which seeks to describe what is likely to occur under a given set of circumstances at a future time.

Andrew Lang, British literary scholar, purportedly described a man

---

Table 1. Proportion, Percentage, Ratio

Total Reference Transactions: 4,000

	Proportion	Percentage*	Ratio
Directional (2,000)	.50	50	2:1[†]
Informational (1,000)	.25	25	1:2[‡]
Research (1,000)	.25	25	1:2[‡]

*Multiply proportion by 100.
[†]To informational or research questions.
[‡]To directional questions.

thusly: "He uses statistics as a drunken man uses lamp-posts—for support rather than illumination." For support or illumination, a library statistics program is crucial in austere times.

A Statistics Program for Individual Academic Libraries

A satisfactory statistics program should be grounded on a lucid distinction between what data an individual library requires to fulfill its responsibilities and what data associations, library groups, state and federal governments need to fulfill their responsibilities. Thus, statistical information can be divided into two classes: data for internal management and data for satisfying reporting requirements from external bodies, such as parent institutions, government agencies, and associations. However,

The diverse purposes of these efforts have often led to the use of varying categories and conflicting definitions. . . . [The] lack of standardization, as well as the unique nature of such surveys, has prevented comparison of the resulting information. Of equal concern has been the burden placed on libraries to collect data which often do not conform to the types of data collected internally. Ideally, these external survey efforts would be based upon standard terminology and data categories similar to those used for internal library data systems. The benefits of standardization among these diverse survey efforts include: the possibility of comparing and combining data from different survey projects, the reduction of response burden and the avoidance of redundant data collection by various organizations.[27]

The ANSI Z39.8 Committee is also concerned about satisfying both the information needs of individual libraries and of external bodies. In its draft *American National Standard for Library Statistics* appears this statement of purpose and objectives:

This document has been prepared to assist librarians and researchers by indicating and defining useful quantifiable information to measure the resources and performance of libraries and to provide a body of valid and comparable data on American libraries. . . . The current revision differs from the previous standard in standardizing reporting for various types of libraries except where evidence justifies variations; by dealing with non-book material, including audiovisual, microform, and machine-readable material, on a basis comparable to that for books; by including measures of services, availability of material, and other performance, in order to report the outputs from budget, staff, and collections; by including cooperative relationships and the functions they serve for libraries; and by financial reporting that promotes accountability and an understanding of assets and liabilities. Sampling is treated as the regular means of gathering certain types of data, and sampling methods are provided. The current revision goes beyond the minimum needs of national data collection and publication, and provides standardized concepts and measures of library resources and services for state and local use, and for library research, in order to promote a common vocabulary for the exchange of information about libraries.[28]

ANSI advances six general principles as the basis for its standards; in the NCES *Library Data Collection Handbook* these same principles appear along with several useful comments as well:

1) *Accountability of Categories.* Reporting should be in mutually exclusive categories insofar as possible, so that totals of resources, expenditures and other categories can be derived from subtotals.

2) *Collections as Resources.* Collections are to be reported as intellectual and as physical resources. Generally, the title or bibliographic unit is the unit for intellectual resources and the volume or equivalent library material unit is the unit for physical resources. The concept of the volume equivalent provides, for example, in the case of microforms, for reporting a series of twenty volumes in microform as the resource equivalent of the same series held in volumes or another format.

3) *Equipment Required for Audiovisual and Other Material.* For material whose content can be received by users only when amplified, projected, or magnified, the availability of the necessary equipment is to be reported as well as the library material.

4) *Agreement of Expenditure Categories with Other Reporting Categories.* The same categories should be used for expenditures as are used in the rest of the report for staff, resources, services, etc. Every category in which expenditures are to be reported should also be separately identifiable.

5) *Need for Estimates.* If an exact figure is not available for a particular item, but the amount is known to be greater than zero, the library should make the best estimate available from its records, or from the expenditures of institutions in comparable circumstances for comparable goods, services, utilities, and the like. Estimates of collection size, utilization of services, and the like may be derived by sampling, prorating or extrapolation as appropriate.

6) *Frequency of Collection and Publication of National Library Statistics.* Except where specified otherwise, the statistical data identified in this standard should be collected annually and published promptly, in no case longer than twelve months after the end of the report period.[29]

This is all well and good, but an appreciable portion of the data categories specified to be collected and analyzed requires a faith in future human behavior not supported by past conduct. Furthermore, too much data are already clogging information interchange; for example, principle 6 is totally unrealistic. Few statistical data need be published annually. The *Library Data Collection Handbook* approaches the matter with sensible objectives:

The *Handbook* is intended for managers in all types of libraries and for persons concerned with library resources and programs at all government levels . . . and in associations. It is hoped that the collection of information suggested here will: provide a sound basis for library management and planning, enhance exchange of information about libraries, and facilitate reporting by libraries to external agencies and organizations. This *Handbook* provides library managers, boards of trustees, and other library decision makers with guidance in identifying factual and comparative data useful in developing policies and making decisions. It also identifies data useful in communicating with constituencies, legislative bodies and governing organizations and in fulfilling information requests from external agencies. The wide acceptance and use of data categories defined in this *Handbook* will enhance the comparability and compatibility of data collected for a variety of reasons by a variety of organizations and will reduce the response burden associated with diverse data-collection activities. It is hoped that the structure and definitions provided in this *Handbook* will become a standard language for intra-library and inter-library communication.[30]

It seems then that the information needs of administrators and policy makers should come first in any sound statistical program. Moreover, this program should be inseparable from an integrated on-line information management system even though relatively few libraries have such capabilities now. Runyon declared that:

One major impediment to effective library administration is the lack of a comprehensive management information system (MIS). Some investigators in this area seem to have become fascinated with the potential value of various elusive and fugitive statistical measures, but they have given little attention to the operational systems that would be required to assemble these data.[31]

Individual libraries are currently faced with the almost intractable problem of quantifying their objectives to measure effectiveness. But the effectiveness problem is only a portion of the overall management problem. In brief, directors require data to achieve these management objectives:

1. Identify and serve the target group (users);
2. Direct activities and services;
3. Maintain resources and facilities.

The ANSI *Standard,* the *Handbook* and Runyon suggest the kinds of statistical data which managers should collect and analyze. Table 2 sets forth a suggested minimum statistical information system arranged under the three categories designated above.

Since a library has its own particular objectives, it needs to know how well or ill it does its job of achieving its objectives. Two fundamental measures are involved: effectiveness, which signifies in quantitative terms at what level a specific objective is being attained, and efficiency or cost-effectiveness, which signifies the costs incurred in achieving specific objectives. Of course, measuring effectiveness requires precise quantifiable goals. Lancaster warned that:

Table 2. Library Management Statistical Information System

Category	Frequency
I. TARGET GROUP	
1. Total Population (students, staff, faculty)	Annually
2. Users, turnstile count	Daily
II. ACTIVITIES & SERVICES	
Technical Services	
1. Orders	Annually
2. Titles cataloged	Annually
a. original	Annually
b. copy	Annually
3. Serials control, check-in	Annually
4. Physical processing	Annually
5. Filing	Annually
6. Binding	Annually
Public Services	
1. Circulation	Daily
2. Circulation, discharges	Daily
3. Holds	Daily
4. Recalls	Daily
5. Reserves	Daily
6. ILL	Monthly
7. In-house use	Sample
8. Reference transactions	Sample
9. Database searches	Daily
10. Tours and bibliographic instruction	Annually
III. RESOURCES AND FACILITIES	
Resources, Print	
1. Volumes added	Annually
2. Titles added	Annually
Resources, Nonprint	
1. Microform	Annually
2. Sound recordings	Annually
3. Films & Videorecordings	Annually
4. Other	Annually
Facilities	
1. Shelving in feet	Once
2. Seating	Once
3. Carrels	Once
4. Net assignable sq. ft.	Once

Over the years various individuals and groups have published statements of objectives for various types of libraries. These published objectives vary widely in scope. Some are specific and practical, while others, especially those relating to public libraries, are somewhat nebulous and even platitudinous. . . . [Such objectives] certainly do not relate directly to the immediate function of the library, are not easily (if at all) measurable, and are too vague and impractical to be used as criteria by which one can readily evaluate a library or its services.[32]

He concludes that:

Fortunately, all libraries have one overriding objective that is practical, that, to a certain extent, is measurable, and that may be used as a basis for evaluation . . . the library exists as an interface between the universe of bibliographic resources (using "bibliographic" in the widest sense) and a particular user population (restricted geographically or by institutional affiliation). The overall objective of the library is to make this universe (or at least that portion having the most immediate relevance and interest) maximally accessible to its users.[33]

Other writers have also wrestled with "effectiveness".[34–38] The fundamental problem is beyond effectiveness per se and lies in whatever social and cultural values persons place on library activities. What is really involved here is "cost-benefit analysis" which seeks to justify library costs on the basis of social and personal enrichment. The *Library Data Collection Handbook* suggests nine possible performance (level of effectiveness) measures:

1. *Accuracy:* percent of reference questions answered accurately; percent of items reshelved correctly; error rate in circulation records; error rate of catalog entries; percent of total collection recataloged due to inaccuracy.
2. *Budgetary Control:* percent of total budget spent during year; percent of material acquired at less than publisher's stated price; operating surpluses arising from provision of user copying service.
3. *Financial effectiveness:* percent of grant/contract applications awarded; percent increase of current year revenues over previous year.
4. *Operations effectiveness:* user satisfaction with library programs; percent of interlibrary loan borrowing requests filled through first channel queried; number of order requests by users for material already on order or in collection; percent of purchases which circulate within a year of receipt.
5. *Policy effectiveness:* percent of questions answered by reference collection; percent of circulation that is renewed; user satisfaction with circulation policy.
6. *Productivity:* amount of activity performed per dollar expenditure or service month or personnel.
7. *Staff competence:* experience in job; user satisfaction with library-employee attitudes.
8. *Timeliness:* lag time between receipt of reference question and response; percent of interlibrary loan borrowing requests filled within user specified time; percent of total purchase orders issued that are out-of-stock; number of days required to catalog the backlog; percent of items requested while in cataloging process; median/model elapsed time required for physical processing of new material.

9. *Work environment/staff morale:* employee satisfaction; average number of sick days taken per employee; employee turnover rates.[39]

To be effective, a systematic statistical program requires full administrative support. Particularly important is the faculty/student advisory committee's cooperation. But above all, full staff participation is imperative. Depending upon the library size, the following departments and services will be involved: administration, acquisition, collection development, cataloging, serials control, circulation, reference, interlibrary loan, special collections, and divisional/departmental libraries.

The library should establish a standing committee whose job is to determine what statistics should be collected and reported and how often. The committee should supervise the design of forms, their distribution and instructions for completion, and specify who should do the tallying, tabulation, analysis, and evaluation. Orientation sessions should be conducted so responsibilities and assignments are clearly delineated. The committee should also plan and execute special statistical investigations whenever required including comparison with peer libraries. Of course, computer use will eliminate much tallying and tabulating drudgery. In brief, the library should have a management information system second to none on the campus.

Data Collection and Analysis Program Examples

Due to HEGIS surveys, all libraries collect and report statistical data on three common variables: expenditures, collection, and staff member size. A considerable number collect data on circulation and reference transactions. Moreover, the literature contains many special investigation reports. A recent example of one user study phase is, "Planning a User Study—The Process Defined."[40] Especially helpful are the surveys and reports issued by the Systems and Procedures Exchange Center of the Association of Research Libraries and the quarterly journal, *Library Research.*

Data and Research Needed

Sheer statistic quantity frequently defeats its own purposes: a statistical data item is useful only if it can lead potentially to a change in behavior or a course of action. Fortunately, more libraries are automating routine activities, so they should program needed data at the automation planning stage. A problem is that inhouse statistics serve particular administrative purposes, many of which are at variance with state, regional or national purposes. Each library is involved in continually defining what it is: its facilities, its budget, its staff, and its collection. The total framework encompasses three components: resources, activities, and environment. The first component is the sum of library assets—staff, collection, facilities, equipment, and expenditures (input measures); the second component covers all the things which the library does with its assets—ordering, cataloging, referencing, binding, circulating material, etc. The last component includes all relevant external social, economic, political, and educational forces which affect a particular library.

Given the constraints of time, money, and utility, libraries should collect only essential statistics about resources, activities, and environment. Neither the ANSI *Standard* nor the *Library Data Collection Handbook* have provided ultimate answers. Both suffer from an immoderate desire to measure almost everything. Parkinson's law applies here as it does to almost any activity which seeks salvation in numbers. The faith in excessive counting is reminiscent of past faith in examining sacrificed beasts' entrails for clues to the future. Today's futurists proclaim both dire and paradisiacal times ahead.[41] It seems certain, however, that more information will be stored electronically, so both the wealth and the garbage formerly stored in books and journals will be stored in another format. T. S. Eliot's basic conundrum (in *The Rock*, 1934, I) cannot be answered by statistics:

Where is the wisdom we have lost in knowledge?
Where is the knowledge lost in information?

References

1. *National Inventory of Library Statistics Practices*, by S. Herner. Vol. 1: *Data Collection on National, State and Local Levels* (Washington, D.C.: U.S. Office of Education, 1974); Vol. 2: *Agency Profiles and Individual Site Descriptions* (Washington, D.C.: U.S. National Center for Education Statistics, 1972).
2. *ALA Handbook of Organization, 1981–82* (Chicago: American Library Association, 1981), pp. 84–85.
3. American National Standards Institute. *American National Standard for Library Statistics* [Draft] (Washington, D.C.: Institute, 1982).
4. Association of Research Libraries. *ARL Statistics* (Washington, D.C.: Association, 1961–).
5. George Piternick, "ARL Statistics—Handle With Care," *College and Research Libraries* 38 (September 1977), pp. 419–23.
6. N. A. Radford, "The Problems of Academic Library Statistics," *Library Quarterly* 38 (July 1968), pp. 231–48.
7. W. S. Baumol, *Economics of Academic Libraries* (Washington, D.C.: American Council on Education, 1973).
8. R. Beazley, *Library Statistics of Colleges and Universities: Trends 1968–77, Summary Data, 1977* (Washington, D.C.: National Center for Education Statistics, 1981).
9. S. Bentley, "Academic Library Statistics: Search for a Meaningful Evaluation Tool," *Library Research* 1 (Summer 1979), pp. 143–52.

10. M. K. Brown, "Library Data, Statistics and Information: Progress Toward Comparability," *Special Libraries* 71 (November 1980), pp. 475–84.

11. Thomas Childers, "Statistics That Describe Libraries and Library Service," in *Advances in Librarianship* (New York: Academic Press, 1975), Volume 5, pp. 107–21.

12. F. Machlup, "Our Libraries: Can We Measure Their Holdings and Acquisitions?" *AAUP Bulletin* 62 (Autumn 1976), pp. 303–7.

13. A. D. Pratt, "The Analysis of Library Statistics," *Library Quarterly* 45 (July 1975), pp. 275–85.

14. *Library Data Collection Handbook: A Report Prepared for the National Center for Education Statistics* (Chicago: American Library Association, 1981).

15. American National Standards Institute, *op. cit.*, pp. 23–40.

16. Brown, *op. cit.*, p. 477.

17. F. W. Lancaster, "The Cost-Effectiveness Analysis of Information Retrieval and Dissemination Systems," *Journal of the American Society for Information Science* 22 (January–February 1971), p. 12.

18. Association of Research Libraries. Systems and Procedures Exchange Center. *User Surveys and Evaluation of Library Services* (Washington, D.C.: Association, 1981), p. 1.

19. Ray L. Carpenter, *Statistical Methods for Librarians* (Chicago: American Library Association, 1978).

20. R. B. Ellis, *Statistical Inference: Basic Concepts* (Englewood Cliffs, N.J.: Prentice-Hall, 1975).

21. W. I. Hays, *Statistics for the Social Sciences* (N.Y.: Holt, Rinehart and Winston, 1973).

22. M. G. Kendall and W. R. Brekland, *A Dictionary of Statistical Terms* (N.Y.: Hafner, 1971).

23. D. W. King, *The Evaluation of Information Services and Products* (Washington, D.C.: Information Resources Press, 1971).

24. Ching-Chih Chen, ed., *Quantitative Measurement and Dynamic Library Service* (Phoenix: Oryx Press, 1978).

25. I. S. Simpson, *Basic Statistics for Librarians* (London: Clive Bingley, 1975).

26. Chen, *op. cit.*, p. 33.

27. *Library Data Collection Handbook, op. cit.*, p. 2–3.

28. American National Standards Institute, *op. cit.*, p. 2.

29. *Library Data Collection Handbook*, pp. 94–95.

30. Ibid., p. 1.

31. R. S. Runyon, "Toward the Development of a Library Management Information System," *College and Research Libraries* 42 (November 1981), p. 539.

32. F. W. Lancaster, *The Measurement and Evaluation of Library Service* (Washington, D.C.: Information Resources Press, 1977), p. 4.

33. Ibid., p. 5.

34. Rosemary R. DuMont, "A Conceptual Basis for Library Effectiveness," *College and Research Libraries* 41 (March 1980), pp. 103–111.

35. Rosemary R. DuMont and P. F. DuMont, "Measuring Library Effectiveness: A Review and an Assessment," in *Advances in Librarianship* (New York: Academic Press, 1979), Volume 9, pp. 103–41.

36. Rosemary R. DuMont and P. F. DuMont, "Assessing the Effectiveness of Library Service," *University of Illinois Occasional Papers*, no. 152, December, 1981.

37. Daniel Gore, "The Mischief in Measurement," *Library Journal* 103 (May 1, 1978), pp. 933–37.
38. D. M. Morse, *Library Effectiveness: A Systems Approach* (Cambridge: MIT Press, 1968).
39. *Library Data Collection Handbook*, pp. 34–35.
40. Meredith Butler and Bonnie Gratch, "Planning a User Study—The Process Defined," *College and Research Libraries* 43 (July 1982), pp. 320–30.
41. Edward M. Walters, "The Future of the Book: A Historian's Perspective," *Information Technology and Libraries* 1 (March 1982), pp. 15–24.

Bibliography

American Library Association. *Library Effectiveness: a State of Art: An ALA Preconference . . .* (Chicago: Association, 1980).
American National Standards Institute. *Compiling Book Publishing Statistics* (Z39.8–1977) (Washington, D.C.: ANSI, 1977).
Association of College and Research Libraries. *New Horizons for Academic Libraries: Papers Presented at the First National Conference* (N.Y.: K. G. Saur, 1979).
Association of Research Libraries. Systems and Procedures Exchange Center. *Library Materials and Cost Studies* (Kit no. 60) (Washington, D.C.: Association, 1980).
Association of Research Libraries. Systems and Procedures Exchange Center. *Preparation and Presentation of the Library Budget* (Kit no. 32) (Washington, D.C.: Association, 1977).
Association of Research Libraries. Systems and Procedures Exchange Center. *User Statistics and Studies* (Kit no. 25) (Washington, D.C.: Association, 1976).
Association of Research Libraries. Systems and Procedures Exchange Center. *User Surveys* (Kit no. 24) (Washington, D.C.: Association, 1976).
Brooks, Terrence A. *The Systematic Nature of Library-Output Statistics* (To be published).
Brooks, Terrence A. *An Analysis of Library Output Statistics*. Unpublished Dissertation, University of Texas, Austin, 1981.
Buckland, M. K. *Book Availability and the Library User* (N.Y.: Pergamon, 1975).
Cronin, Blaise. "Taking the Measure of Service," *Aslib Proceedings* 34 (June/July 1982), pp. 273–94.
De Gennaro, R. "Library Statistics & User Satisfaction: No Significant Correlation," *Journal of Academic Librarianship* 6 (May 1980), p. 95.
Dougherty, R. M. and F. J. Heinritz, *Scientific Management of Library Operations* (Metuchen, N.J.: Scarecrow Press, 1966; 2nd ed., 1982).
Drake, M. A. "Forecasting Academic Library Growth," *College and Research Libraries* 37 (January 1976), pp. 53–59.
Emerson, K. "National Reporting on Reference Transactions, 1976–1978," *RQ* 16 (Spring 1977), pp. 199–207.
Fussler, H. H. and J. L. Simon, *Patterns in the Use of Books in Large Research Libraries* (Chicago: University of Chicago Press, 1969).
Goodell, John S. *Libraries and Work Sampling* (Littleton: Libraries Unlimited, 1975).

Gore, Daniel, ed. *Farewell to Alexandria* (Westport: Greenwood Press, 1976).

Gough, Chet, *Systems Analysis in Libraries* (London: Clive Bingley, 1978).

Hayes, Robert M. *Handbook of Data Processing for Libraries* (Los Angeles: Melville, 1974).

Katzer, J. "The Evaluation of Libraries: Considerations from a Research Perspective," *Drexel Library Quarterly* 13 (July 1977), pp. 84–101.

Ladd, Boyd. *National Inventory of Library Needs, 1975.* (Washington, D.C.: National Commission on Libraries and Information Science, 1977).

Library Management: Quantifying Goals, edited by Choong M. Kim (Terre Haute: Indiana State University, 1973).

Library Planning and Decision-Making Systems, by Morris Hamburg, et al. (Cambridge: MIT Press, 1974).

Lyle, Guy R. *The Administration of the College Library* (N.Y.: H. W. Wilson, 1974).

Magrill, R. M. "Conducting Library Research," *College and Research Libraries* 41 (May 1980), pp. 200–206.

Maher, W. J. "Measurement and Analysis of Processing Costs in Academic Archives," *College and Research Libraries* 43 (January 1982), pp. 59–67.

Martin, M. S. *Budgetary Control in Academic Libraries* (Greenwich: JAI Press, 1978).

Martyn, J. and F. W. Lancaster, *Investigative Methods in Library Information Science: An Introduction* (Arlington: Information Resources Press, 1981).

Measuring the Quality of Library Service: a Handbook (Metuchen, N.J.: Scarecrow Press, 1974).

Mitchell, Betty Jo. *Cost Analysis of Library Functions. . . .* (Greenwich: JAI Press, 1978).

Mosborg, T. S. "Measuring Circulation Desk Activities Using a Random Alarm Mechanism," *College and Research Libraries* 41 (September 1980), pp. 437–444.

Nachlas, J. A. and A. R. Pierre, "Determination of Unit Costs for Library Services," *College and Research Libraries* 40 (May 1979), pp. 240–247.

Orr, R. H. "Measuring the Goodness of Library Services: A General Framework for Considering Quantitative Measures," *Journal of Documentation* 29 (1973), pp. 315–332.

Palmer, David C. *Planning for a Nationwide System of Library Statistics* (Washington, D.C.: U.S. National Center for Education Statistics, 1970).

Raffel, Jeffrey A. *Systematic Analysis of University Libraries* (Cambridge: MIT Press, 1969).

Rodgers, R. and D. C. Weber. *University Library Administration* (N.Y.: H. W. Wilson, 1971).

Salverson, C. A. "The Relevance of Statistics to Library Evaluation," *College and Research Libraries* 30 (November 1969), pp. 352–62.

Sargent, S. H. "The Uses and Limitations of Trueswell," *College and Research Libraries* 40 (September 1979), pp. 416–423.

Schick, F. S. "Library Statistics," In *Encyclopedia of Library and Information Science* (N.Y.: Marcel Dekker, 1975), vol. 15, pp. 63–74.

Steady-state, Zero Growth and the Academic Library (London: Clive Bingley, 1978).

Stubbs, K. "University Libraries: Standards and Statistics," *College and Research Libraries* 42 (November 1981), pp. 527–38.

Trueswell, Richard W. "Article Use and Its Relationship to Individual User Satisfaction," *College and Research Libraries* 31 (July 1970), pp. 239–45.

Trueswell, Richard W. "Determining the Optimal Number of Volumes for a
   Library's Core Collection," *Libri* 16 (1966), pp. 49–60.
Trueswell, Richard W. "An Experiment in Measuring Certain Aspects of the
   Information-Searching Behavior of X-Ray Crystallographers. Technical
   Report 2 (Final Report)," March 1968. NASA Grant NSG-495.
Trueswell, Richard W. "Growing Libraries: Who Needs Them? A Statistical
   Basis for the No-Growth Collection," in Daniel Gore, ed., *Farewell to Alex-
   andria* (Westport: Greenwood Press, 1976), pp. 72–104.
Trueswell, Richard W. "A Quantitative Measure of User Circulation Require-
   ments and its Possible Effect on Stack Thinning and Multiple Copy Deter-
   mination," *American Documentation* 16 (January 1965), pp. 20–25.
Trueswell, Richard W. "Some Behavioral Patterns of Library Users, e.g., The
   80/20 Rule," *Wilson Library Bulletin* 43 (January 1969), pp. 458–61.
Trueswell, Richard W. "Some Circulation Data from a Research Library," *College
   and Research Libraries* 29 (November 1968), pp. 493–95.
Trueswell, Richard W. "Two Characteristics of Circulation and Their Effect on
   the Implementation of Mechanized Circulation Control Systems," *College
   and Research Libraries* 25 (July 1964), pp. 285–91.
Trueswell, Richard W. "User Circulation Satisfaction versus Size of Holdings at
   Three Academic Libraries," *College and Research Libraries* 30 (May 1969),
   pp. 204–13.
Unesco. *International Standardization of Library Statistics* (Paris: Unesco, 1970).
Urquhart, J. A. and J. L. Schofield, "Measuring Readers' Failure at the Shelf,"
   Journal of Documentation 7 (1971), pp. 273–86.
Use of Library Materials: the University of Pittsburgh Study (N.Y.: Marcel Dekker,
   1979).
White, G. Travis. "Quantitative Measures of Library Effectiveness," *Journal of
   Academic Librarianship* 3 (July 1977), pp. 128–36.
"Zero Growth: When is NOT-Enough Enough? A Symposium," *Journal of Aca-
   demic Librarianship* 1 (November 1975), pp. 4–11.
Zwezig, D. L. "Measuring Library Use," *Drexel Library Quarterly* 13 (July 1977),
   pp. 3–15.

11. Austerity Budget Management

Gerard B. McCabe

AUSTERITY BUDGET MANAGEMENT has become a national concern, perhaps our national preoccupation, as the severity of declining budgets increases. Careful planning in preparation for local decline is essential to avoid the need for hasty decisions.[1] No large body of library literature addresses this issue. However, several papers deal with the larger austerity management issues facing government agencies. Such basic issues often arise and end with these agencies.

Normally, an academic institution has a mission and an objectives statement. The library should have a statement of its own mission and objectives for fulfilling its institutional role. From this statement, the library should set operation priorities. In the future, the institution will either remain static or shrink and find a new service base.[2] A new mission statement can be inferred. If the institution is shrinking and redefining its role, the library must also shrink and redefine its role. The library may bear an extraordinary share of institutional budget reduction.

The budget is the controlling vehicle for pursuing objectives and priorities. Austerity budgeting stresses priorities and forces reassessments. Staff members should review all operations and propose areas for curtailment.[3-4] Possible curtailments should be reviewed with faculty advisors for suggestions and support. A state of readiness for the unwanted is the best preparation. Austerity management requires assembling what we have learned and providing more effective service in spite of fund curtailment.

All libraries have service improvement plans. Applying the converse, asking what can be curtailed and arriving at a sound plan in a ready state, is the requirement in austerity. A well-prepared organization will absorb the shock of sudden and drastic budget reduction. Preparing the library to face funding and staff losses is this chapter's subject.

Budget Planning

Higher education austerity's general theme is that budgets will tend to remain constant, almost static. Even with an added inflation factor, increases will be modest. Sound and productive fiscal management will be required of every library director, and emphasis will be on trying to obtain greater value from the funds available.

Automated operation and cost effectiveness became important during the 1960s and 1970s. Time and cost studies were common and procedures were analyzed step by step. These actions were and are important because a good understanding of library operation economics is essential. Drake and Olsen emphasized this understanding and advocated greater innovation.[5] Increasing public demand will not yield to a declining budget. Librarians must find innovative ways to increase service capability without raising costs. Staying even with demand may force further internal economies.[6] Even if change involves risk, we should forge ahead.[7] In responding to curtailment mandates, the staff must defend its proposals vigorously.

Individuals in other university departments will pursue reduction plans vigorously also. The debate will be intense and the planning environment may become hostile. With jobs at stake, critical analyses will be required, and library defenses must be full, clear, and precise. The situation may vary by institution size. In a medium-to-large library, to effect staff reductions non-librarian planners will attack certain positions persuasively. They will offer seemingly attractive substitutions which may beguile academic administrators but which should leave library directors wary. The positions attacked may include all administrative support staff members—systems librarian, space planner, budget planner, administrative services librarian, personnel librarian, and collection development librarian, for instance.

The entrancing proposal will simply state that another institutional department will provide each one of these services. Staff members in the other departments have been trained to carry out similar duties and faculty members can select material. Academic administrators will not dismiss the idea simply on a mere retort of unworkability or lack of library background. The staff members who can best provide the new library plan and make it work could be lost in this situation, also.

A review of the library's current situation, recent history, and objectives are in order at this point. Identify objectives very precisely and evaluate performance against them. Many libraries have substantial investments in automation and other presumably cost-effective operations. Before attempting to introduce newer approaches, the director must study current financial data. Time and cost studies should be updated in order to test current procedures vs. newer automated methods. A recent study compared the operating cost of an automated circulation system to that of the previous manual system.[8] New system costs were higher, but benefits seemingly outweighed the added expense.

Libraries converting from an obsolete automated circulation system, for example, to a newer one can seldom reduce costs but must strive for other tangible cost benefits. Another example reported using a modification of the job analysis method in a team study of staff work.[9] Drake and Olsen foresaw greater automation commitment and decreasing dependence on manual tasks with people-performed duties being converted to machine assignments.[10]

A word of caution may be useful here. If not used properly automated activities can produce frustration. Thompson chided interlibrary loan staffs for sending out requests without locator codes.[11] If staff members are not trained to use new systems effectively, considerable waste will occur. In traditional service areas, present operation cost must be compared to automated cost.[12] Other potential conversion advantages such as greater accuracy and excessive record elimination must also be reviewed.

The director's objective is a plan permitting effective development. This is why we upgrade circulation to information systems and catalogs to bibliographic data bases and strive to improve staff information-obtaining capacities. In the future, fewer staff members will be available so they must individually have improved service abilities. If central computer service is available, arrange for a detailed annual expenditure analysis through use of a standard budget analysis program. A standard program package can aid in reduction planning through cost-effectiveness analysis at a considerable time saving. Such analyses can be helpful in deciding to continue or close a service facility, for instance. In addition, objective outside consultant assistance can be beneficial in developing austerity solutions.

With sufficient planning time the adjustments necessary to preserve library balance can be made. Staff reduction can be obtained through attrition if time permits, or termination if it does not, the latter being inequitable and probably creating service imbalances. Different areas will be afflicted at varying rates.[13] Service loads will become disproportionate and disorder will result as the director attempts to patch up critical areas. The institutional administration may compound the difficulty by advising that such quick responses as reducing service hours or leaving desks unstaffed for lengthy time periods will incur its displeasure. The responsible library departmental administrators must be in charge of planned reductions.[14]

Consider this example. With an austerity budget, a mythical library's reference department, sufficient to meet present service needs, loses two staff members by resignation with replacement ruled out. Departmental service demands remain level. The obvious solution is to pass on the inconvenience directly to the user. There is no support for such a decision. With adequate planning time, the crisis solution deemed most satisfactory can be implemented. A good answer might rearrange the department's work—shifting some work out, dropping low demand service, and pulling back from certain assignments. The department could then absorb most of the effect of its own attrition. Such planning provides for equal misfortune sharing.[15] Considering the known probability of resignations or retirements occurring also in other departments, they can absorb their own losses. The entire library can shrink as staff leave and service potential diminishes.

Another solution may require borrowing somewhat qualified staff members from other departments for part-time assignment to fulfill service obligations. This involves administratively reassigning personnel loss to other areas.[16] However, this solution can suddenly become infeasible if staff losses occur elsewhere and institutional staff reduction requirements have not yet been met. For this example, an attempt may be made to retain the previous staff support level for reference service, with capability elsewhere diminished. Depending on circumstances, the first option appears to be the better choice until the institution's enforced requirements are met and restructuring can occur through a priority system. A system of flexible priorities can be developed to offset attrition effects, also.

Budget Proposal Preparation

In austerity, institutional budgetary planners will examine overall needs. Acting under the president's directive, they will formulate a plan to apply austerity management principles throughout the organization. They will criticize as duplication work which can be done elsewhere. When the institutional plan is presented, the director must try to ameliorate its library effects. Response must represent the best staff thinking.

In obtaining helpful information from library supervisory personnel, institutional administrative constraints must be carefully delineated even though final decisions will be negotiated. Ask that requests be submitted in terms of library objectives and present both potential affirmative and negative results. The director can then review reports and assign priorities in terms of achievable objectives, thereby facilitating later negotiations with administrators.

Institutional Austerity Budget Reactions

When asked to prepare an austerity budget adjustment plan, without consulting service units, planners frequently devise devastating changes.[17] Three currently popular plans of this type can affect libraries adversely. They are the central pool concept, the salary/wage line ceiling, and the summer session budget allocation rollback. The first two are budgetary devices to increase staff and funding size when no increase is provided by the higher authority. The summer rollback is an operation expense adjustment.

In a financially difficult time when institutions face greater demands as well, often their only response is an instructional program change. If a program does not meet society's needs and enrollment declines, the only answer is cancellation, revision, or addition. For the private institution, a tuition raise may be an early response; lost revenue can be recouped by a price increase passed on to those persons still buying the product, a questionable policy.[18] For the public institution, a tuition increase provides only a partial answer; new programs quickly emplaced are another answer. The community expects a prompt response to its stated needs.

The alternatives are clear. Faculty members teaching in poorly attended programs must be terminated or transferred to other disciplines and vacancies must be left unfilled until the revisions are clear and new programs formulated. Then, funding must be found for faculty recruitment and new curriculum development. How can the resulting funding and faculty shortage be resolved? In the central pool device, the university administration collects money and staff positions on a percentage basis from the operating budget and from existing or forced staff vacancies. The library's material budget is left almost untouched, perhaps not increased but at least not significantly decreased. All other expenditures are subject to a percentage rollback. The balance between staff and material expenditures is not disrupted severely, but library staffing cost is reduced.[19] The potential for disproportionately large staffs and declining material acquisitions is obviated.

The institution's purpose in building the central pool of funds is to support new and expanded programs. All departments must justify their requests for fund and staff assignment from the central pool. Those assigned the highest priorities will receive all or part of their requests up to the pool's limits. Reductions will be made in all academic and support unit budgets. The library director must review all services: training, teaching, reference, literature searching, technical service, special collections, and collection development. The library must weigh budget reduction and expansion including collection and service addition in support of new programs. In personnel budget planning, the library director must detail future public, administrative and technical staff service needs and the degree of specialization required.

A central pool concept variation is found in certain institutions where the university administration designates ceilings for salary wage expense lines, the second plan. This can be done many months before the fiscal year begins. In this plan the new salary budget includes salary increases, either across the board, merit, or a combination. The university administration may instruct departments to allocate the salary increase among their staffs while taking such factors into consideration as competitive wages, rewarding good performance, the possible need for new subject competence due to an academic program addition, across-the-board percentage increases, and the value of the services provided by each employee group.

The library director may find that all of the above cannot be done without a staff reduction, and so he/she is forced to terminate or transfer staff members to produce needed funds. Consequently, the result is the same. Either this plan or the central pool plan is likely to result in the library making a substantial net contribution to the university administration.

The Summer Rollback

Where library faculty members have nine-month contracts, summer operating budgets, usually at 30 to 40 percent of regular session budgets, are now being reduced to 20 percent or less. Institutional administrations have chosen this alternate as a means of reducing expenses in lieu of directing staff reductions and regular session economies. Frequently, however, this proves to be only a stopgap measure and the steps necessary to reduce regular session expenses are merely postponed. The director will have bought time but must develop a supplementary plan which will enable the library to operate with fewer staff members, provide adequate summer service and meet basic growth requirements.

Rollbacks in whatever guise only emphasize the importance of maintaining a well-educated staff with competitive salaries. Staff reduction removes promotion opportunities; with future rank advancement improbable, salaries become critical.[20] Staff member salaries, especially those for supervisors, must be strongly competitive. Considering normal turnover, this is the only way to forestall severe staff problems. The recruiting effort necessary for replacement can be very demanding. Low salaries have an adverse effect on recruiting into the field.[21] The loss of many key positions can reduce the library to basic service levels, and several years may pass before the staff is restructured.

In building a plan, a problem is to reassign priorities to fit the probable remaining staff and funding. The director can infer that the staff may never regain its previous size and that certain of its previous components will not return.[22] Once lost, staff slots will not be replaced in the foreseeable future, and alternate means must be found for service provision. Other library departments, other institutional departments, machines, or vendors under contract may be used to replace them. Options must be studied and choices made.

Resource Allocation

Budget allocations must be worked out. Probably the institution will impose limits on certain operating expenses, such as supplies, equipment, and telecommunication. Library guidelines must be tight. Normally the material budget receives the most attention and deservedly so. This is the fund through which the collection grows and the service rationale is provided. The welfare of most academic and research programs depends upon a strong material budget. Faculty members will accept many radical changes as long as funds are available with which to buy essential material. This is an area where miscalculation can bring disaster; if allowed to grow haphazardly, this budget will devour other funds.

If material budget controls have not yet been instituted, policies should be prepared at once and reviewed with faculty advisory committees and institutional administrators. Controls should regulate monograph acquisition policies, duplication, journal subscriptions, and current vs. retrospective purchases. Responsible staff members should have full authority to enforce policies.

For certain libraries, interlibrary cooperation is a satisfactory solution to the excessive journal cost problem. Cooperative agreements can be formulated, such as the one at the Richmond Academic Library Cooperative (Virginia). There, each library has its own basic subscription list, but major expensive title cost is spread over the membership. Each member library's collection development policies and strengths are tabulated according to ALA's Resources and Technical Services Division's guidelines, so each collection development librarian can easily determine the likelihood of another institution's acquiring a specific expensive monograph or journal. Cooperative resource sharing agreements help to ease faculty pressure on material budgets. Such an effort should expand to cover all institutions in the state and cooperative purchasing service should be added as well.[23]

A greater future dependence on networking can be predicted to provide further material budget relief.[24] The national networks built for shared cataloging now offer interlibrary loan service. Libraries can transmit loan requests regionally over OCLC cataloging terminals. Center for Research Libraries membership offers access to extensive holdings, also.[25] These options offer means of controlling and developing the material budget to improve service.

The Contingency Rollback

When austerity strikes, common practice among public institution governing bodies is to apply percentage rollbacks to gross budgets. With forewarning, the library director can review the budget and change priorities. A judicious solution to the potential reduction of student wage allocations was presented recently.[26] Student assistants perform a considerable variety of library duties. The importance of each duty was evaluated and significant duties were assigned higher priorities than others. Any budget cut could then be answered by a corresponding reduction of less significant duties.[27]

Often operating and salary budgets are attacked first, and the travel allocation may be the first item reduced. Typically, a travel budget supports representation at the meetings of cooperative organizations (e.g., OCLC's user groups and training workshops); automated system training sessions (e.g., computer-assisted literature searching); potential donation and large purchase review sessions; or educational conferences and other activities. Travel funds are spent primarily for staff development, a critical area for active system and procedure advancement.

Supply and equipment budgets can profit from controls. Supply controls can be applied by establishing a commonality of items consumed. Quality standards are set for certain items, e.g., ball point pens, pencils, and bond paper. When supplies are diminishing, items may be bought in a sufficient quantity for a specified time period. Deviations from standard are rejected. This method requires elimination of choices from the supply order—everyone uses the same supply items in their work.

Institutional equipment budget confiscation is a grim austerity reality. It is put under central control, new purchase justification is required and reallocation is by broad division. Institutional priorities may place equipment needed for scientific teaching and research and for new programs at the top. The library may not receive a direct allocation but will share one with other academic support departments. At the worst, the library portion will allow only minimal replacement of worn public service equipment, stolen items, or an occasional new item because it provides cheaper service. Library needs can be defended by use statistics. They require only easily understood tabulation methods, e.g., a simple piece count (microfiche, film reels), used daily.

Equipment policies should include amortization, brand consistency, and regular maintenance. Typically, no savings occur from a refusal to buy new typewriters when needed. Repairing them beyond a reasonable service life drives costs higher. Changing brands forces up supply and maintenance costs through non-compatible ribbons and separate service calls. If major new equipment is required, no immediate savings may occur. An automated circulation control system is a case in point. A justification illustrating major potential savings will be required. When production equipment is desired, commercial availability and cost must be compared with inhouse production and cost. A postal manual can be obtained from the local postal supervisor. The library may also compose its own manual from rate information provided by the post office and thereby establish cost control policies. Certain institutions may ban long distance telephone calls. However, time and cost studies can indicate where calls offer advantages over correspondence.

User Analysis

Often an academic institution's service community appears to be limited to students, faculty members, and staff. In projecting service it is important to identify the users and know their library needs and demands. A user survey can elicit the desired information. Frequently, a survey reveals a noticeable percentage of non-affiliated persons using services. A sense of the institution's service commitment to the surrounding community is needed. In recent years, certain urban private universities have refused service to outsiders. Others have introduced fee-based services for non-affiliated users, but this action's side-effects on potential community support must be considered.

Business and industry, accustomed to the matching fund donation concept and to service fees, may not be willing to make outright library donations. Many institutions prefer to offer free library service as a way of thanking major corporate donors. Business and industry face austerity, also, and need to control costs. Tenopir suggested that corporate librarians borrow from neighboring academic libraries as a way of reducing material purchases.[28] On occasion, business and government libraries use neighboring academic libraries heavily. With survey evidence justification, the library may obtain supplemental budgeting through fee-based services, including circulation privileges. It is critical, too, for the institutional administration to establish the library's right to the new income through reallocation or advance credit.

In suburban areas, white collar workers may swarm in on weekends to claim privileges based on personal need only. An access fee or paid resident borrower's card may be the answer here. Another device is to establish a Friends of the Library group with a nominal membership fee sufficient to cover the usual services. In a Friends group established as a foundation controlling its own finances, income can be used for the library. After a decision is made on the scope of fee-based service, estimated recoveries can be projected in the budget planning process.

Conclusion

In recent times, financial austerity seemed to have historical and foreign connotations to Americans. It was a condition known in the Great 1930s Depression and after World War II in certain countries—a time of lean budgets, extensive unemployment, and little growth. Today, in American academic libraries it means rolling back budgets, cutting expenses, and reducing personnel. When the time comes for curtailment, budget response should not be spontaneous or ill-conceived, but must be a well prepared and reasoned statement. The library's budgetary management plan must be presented with firmness and demonstrably be achievable.

Reading general management literature will assist in understanding the views of academic budget officials, who, following mandates, try to reduce institutional and library operating costs. They may impose the same reduction criteria on all institutional units and force the library into an uncomfortable pattern.[29] Convincing curtailment planners that a science bibliographer will give more effective collection development service than a random science faculty member group may be difficult. Triennial surveys help to identify user service perceptions and needs.

The library collection must at least maintain a semblance of currency, and new instructional programs will require new resources. An effective plan must enable the library to maintain a degree of equilibrium, collection growth, and staff development, and to remain an effective service agency. The austerity budget management plan must emphasize positive action and not be a holding action formula but lead to continued progress.

References

1. Nancy E. Gwinn and Warren J. Haas, "Crisis in the College Library," *AGB Reports* 23 (March/April 1981), pp. 341–45.
2. Richard M. Cyert, "The Management of Universities of Constant or Decreasing Size," (A Symposium on Organizational Decline and Cutback Management) *Public Administration Review* 38 (July/August, 1978), pp. 344–49.
3. Joan Repp and Julia A. Woods, "Student Appraisal Study and Allocation Formula: Priorities and Equitable Funding in a University Setting," *Journal of Academic Librarianship* 6 (May 1980), pp. 87–90.
4. Charles H. Levine, "Organizational Decline and Cutback Management," (A Symposium on Organizational Decline and Cutback Management) *Public Administration Review* 38 (July/August 1978), pp. 316–405.
5. Miriam A. Drake and Harold A. Olsen, "The Economics of Library Innovation," *Library Trends* 28 (Summer 1979), pp. 89–105.
6. Levine, *op. cit.*, p. 321.
7. Drake and Olsen, *op. cit.*, pp. 97–98.
8. Edward C. Jestes, "Manual Versus Automated Circulation: A Comparison of Operating Costs in a University Library," *Journal of Academic Librarianship* 6 (July 1980), pp. 144–50.
9. Repp and Woods, *op. cit.*, p. 88.
10. Drake and Olsen, *op. cit.*, p. 95.
11. Dorothea M. Thompson, "The Correct Use of Library Data Bases Can Improve Interlibrary Loan Efficiency," *Journal of Academic Librarianship* 6 (May 1980), pp. 83–86.
12. Drake and Olsen, *op. cit.*, p. 98.

13. Levine, *op. cit.*, pp. 321, 322.
14. Ibid., p. 320.
15. Ibid., p. 320.
16. Ibid., p. 320.
17. Gwynn and Haas, *op. cit.*, p. 41.
18. Cyert, *op. cit.*, p. 345.
19. David H. Eyman, "Library Budgets in the Independent Liberal Arts College," *Liberal Education* 65 (Fall 1979), pp. 371–82.
20. Levine, *op. cit.*, p. 322.
21. Gwynn and Haas, *op. cit.*, p. 44.
22. Cyert, *op. cit.*, p. 347.
23. Gwynn and Haas, *op. cit.*, p. 44.
24. Drake and Olsen, *op. cit.*, p. 101.
25. Gwynn and Haas, *op. cit.*, p. 43.
26. Repp and Woods, *op. cit.*, p. 89.
27. Levine, *op. cit.*, p. 321.
28. Carol Tenopir, *Realistically Reassessing the Costs and Functions of Special Libraries*, ERIC Document Reproduction Service, ED 194088. 1980.
29. Gwynn and Haas, *op. cit.*, p. 42.

12. Cost-Benefit Analysis for Austerity

Murray S. Martin

THE PRIMARY WEAKNESS of non-profit institutions is that they are budget-driven. A few statements will show why such tools as Program Budgeting, Cost-Benefit and Cost-Effectiveness Analysis have become popular in government and education. Most non-profit institutions do not create their own incomes from product sale.[1] Many institutions are created to provide service for which cost assignment is difficult, nor is it easy to separate off these services since they are often interdependent. Hence it is usual to define their service statistically—so many interviews, so many books circulated, etc.—and to match them to expenditures. Sometimes, as an added protection, comparative figures from similar institutions are used to provide a normative background. The intention is to defend the budget, and if possible bring back a little more next year.

Now, however, beginning with the public sector—which includes most libraries—the money supply is drying up. For reasons well explained by Baumol and Drucker, the cost of providing service has risen faster than general costs, which has meant that governments at all levels are faced on the one hand with a need to increase revenues and on the other with increased taxation resistance.[2,3]

There is a drive to cut costs in the present federal administration. This goal can be achieved in only two ways. The first is to find cheaper operating methods, and the second is to reduce the number of services provided. In the long run both approaches will be used, but the mix will differ according to the controlling body's philosophy.

In general terms, libraries are labor-intensive organizations. For this reason, the typical operating cost distribution shows 60 percent for personnel, 30 percent for library materials, and supplies and expense costs about 10 percent. If cost reductions are necessary, such cuts must be in the larger cost centers, since the supply and expense category would not provide enough savings. This will undoubtedly lead to cuts in personnel and perhaps to cuts in services. The second approach might be cuts of the materials budget, which is likely to lead to an erosion of the quality of collections needed in support of the academic programs of the institution. Like the approach used by the federal government, academic libraries will adopt both approaches, but the mix of budget reductions will differ according to the philosophy of the controlling institution. The need to cut costs has brought most non-profit institutions to face self-analysis since they can no longer consider themselves to be self-justifying.

What is the meaning of words like cost, benefit, efficiency, and effectiveness, which have recently been added to the library vocabulary? Cost seems relatively straightforward, but when you ask the cost of what, it is clear that we must rethink previous categorizations. Circulation, reference, cataloging, and acquisitions are no longer sufficiently clear terms to deal with cost. Benefit is even more difficult. What is the benefit? Who received it? What value does it have? What does being efficient mean? Does it mean doing things faster or better or simply at less cost? Effectiveness relates not only to service quality but to the mix provided and is sometimes not consonant with efficiency. For example, it is efficient to centralize all circulation activities to profit from scale economies, but this may result in decreased effectiveness, whether in terms of book shelving times or services not sought because of distance. Librarians must now try to answer these questions and more.

One caution should be presented, however. When the words above are used in combination they have very specific meanings. Cost-effectiveness analysis determines whether existing activities are being carried out efficiently. To that extent it accepts existing goals and concentrates on how they are met. In a way it resembles the older Taylorism goals and uses such tools as time and motion studies, job analysis, and comparative analysis of alternative ways of doing the same thing. On the other hand, cost-benefit analysis is user-oriented and examines alternative services while seeking to determine whether new tasks should replace existing ones. Its tools are market and opinion surveys and it often relies on value judgments in choosing among alternatives.

Neither analysis system can answer all questions. Each one must be used only when appropriate, in a supportive setting. For example, it is appropriate to use cost-effectiveness analysis to determine whether automated will be cheaper than manual cataloging. It is inappropriate to use that method to decide whether or not to automate. Instead, that is the proper sphere of cost-benefit analysis with its greater emphasis on user expectations and reactions.

No analysis is cheap. It requires work, time, and commitment. Therefore, the goals of any analysis should be clearly stated and thoroughly understood by all participants, and those goals should be worth its cost.[4]

A budget cut frequently spurs self-examination. Such an examination begins with severe limitations. Certain of its objectives are set already. The best results are achieved by anticipatory studies providing clear alternatives which can then be matched to budgetary facts.

Self-study preparation includes listing the activities to be studied. Codifying intra-library relations, determining environmental conditions (i.e., parent institution objectives and priorities), and creating a positive attitude toward change. The latter is important since staff co-operation will be essential to successful change implementation.

When undertaking a self-study, most libraries discover that they know too little about present activities. For example, it may be necessary to update manuals or gather new statistics.[5] A common example is the discovery of the library's fulfillment rate—how often a user finds a needed book.[6] It is always necessary to recompute budget figures to allocate costs more precisely, particularly when a line item budget is used. It may also prove necessary to compute indirect costs and to analyze space use. Such analyses are seldom included in budgets now, but they may be major determinants in choosing between alternates. Most libraries are far from being in control of their destinies now.

No analysis should be undertaken lightly, since its objective is to influence the future. Among the discoveries likely to be made are that library priorities must be reordered, that certain services should be modified or discontinued and that resource allocation should change. All changes have long-reaching effects, so all analyses must extrapolate short- and long-term futures.[7]

The next stage is to develop an analysis project and to determine its scope. Although a total evaluation is best, time and cost may require something more limited. Adequate personnel resources must be available for the study, either by using consultants or providing released staff time. The project leader must have the requisite authority, and limitations must be clear. Although many chief librarians are tempted to undertake the job themselves, that is generally unproductive.[8] He/she should be supportive and visibly involved, but the primary objective is to produce a plan which is freely supported by the staff, not directed from above. The recommendations are advisory and subject to the usual political and financial pressures. An independent chief librarian can be a more effective advocate.

Any study must be used. Nothing is worse for morale than to see such an effort ignored. Every recommendation need not necessarily be implemented, but non-implementation reasons should be real, acceptable, *and* explained to the staff. Nor can every recommendation be implemented at once. The study should conclude with an action plan related to the new priorities and with realistic timetables. Overoptimism is the cause of most unhappiness with innovation plans. Nevertheless, fiscal realities may speed up action.

What is a Cost-Benefit Analysis?

A cost-benefit analysis studies some or all programs to determine whether or not they are being carried out efficiently.[9] Such an analysis is easiest to conduct on a well defined product, since it depends on measurement. Most cost-benefit analyses have concentrated on cataloging or circulation with easily recognizable products rather than on reference or instruction with more heterogeneous results. A well-known example is the University of Pittsburgh *Study of the Use of Library Materials*. Its rebuttals and supporting statements revealed the degree to which opinions differed on study technique and values.[10]

Clearly, broad issue examination will result in broad answers helpful in setting general policies, but it will not settle questions about specific activities. Nevertheless broad analyses are necessary to help determine whether or not the library's goals are still in line with reality. A problem is that they are time-consuming, require considerable skill and may simply confirm known trends.

More immediate benefits may be gained by concentrating on subordinate activities where the variables are easier to isolate and the products simpler to measure. Ultimately, however, all studies require the same approach and it will be useful to review that approach in some detail. The first step is to list activities. While this may appear simplistic, a clear definition of what is being studied is required. It is not sufficient to list departments, since most departments carry out activities unrelated to their principal activity, while, on the other hand, certain other activities may be carried out in several departments.[11]

There is no generally accepted taxonomy for this task. General taxonomy development is a monumental but long-overdue task. In another context, the author developed a somewhat primitive output model which resulted in five broad activity groupings: Volumes Added (acquisition); Collection Usage (including circulation); Reference Service; Interlibrary Loan; and Catalog Maintenance.[12] This is not cited as a model but as an indicator of the way in which activities should be analyzed.

For a cost-benefit analysis, more detail will be required. For example, if the goal is to study library use, each kind of use will require separate consideration. General differs from reserve circulation while book use inside the library falls into yet another category. Different materials need to be considered. Microform use requires a different response than does book use. Similarly, periodical borrowing for photocopying has a different library impact than simply borrowing for reading.

The resulting matrix produces the following list of possibilities:

1. By type of circulation, e.g. general, reserve, special permission (including use in-house);

2. By type of borrower, e.g. faculty/student; member/non-member;
3. By location, e.g. branch library, reserve book desk;
4. By type of material, e.g. books, periodicals, documents, microforms;
5. By purpose, e.g. photocopy, research, class reading;
6. By time of day, term, year.

This careful activity articulation facilitates proceeding to the next step, cost calculation.[13] All of the activities listed above have different costs and the blurring of these costs may eliminate a worthwhile outcome. What costs should be considered? Ideally, all costs, both direct and indirect, but in most instances indirect costs, such as utilities, will be constants and can be ignored. This is not so in two important instances: when a library is considering remodeling or automating. These situations will be considered later.

The principal costs are people, equipment maintenance, supplies, and communication, e.g., telephones. Equipment and furniture cost becomes a factor if change is contemplated. While these are conventional terms, they have other definitions, also. People costs are essentially time costs, but time is also a function of distance covered per transaction, so an operation's layout must be accounted for. Administrative costs are frequently overlooked, but they are real.

Cost quantification is a difficult procedure and requires careful time study. Gross circulation department personnel costs can give a general idea of each transaction's cost, but a better analysis would show how time is divided among renewals, problem-solving, discharging, overdue collection and fines, as well as charging. Since each one of these procedures can be improved, each one must be considered separately and costs assigned appropriately.

From the information gathered it is then possible to derive a cost per activity unit. Costs are not equally distributed across all transactions, however. To provide any service there must be some determinable outlay—a minimum staff, equipment, and space. In certain settings, for example a branch library or reading room, the minimal costs may exceed those directly attributable to the circulation function with the remainder being the price paid to ensure a value, that of a separate facility, by providing security. In cost-benefit analysis, we examine marginal costs—the costs of adding or subtracting activity units—and compare them with the marginal benefits accruing therefrom to users.

Therefore, it is necessary to identify those benefits. In circulation, the chief user benefit may not be book borrowing, but the speed with which it can be done. Waiting in line is seen as a disbenefit. This is where the interplay of cost and benefit appears. What would be the cost of ensuring that no borrower ever had to wait in line? Is the benefit great enough to offset the fact that the money spent to achieve it must be taken from other services? This decision is a value judgment which cost analysis can support but not determine. It must be made against the whole spectrum of competing demand and supply situations. An interesting user-preference determination example is that of Raffel and Shishko at M.I.T. where respondents were asked to choose between services at various funding levels.[14]

Such a survey provides a user-generated framework within which to examine alternatives by indicating those which they would find unacceptable. However, any population includes groups whose goals are in conflict. For example, students may prefer study space while the faculty prefers added resources. Here one must consider the degree of benefit. How many people will receive the better service? Which service will give what population greater benefit? What is the trade-off, in such terms, between one service and another?[15] Increasing the number of reserve book copies may increase the satisfaction of a high population proportion, but reducing the number of new titles purchased in the rest of the collection may increase user dissatisfaction in a powerful group, the faculty, and result in increased interlibrary loan cost.[16]

The same questions must be answered whatever the service examined and Lancaster has provided a valuable source of assistance.[17] Service evaluation raises the question of evaluating the benefits received. Neither services nor benefits are equal in value. Based solely on funds, the decision would be relatively simple, but it must be based on values. Because many values are intangible, librarians face the same kinds of difficulties as engineers required to provide an environmental impact statement. Engineers' values differ from those of ecologists, environmentalists, health planners, and others who will read and dispute the statement so engineers must try to build these values into the study and try to reduce them to quantitative, funding terms. Librarians deal mostly with intangibles. In economic terms, their product is an added value. But how much is the value of a student increased by his/her reading? We know only that reading appears to accompany education and that the better read appear to be the better students.

We have always provided quantitative statistics and have used them to foster a growth ethic. However, "it is time to put quality and user satisfaction ahead of big numbers as the goal and guiding concept of library management."[18] Circulation statistics and user satisfaction are quite different. "These are things we can count, but that doesn't make them appropriate measurements of results."[19] There are innumerable studies on collection use, journal evaluation, and obsolescence, but they give only generalized mathematical future use approximations. They cannot predict what future books will be read.[20] Nor can they predict what value any particular reader use will have. What is the difference in value between reading a reserve book and a reference book? Is a faculty member use superior to graduate student use and that, in turn superior to undergraduate use? There are no simple answers to these questions, but all evaluation systems must use some kind of weighting. No known system can provide for the use that assists the user toward a Nobel Prize.

Librarians must be aware of the parent institution's goals and values since they will determine its willingness to support library programs. Program priorities must be known if the library is to serve institutional purposes. Classics and philosophy may need to rely on borrowed resources if the university emphasizes the sciences with their expensive needs. The conflicting claims of librarians, students, faculty, and administrators must be evaluated if quality questions are addressed.

The Nature of Benefits

Since a cost-benefit analysis's object is to assess the degree of benefit deriving from any particular course of action, the nature of the benefits involved and a way of quantifying them must be established beforehand. Certain of them concern the nature of the institution itself and could be put in very basic terms. If a private college student pays $12,000 a year to attend and the library expenditure is 5 percent, is the average student receiving $600 worth of library benefits? Undoubtedly some students will receive more, some less, if measured by number of book uses, reference questions, or library visits, but the figure can at least be used as a touchstone.[21]

A similar approach can be used when examining library expenditure distribution. Distribution by branch or academic department can frequently reveal disparate priorities that must be corrected. Many formulas exist for distributing book budget expenditures, but few of them are useful when the library faces a stable or shrinking budget and rising costs. Library investment in academic departments should roughly parallel institutional investment, excepting the hard sciences where astronomical journal subscription prices distort distribution. Even so, this distribution can be used as a means of getting administrative support for unpopular moves such as cancelling journal subscriptions.

For instance, in a small university the Chemistry Department may receive 10 percent of the assigned material budget (because of *Chemical Abstracts* and *Beilstein* subscriptions) and 7 percent of the total expenditure. Is this proportion justifiable for a department with only a mediocre use record? The administration may agree that the proportion should go no higher and that it will support restrictions. The library can correct other internally glaring mis-matches between academic programs and collections, while leaving to higher authorities the decisions on such academic changes as creating or discontinuing major or degree programs.

Despite their differences, most college and university libraries show roughly the same expenditure distribution.[22] Larger institutions tend to spend more on staff, and smaller ones more on material. This normative pattern appears to work well enough and dramatic change should not be expected. The only possible exception is the long-term effect of integrated automation, but budgetary difficulties and institutional financial policies may change this pattern, in particular because permanent staff members represent a significant long-term investment. Therefore, libraries need to examine what happens when the proportions change significantly. Can a library continue to function with 50 percent spent on staff, 35 percent on material and 15 percent on other?

Few studies have been carried out on the processing cost shifts consequent upon automation. It is likely, however, that such a shift will affect public service more than technical operations, because the former's costs are almost entirely personnel-related. Such a shift's benefits would need to be substantial indeed to justify its implementation, but the effects of such changes can be measured in order to demonstrate the consequences to the university administration. For example, public desk service hours might need to be reduced or specific service points closed. Unfortunately, question response deterioration is likely to occur, also, e.g., short answers because of lack of time. Such a deterioration cannot be demonstrated without a significant survey time investment.

The presumed principal library use benefit is added knowledge enabling a student to pass an examination or a faculty member to publish a paper. Whether or not this goal is achieved via specific library transactions can only be determined by a user survey.[23] Most libraries must rely on more pragmatic measures such as fulfillment rates. Lancaster claimed that the average fulfillment rate was about 40 percent.[24] Presumably an increase to 45 or 50 percent would represent an increase in user benefits, and this could become a library goal.

Space Consideration

Space is rarely considered in program analysis, but in fact the space required by an activity is one of its principal costs. Universities have become more space conscious as construction, renovation, and maintenance costs have soared. "Because colleges and universities have traditionally funded space needs through private gifts, federal grants, or state financing, space has come to be regarded almost as 'free goods.' Yet space is a measurable asset with a cost, and this unrecognized cost absorbs money that could be used for staff or another vital component of our institution."[25] Not only could the funds represented by the space be better used, frequently the space itself could be better used.

For librarians accustomed to growing collections, the likely inability to expand physical plant in the near future represents a significant change. According to one consultant, furnished library space now costs about $200 a square foot. Wasted space is a matter for serious concern. It is also clear that the best space (i.e., the most accessible or the most flexible) must be allocated to the most important activities. Hall described a library space use methodology which can help in determining both relationships and relative importance.[26] Such a tool can be useful when contemplating renovation or construction. Equally, the cost and benefit of transferring material to storage can be weighed against providing greater seating space. These should be part of any cost-benefit analysis.

The Implications of Automation

The advent of practical automation systems has revolutionized libraries. Most university libraries have installed some kind of automated system. Of course, we recognize that people will continue to be involved and that costs will not diminish. Automation proposals should be viewed soberly. While they are unlikely to decrease costs, they may change their incidence. They can also increase individual productivity, particularly because computerized catalog records are no longer location-bound, which implies considerable savings possible in internal staff and user travel time. Access time cost in obtaining information is frequently overlooked. To this can now be added the complexity of computer-accessible information which may require extraordinary skill to manipulate in user-agreeable form.[27]

Automation implications for service point reorganization are startling and have scarcely begun to be grasped, yet they are more important in managing scarce resources than the long-hoped-for direct catalog and circulation personnel savings.[28] The new element is information fluidity which makes the same information available simultaneously at widely dispersed points *and* enables the user to manipulate that information according to need. Such a change can result in major time-savings but only if the system is planned to permit it. An automated system that replicates an existing manual system is unlikely to return all the benefits and savings possible from a more innovative approach.

Automation projects should be preceded by a cost-benefit study which is directed not only to determining the kind of system needed but how it should be deployed and exploited. The latter is an impact study and should include such alternatives as locating terminals in offices outside the library. Unless that is done, the study will be self-limiting. Because of each campus's unique character, other libraries' studies are not easily used. Nevertheless, others' experience can be helpful. For example, Dwyer's and Blackburn's reports are useful evaluations against which to measure the library's proposals and predict their effects.[29,30]

All automation projects are concerned with capital equipment depreciation and amortization. One of the side-effects of being budget-driven is that institutional budgets make no provision for depreciation. Instead they extract capital expenditures from operating income or seek endowment funds for specific purposes. None of these styles can take care of equipment replacement. Any library installing an automated system must be prepared at regular future times to replace worn-out equipment or upgrade the computer. In certain instances, therefore, leasing or simple contract payment for service is preferable to buying. OCLC cataloging is an example. The decision should be based on a financial analysis, but institutional budget control conditions may override other considerations.

A small example of these problems was the apparent generosity of foundations and state libraries which made 1970s funds available for OCLC terminals, to be installed free, in order to encourage small libraries to participate. Unfortunately, many of them had insufficient traffic to justify a terminal, nor did they have the budget resources for maintenance. Many terminals were seriously underused. Fewer but properly worked out automation programs would have been better, perhaps including the establishment of processing centers or similar mechanisms to encourage cooperation. It was forgotten that in small libraries the amount of money that can be transferred between operating units is small, and that the staff is not large enough to generate savings to cover added costs.

The automation decision should be based on a positive response to the following conditions:

    a. The money is available for the initial outlay;
    b. Maintenance and upgrading costs can be met within the budget or by substitution for other expenditures;
    c. The new system will improve on existing systems' performance;
    d. Necessary physical plant and personnel changes to the new system can be made; and
    e. Long-term user benefits are unattainable in any other way.

These conditions should be met before a decision is made to proceed. If they cannot be met, then other alternatives should be pursued. Although this is true of any proposed change, it is especially important in automation because the changeover is irreversible.

It is not necessarily true that automation costs will continue to decrease. Actually, unit cost, i.e., what it costs to carry out a particular activity once, is decreasing because the machines become increasingly efficient. You can get more equipment for the buck, but you must still spend the buck, or more often the kilobuck or even the megabuck to make the system function.

Possibilities and Problems

The range of possibilities is broad, but the following examples have been chosen to show what might be done to meet given problems. The preceding part of this chapter was based on the premise that, properly applied, cost-benefit analysis can lead to improved performance without necessarily increasing expenditure. It is a slow tool, unless the librarian maintains a constant state of alert, and therefore is not always ready to cope with a crisis. On the other hand, if the proper analyses have been conducted, the librarian can begin with half the job done by using the results of earlier studies as stepping stones to the newly needed solution. The response must be determined by the way in which the institution presents the problem.

No handy ground rules exist for coping with an instruction to reduce costs by 10 percent, nor with a severe cut in a particular area. There is seldom much lead time and the library response must be based on previous planning. The one certain rule for failure is to apply the cut across the board. Such a cut would not lead to a meaningful reconsideration of library departmental goals. A set of service priorities provides the only guide. In all cases, however, the results of cuts must be explained to the staff and constituency. If, for example, it means eliminating one service point during evening and weekend hours, alternatives should be pointed out or means for obtaining replacement help.

Centralization vs. Decentralization

Given a budget reduction, no library can maintain all services at previous levels. The question seldom arises in pure form. Wheaton College, however, when faced with deciding how to renovate facilities, conducted a branch library survey and determined that centralization would better serve its needs.[31] Seldom can so pure a solution be found, and faculty pressures are in the opposite direction. On the other hand, Atkinson, at both Ohio State University and the University of Illinois, Urbana/Champaign, advocated service point dispersion and document delivery improvement as the better alternative. For most institutions, the question is likely to be whether a less than adequate branch facility should be upgraded, downgraded, or disbanded.

In looking at a specific case recently, I saw that the facility was completely full, had no load-bearing capacity for space increase and carried a relatively low reference service load. The proposed solution was a restricted collection, a special hotline reference service and ultimately computer terminal service with solely clerical security-oriented personnel. More demanding service would be provided from another branch. This solution was accepted only because of the floor load problem, but it represented also an alternative lower-level and less costly service solution. At a later date, if further renovation money is obtained, this branch will be completely amalgamated with another one. Compromises of this kind are likely outcomes on most campuses.

Severe budget cuts (circa 20 percent) may require much more drastic approaches though attention must be paid to institutional priorities. All branches could be limited in hours and personnel categories with central telephone reference service picking up the slack. It would be better, however, to close one or more service points entirely and amalgamate service. Self-maintaining honor-systems are ineffective and should be considered only when all other alternatives fail. Size, geographic concentration, academic shape, and institutional style are the decision determinants.

Access vs. Ownership

The level and scope of the library's collecting policies is one of the most critical austerity decisions. Apart from increasing serial cost pressures, electronic publishing's emergence makes library goal reconsideration mandatory. Response will depend on each institution's stance and financial capabilities, relations with other libraries, and geographical position. Response may vary from reducing the collection to core level (in a small and homogeneous college) to cutting back areas with low academic investment. For some years, many libraries have insisted that any new subscription be balanced by matching cancellations.

Much can be gained by a consortium agreement on where less-used serial backfiles will be housed. Although such arrangements have previously been difficult to work out, new stringency gives the task urgency. Wholesale microform conversion is not the answer. It does not save space, unless the material converted is never used, in which case the material should be discarded. A planned serial program may be useful, however. Gleaves and Carterette presented such a proposal based on a space and maintenance cost-benefit analysis.[32] Judiciously used, such a plan can save money.

The question is deeper than this, however. We must shift attention from providing artifacts to providing information access.[33] Increasingly, that access now comes thru telephone line and terminal and the information volume so available is increasing rapidly. The library's greatest cost is not for acquiring information but for recording and storing it. While no one would suggest, except in a non-academic special library, a complete shift to on-demand purchasing, that style must increase in the future.

In combination with increased interlibrary loan and reciprocal borrowing use, where possible, a library's acquisitions can be trimmed heavily without reducing its ability to provide information access. This change requires shifting budgetary resources from things to people and presupposes that other libraries or commercial services will supply what is needed.[34] Many libraries are consciously doing this already but have not capitalized on the fact. Access to OCLC, RLIN, etc., is the equivalent of buying an entire range of bibliographic service but receiving it as a free adjunct to purchasing cataloging service. This kind of two-in-one purchase makes electronic service very desirable. Little research into this information approach exists, and proper management system development for resource sharing is overdue.[35]

What Success Rate?

What kinds of marginal costs is the library prepared to accept? The 90 percent library concept, a variant on the old 80/20 rule (80 percent of the profit arises from 20 percent of the business) is based on the fact that attempting to fulfill 100 percent of user needs can be very costly.[36] The concept's proponents claim that, since no library can ever hope to own and provide everything, finding a way of establishing specified kinds of expectations is more rational than leaving expectations to chance. The trade-off between waiting lines and staff/equipment costs is an example of the problem which the 90 percent solution is designed to solve. Which 10 percent of expectations will not be fulfilled, is, of course, the most difficult problem. In this context, a library might decide to cut periodical holdings to the core titles established in various disciplines. However, this merely transfers unsatisfied needs to interlibrary loan, where the per transaction cost can be large. This solution is likely to work well only in an institution where research is not stressed.

It is more difficult to achieve similar results in public service areas. The commonest result is simply failing to answer questions or else arbitrarily limiting staff time which restricts the number of service requests. A more rational approach would require service desk activity reorganization either to channel various kinds of need or amalgamate under-used desks. A method which can be effective and efficient is to provide a screening mechanism via an information desk designed to absorb as many as possible of the basic questions and direct users with more difficult needs elsewhere. Branch hotline telephone use is a variant. Automated systems must make this kind of choice, also. To reduce costs, terminals or work-stations should be provided only to meet high average work loads, not peak loads, thereby balancing cost against small waiting time increases.

Service Elimination

All services deteriorate over time and must be reviewed at least every 4–5 years. It is not that they become too costly or are badly carried out, but that they become irrelevant to the library's main goals. In another context, Crompton and Lamb advocated a formal program evaluation and elimination strategy.[37] Libraries could well apply their methodology which is akin to zero-base budgeting. Both seek a ground-up evaluation with a view to eliminating certain programs rather than trimming them all. A good example would be the reference/acquisitions effort put into decreasingly emphasized academic areas. The acquisition rate could be cut to basic material and research needs met by borrowing. Sometimes, however, what at first seems to be a very sensible money-saving proposal turns out to be the opposite.[38] Proposals for making money by selling off stock should always be treated with skepticism. Also, closing facilities is very difficult except in a general crisis and savings can better be effected by lowering staff service levels or shortening hours.

Cost Recovery

User service payment is a "hot" topic in a field which has maintained the importance of free information access. The attitude is variable by subfield, however, since special and medical libraries have long been accustomed to a commercial approach. The debate has shown that there are different access levels and different kinds of information. The principle has emerged that substitute service, i.e., that for which a self-service alternate exists, is properly chargeable. In any case, decisions should be made in accordance with a coherent information access philosophy and should not be arbitrary or ad hoc.

Most libraries charge for extended data-base searches and their products, in the same way that they do for photocopying, because these are substitutes for manual searches or reproduction of originals. On the other hand, terminal use for quick reference is usually not charged for, the benefits being improved service and enhanced productivity. However, libraries do face future problems when the basic service will be electronic.

It may, for example, be cost-effective to cease subscribing to *Chemical Abstracts*, even while providing free searches as a substitute, because use volume is low and the library has terminated the alternative access means. These questions are intricate. Pfaffenberger and Echt reported on a project where decisions were made between paper and electronic access.[39] Their evaluation method may be useful to study. At the other extreme, the library must determine whether or not existing service is still effective. An unused service is a useless cost and should be terminated. Kiewitt developed an ERIC search evaluation tool which set out the facts needed, and it can serve as a model.[40] Search-based services may also be sought as a way of meeting demand and generating income.

Circulation automation facilitates overdue and lost book cost recovery because a better control system can be implemented. Certain libraries have developed series of cost recovery models. This approach has proved more acceptable than the old method of levying punitive fines which alienate users. Although it is only a name-change, the concept of recovering costs which should not have been incurred is much more acceptable than levying fines.

Income Generation

Until recently libraries seldom sought outside income actively. It is now necessary to do so. Two routes can be followed. The first is through fund-raising which is the subject of another chapter. The second is through marketing service. We can charge non-members of the academic community for library use. Membership or use fees are common. They range from a small registration fee to amounts intended to discourage all but the most serious potential users and include carefully graduated scales for kind of user and kind of service. The latter is well exemplified by the latest Harvard University Countway Library of Medicine charge scale.

An alternative approach, with much to commend it, is the sale of service to industrial and business firms, either for a fixed associateship fee or according to a charge scale. The goal is to achieve income at a chosen expenditure percentage, say 10 percent, although the figure may be revised after a market survey of the degree of external involvement possible without disrupting existing service. Both Rice and Lehigh universities report success in this outreach.[41] Other services, such as contract cataloging, can also be marketed as well as back-up reference service provided in return for access to other collections. Sale of publications and products such as a COM catalog should also be considered if collection importance attracts outside interest. However, many of these activities must be carried out in relation to existing consortium commitments. Although it is uncommon, rental charges for facility use by outside groups, such as meeting rooms, should be considered. Contracts may be offered to other libraries for facility use.

The goal in these explorations is to identify what works best in a given library. The chosen course should maximize benefits and minimize costs. To some extent, academic libraries are protected by the long-held belief that the library is the heart of the university, even though it may have been starved for years. However, it is no longer possible to rely on that belief as a cushion for inefficiency. Librarians can expect to spend more time in self-evaluation, and cost-benefit analysis can make this process more effective.

Research Needed

Because libraries have only recently begun analyzing cost and income, many needed models and techniques are lacking. More effective means for evaluating user need and satisfaction are needed. Further research into the added benefit of library use is needed. Statistical analysis methods should be reviewed since some are based on untested assumptions and none have been developed to cover the whole library service range.[42] Simulations and models for projecting futures under varying conditions are emerging, but are not yet in common use. Further study of automation's cost and service impact is desirable. Though these studies may sound general and of little value in specific instances, only from such studies can general rules, standards, and methodologies emerge.

References

1. Private colleges and universities are partial exceptions to this rule, inasmuch as tuition bears a close relationship to costs, but sometimes they defy the ordinary marketplace rules, also.
2. Douglas M. Knight and E. Shepley Nourse, *Libraries at Large* (N.Y.: R. R. Bowker, 1969), Chapter 5, "The Costs of Library and Information Services."
3. Peter F. Drucker, *Management: Tasks, Responsibilities, Practices* (N.Y.: Harper and Row, 1973).
4. Limited analyses present problems. In an interesting commentary on an experiment, Lewis pointed out in "Management by Objectives," *Journal of Academic Librarianship* 6 (January 1980), pp. 329–334, that the application of MBO principles (a process parallel to cost-benefit analysis) to a single department resulted in limited improvement, because the application was not extended to related departments.
5. Richard De Gennaro in "Library Statistics and User Satisfaction: No Significant Correlation," *Journal of Academic Librarianship* 6 (May 1980), p. 95, demonstrates cogently that most traditional statistics are useless in determining user satisfaction.
6. Despite the importance of this user satisfaction measure, little has been done to determine ways of measuring fulfillment rates. A useful beginning is Eugene Wiemers, Jr., *Materials Availability in Small Libraries: A Survey Handbook* (Champaign, IL.: University of Illinois School of Library and Information Science, 1981) (Occasional Paper No. 149).
7. In another article, "Budgetary Strategies: Coping with a Changing Fiscal Environment," *Journal of Academic Librarianship* 2 (January 1977), pp. 297–302, I showed the effects of various ranges of decisions on the book budget. Making no decision is the making of a decision that can have expanding consequences. The same effects are encountered in any program. Unless conscious provision is made for them the future will be one of frequent readjustment, a fate which planning is undertaken to avoid.
8. The MRAP experience is valuable here. See Michael K. Buckland, "The Management Review and Analysis Program: A Symposium." *Journal of Academic Librarianship* 1 (January 1976), pp. 4–14 and Edward R. Johnson and Stuart H. Mann, *Organization Development for Academic Libraries: An Evaluation of the Management Review and Analysis Program* (Westport, Conn.: Greenwood Press, 1980).
9. Jacob Cohen, in Chapter 5 of *Use of Library Materials, the University of Pittsburgh Study* (N.Y.: Dekker, 1979) developed a cost-benefit model for library

operation. However, it was based on book-use as the benefit determinant and therefore would need to be supplemented by studies of benefits accruing from other information transfers, such as reference questions answered.

10. Even a partial list is long, but the following will indicate the diversity. Casimir Barkowski and others, "A Reply to the Kent Study," *Library Journal* 106 (April 1, 1981), pp. 710–713; Jasper Schad, "Pittsburgh University Studies of Collection Usage," *Journal of Academic Librarianship* 5 (May 1979), pp. 60–70.

11. Many of the issues were raised by Jerome Yavarkovsky in an address to a conference on research library economic and financial management which will appear in the *Journal of Library Administration*.

12. Murray S. Martin, *Budgetary Control in Academic Libraries* (Greenwich, Conn.: JAI Press, 1978), Chapter 5. Reclassification and Facilities Usage were first included but later dropped as unnecessary.

13. Betty Jo Mitchell and others, *Cost Analysis of Library Functions: A Total System Approach* (Greenwich, Conn.: JAI Press, 1978) is the most complete example of library costing. It presents a taxonomic model for library costs, a methodology for computing them and a complete example. Comparison with other standard cost statements and with the library's own costs would be instructive.

14. Jeffrey A. Raffel and Robert Shishko, *Systematic Analysis of University Libraries: An Application of Cost-Benefit Analysis to the M.I.T. Libraries* (Cambridge: The M.I.T. Press, 1969).

15. A fascinating example is offered by Daniel Traister, "Goodby to All That: A Case Study in Deaccessioning," *Wilson Library Bulletin* 56 (May 1982), pp. 663–668, where he analyzes the Lehigh University proposal to sell the rare book collection. Cost analysis showed that it would be neither effective nor efficient and certainly not profitable, because, while the trustees were looking at the selling price, they did not see the direct and indirect costs involved.

16. Notwithstanding the many studies made of breakdown points for subscribing or borrowing, *e.g.*, M. K. Buckland, and others. *Systems Analysis of a University Library* (Lancaster: University of Lancaster Library, 1970), G. E. Williams and others, *Library Cost Models: Owning Versus Borrowing Serial Publications* (Chicago: Center for Research Libraries, 1968) and the studies carried out by Westat, Inc. for the Association of Research Libraries, it must be stressed that local circumstances always supervene. No study made for one library can be applied directly to another. It is also well to remember that general studies cannot guide specific decisions which must be based on local needs.

17. F. W. Lancaster, *The Measurement and Evaluation of Library Services* (Washington, D.C.: Information Resources Press, 1977), particularly valuable are Chapter 3, "Evaluation of Reference Service" and Chapter 13, "Cost-Performance-Benefits Considerations."

18. De Gennaro, *loc. cit.* See also H. William Axford, "Performance Measures Revisited," *College and Research Libraries* 34 (September 1973), pp. 244–257.

19. Peter F. Drucker, "Measuring the Public Service Institution," *College and Research Libraries* 37 (January 1976), p. 13.

20. This theme emerged at the Conference on Retrospective Collection Development in the Humanities and Social Sciences, Binghampton, July 11–14, 1979. See my reference in the summing up, "Buying, Borrowing and Bibli-

ographies," *Library Acquisitions: Practice and Theory*, p. 118, 1979. There has been some revision of the mathematics underlying the Bradford-Zipf distributions, but no one has moved beyond the prediction of generalities.

21. Admittedly this approach ignores faculty and other use, but student head-counts are used frequently as the college user population without undue distortion. Public colleges lack the same kind of figure but can use a tuition and appropriation combination.

22. Sherman Hayes, "Budgeting for and Controlling the Cost of Other in Library Expenditures: The Distant Relative in the Budgetary Process." *Journal of Library Administration* 3/4 (Fall/Winter 1982), pp. 121–131.

23. A sample of such a survey is available in P. U. Rzasa and J. M. Moriarty, "Types and Needs of Academic Library Users," *College and Research Libraries* 31 (November, 1970), pp. 403–9.

24. Lancaster, *op. cit.*, "Achievements," pp. 26–27.

25. "Space Costing in Colleges and Universities," *American School and University* 49 (April 1977), p. 20. See also, Harlan D. Bareither, "Facilities Utilization," *New Directions for Higher Education* 8 (1980), pp. 55–66.

26. Richard B. Hall. *LSO: The Library Space Utilization Methodology* (Champaign, IL.: University of Illinois Graduate School of Library Science, 1979) (Occasional Paper No. 141).

27. Anthony G. Oettinger. *Elements of Information Resources Policy: Library and Other Information Sciences* (Cambridge, Mass. for the National Commission on Libraries and Information Science, 1976), p. 46 *et passim*.

28. Charles Martell in "Erasing the Past: Technological Shifts and Organizational Renewal," *New Horizons for Academic Libraries* (N.Y.: K. G. Saur, 1979), pp. 175–188, adumbrates certain possibilities.

29. James R. Dwyer, "The Effect of Closed Catalogs on Public Access," *Library Resources and Technical Services* 25 (April–June 1981), pp. 186–195.

30. Robert Blackburn, "Two Years With a Closed Catalog," *Journal of Academic Librarianship* 4 (January 1979), pp. 424–429.

31. Mark B. Mitchell, "Planning for Expansion at Wheaton," *Library Journal* 106 (December 1, 1981), pp. 2290–2292.

32. Edwin S. Gleaves and Robert T. Carterette, "Microform Serials Acquisition: A Suggested Planning Model," *Journal of Academic Librarianship* 8 (November 1982), pp. 292–5.

33. Edmund G. Hamann, "Access to Information: A Reconsideration of the Service Goals of a Small Urban College Library," in *New Horizons For Academic Libraries* (N.Y.: K. G. Saur, 1979), pp. 534–538, and T. Philip Tompkins and Gary J. Bird, "The Urban University Library: Effectiveness Models for 1989," ibid., pp. 577–583.

34. Noelene P. Martin, "Interlibrary Loan and Resource Sharing: New Approaches," *Journal of Library Administration* 3/4 (Fall/Winter 1982), pp. 99–108.

35. David A. Kronick, "Goodbye to Farewells: Resource Sharing and Cost Sharing," *Journal of Academic Librarianship* 8 (July 1982), pp. 132–136. "Libraries also need effective management systems for sharing costs as well as resources." (p. 136) This is an area overdue for study.

36. C. P. Bourne is the most frequently cited. See his "Some User Requirements Stated Quantitatively in Terms of the 90 Percent Library," in *Electronic Information Handling*, edited by Allen Kent and O. E. Taulbee (Washington,

D.C.: Spartan Books, 1965), pp. 93–110. For a brief overview with examples see F. W. Lancaster, *The Measurement and Evaluation of Library Services* (Washington, D.C.: Information Resources Press, 1977), pp. 364–367.

37. John L. Crompton and Charles W. Lamb, "Eliminating Community Services—The Leisure Services Example," *Community Development Journal* 15 (April 1980), pp. 138–145.

38. See note 15 above for an example.

39. Ann Pfaffenberger and Sandy Echt, "Substitution of Scisearch and Social Scisearch for their Print Versions in an Academic Library," *Database* 3 (March 1980), pp. 63–71.

40. Eva L. Kiewitt. *Cost Benefit Analysis of a Computer Retrieval System* (Bloomington: Indiana University Graduate Library School, 1976).

41. Susan A. Cady and Berry G. Richards, "The One-thousand Dollar Alternative: How One University Structures a Fee-based Information Service for Local Industry," *American Libraries* 14 (March 1982), pp. 175–176. Describes a subscription-based search service which includes 40% for general benefits.

42. John Budd, "Libraries and Statistical Studies: An Equivocal Relationship," *Journal of Academic Librarianship* 8 (November, 1982), pp. 278–81.

13. Improving Staff Creativity, Productivity and Accountability

Donna B. Yglesias

STAFF CREATIVITY, productivity and accountability improvement programs may be used by academic library managers attempting to ward off retrenchment's devastating effects. Human resources are the most important library assets. Austerity will bring increasing competition for limited educational dollars, so human resource expenditures must be made more productive. Over two-thirds of library expenditures may be personnel-related.[1] *Creativity* is the application of new ideas to problem-solving and artistic expression. *Productivity* is the ability to generate goods or services in a more efficient and effective manner. *Accountability* refers to employees being held responsible for and answerable to higher authority for specific work results.

This chapter's objectives are:

a. To present a comprehensive statement on improving the creativity of academic library staff members, especially in austere times.
b. To present an analysis of academic library productivity literature and to describe the relationship of employee productivity to economic belt-tightening.
c. To present a review of academic library accountability literature and develop useful accountability, management and austerity generalizations.

The chapter's conceptual framework will attempt to relate creativity, productivity, and accountability concepts so library managers can focus thinking on them in austerity. The manager must relate these ideas to employee performance measurement. He/she must use productivity enhancement programs, accountability measures, and creativity enhancement projects. All relate closely to austerity management, and increased emphasis on them will save many dollars. Indeed, if managers do not seek ways to enhance these activities, library existence may be threatened. The need to improve creativity, productivity, and accountability is shown on the following pages.

Creativity

Creativity plays an important role in any organization; one which fails over time to respond to its constituency becomes static. Libraries may be more formal and stable than most organizations, thus the need for creativity within them.[2] Creative people seek to solve problems in new ways. New austerity problem solutions are necessary in such areas as cataloging, reference, circulation, acquisition, and instructional technology administration.[3]

Creativity may be categorized in four types: 1) *Problem-solving* emphasis is on precise problem definition, from which may emerge a readily apparent solution; 2) *Hypothesis formulation* presents situations and tests hypotheses through experimentation to arrive at the most appropriate resolution to an out-of-balance situation; 3) In *idea linking*, one analyzes a wide range of ideas, experiences, critical incidents, and prior outcomes, and lumps or links all components together to answer the who, what, where, when, why, and how of a given situation; 4) *Free association* or *brainstorming*, perhaps the most popular approach, encourages many individuals to come together and explore ideas in a free-wheeling conversation from which new and original ideas are born. Sometimes brainstorming produces ideas which are so original that no one other than the presentor understands fully what is meant.[4] Creativity and imagination are related in that imagination is required in creating and in setting and testing hypotheses.[5]

Creative library staff members are future-oriented and are not afraid to search for new and bold solutions to old and persistent problems. They exhibit many of the following characteristics: imagination, idea fluency, questioning ability, originality, flexibility, independence, ability to synthesize, ability to abstract, sensitivity, intelligence, challenging personality, persistence, drive, courage, and theoretical and aesthetic values.[6] Uncreative staff members generally exhibit the following characteristics: conformity, fear of failure, resistance to change, lack of confidence, laziness, fear of ridicule, lack of knowledge, pessimism and timidity.[7] Uncreative employees are perhaps the greatest deterrent to library effectiveness and organizational change.

"Creativity can, within certain limits, be encouraged."[8] Research into creativity and its application to academic libraries, however, has been inconclusive. A problem arises in "discussing creativity in the library" in that common work experience there is not always "conducive to creativity."[9] The manager must strive to foster creativity while maintaining organizational conformity. A harmonious balance must be achieved in a systematic and well reasoned manner between the creative process and conformity to organizational needs.[10] An organizational atmosphere favorable toward new ideas will stimulate employee creativity more effectively than any other single activity.[11]

Supervisors must encourage creativity. Evaluation or judgmental cues should be discouraged at the idea-producing stage. Three categories of formats are used in stimulating new ideas: analytical, free-association, and forced-relationship. The *analytical format* utilizes logical, problem-solving methodologies to stimulate new idea formation. The analytical format employs the attribute listing, input-output, and grid analysis techniques. *Attribute listing* consists of listing separate problems in written form while stating each problem's major attributes. After discussion, recommended changes are listed and both changes and attributes are analyzed for their relationships. The object is to generate substantive ideas in large numbers about changes that may occur and to evaluate ideas based on change.

The *input-output technique* differs from attribute listing in that the final output is specified by an individual who is not a group member. Ideas related to factors that generate the final result are discussed and situations are restructured to arrive at the desired output. Emphasis is placed on alternatives in arriving at the final result. A further refinement of attribute listing is *grid analysis,* where attribute lists and problems are placed on a two dimensional grid on which all possible combinations can be considered.[12]

Free association has been widely used at business executive retreats. Only comments pertinent to the discussion topic are permitted. Problem definition is discouraged while comments, reactions, thoughts, and suggestions are encouraged. The brainstorming format's major objective is to maximize idea flow.[13] The *forced relationship* technique relies on small group processes where relationships between problems and attributes can be established and then probability and random occurence stimulate new views and ideas.[14] To stimulate creativity staff members may visit comparable libraries to search for answers to "what else" and "how else" questions regarding operations, functions, activities, processes, tasks, and other service aspects.

Staff members who seek continually to foster, improve and employ creative and productive approaches must be rewarded. Increased productivity and creativity may be rewarded by financial rewards, paid time off, honors, awards, staff newsletter notices, delegation of additional responsibilities and promotions.[15]

Productivity

Productivity includes product manufacture and "improved managerial and employee performance and more effective delivery of service."[16]

In an environment of decreasing revenue and increasing demand and cost, the library must provide better service by improving employee efficiency and effectiveness. There are a number of ways to do this. Work simplification is a tool which graphically details and outlines a job from start to finish. An integral work simplification component is flow charting.[17] Dougherty refers to work simplification as "why is a job performed, who performs it, how is the job performed, where is it performed," and so forth.[18] It is used in simplifying work, improving productivity, and cutting costs.

An analogy of a pyramid, where the base represents work simplification and time and motion studies constitute the remaining angular lines, describes the relationship of these ideas. Once a job is flow charted, a tool is required for determining the time which well qualified employees would spend in doing the job at a normal pace. This tool is the time study, a work measurement component. Motion study aims to eliminate unnecessary steps; it follows time study and both lead to work simplification.[19]

Library managers must standardize operations, tools, forms, records, and material so routine job performance can be made more uniform. Standardization attempts have persisted in spite of the "rugged individualism" of librarians.[20] Employee performance standards are a vital productivity component. They refer to measurement of work quantity and quality produced under normal conditions. Library quality control refers to the accuracy of information given, effectiveness of information presented, and subjective factors such as tactfulness, courtesy, and diplomacy in user relations. Any productivity measure must include a quality control methodology and a process for improving service quality.

In service organizations, systems analysis and work simplification are similar concepts. Industrial management literature describes systems analysis as a way of analyzing organizations in quantitative terms. A systems approach to management forms a relationship between parts and/or subsystems. It begins with setting objectives and proceeds to information feedback and decision-making process development.[21] The organization is systematized, employee performance is standardized, quality control is addressed and the result is that both employee and organizational productivity increase.

Employee productivity is measured by determining the amount of work accomplished, which in turn is determined by setting performance standards and recording how the employee's work compares with them. Increasing employee productivity, hence, is dependent upon the employee's attitude toward performance standards, the performance appraisal process, and organization goals and objectives. The more employees are encouraged to contribute to setting performance standards, participate in the appraisal process, and develop organizational goals and objectives, the more likely that employees' perceptions and attitudes toward their work and organization will be positive.[22]

Job enrichment and innovation are key elements in developing positive employee perceptions and attitudes. Job enrichment strives to make the job more interesting, challenging, and rewarding, thereby improving productivity and general performance. The employee's ability to derive genuine satisfaction and a feeling of truly contributing to the organization's objectives in turn stimulates creativity, initiative, and cooperation.[23] Where "job enrichment programs have been emphasized, increased productivity results even if productivity had not been one of the stated goals of the program."[24]

Innovation is the application of knowledge by individuals within the organization. Innovation has been described as the "lifeblood of productivity."[25] As environmental, social, and technological changes occur, the need for job redesign increases.[26] Employee innovation and its effect on organizational processes require that jobs be redesigned to meet a variety of library changes. To increase productivity, the following job redesign techniques may be used: 1) Adding more and different tasks to the employee's job description which is job enlargement, and 2) moving employees from one to another series of similar activities, known as job rotation.

Task analysis is the process of identifying all discrete functions that must be carried out in satisfactorily completing an activity. An activity is a sequence of several tasks and an operation is a set of several activities. A job is a set of several activities performed by an employee.[27] Job analysis, or its more detailed sibling, task analysis, is utilized to increase productivity. It defines desired employee performance, sets appropriate conditions, and develops acceptable performance standards in behaviorally stated terminology. It is achieved by a detailed analysis of all aspects of all tasks involved in a job.[28] Task analysis is employed to reveal more clearly the nature of the work of the employee and the tasks performed therein in relation to the employee's skills, aptitudes, and knowledge.[29]

Enhancing productivity via task analysis includes correlating costs to tasks performed. Costs must be measured and the costs of performing tasks must be studied. The selection of priorities, service delivery options, employee effectiveness assessment, budgeting, projecting trends, and goal setting are all tied to costs.[30] The relationship of cost to employee tasks is important in developing a productivity enhancement program.

Employees are productive or unproductive. Inability to perform the tasks in a job due to lack of training or intellectual ability characterizes a certain portion of unproductive workers, but the library worker suffers less from these problems than do workers who perform simple and routine tasks. Certain library employees are structure abetted. They

have feelings of security and need satisfaction when there is predictabil-
ity and stability in the organizational environment. Another personality
type is structure-threatened. This individual derives satisfaction from
her/his perception of the organizational environment and her/his ability to control it.[31]

An understanding of employee personality type, the employee's productivity history and employee personal goals within the organization
aid the library manager in structuring a productivity enhancement program on the basis of employee task analysis. There will always be non-
productive employees, and perhaps in austere times, they must be terminated. The productive employee who is unproductive at certain tasks
is worth further discussion. This employee may be counseled, asked to
perform self and peer evaluations, and provided with staff development activities that will improve her/his performance.

If, after the series of events described above, the employee is still
unproductive he/she may be reached, as may other staff members, by
motivational techniques often referred to as work incentives. These
incentives fall into three categories: monetary, performance targeting
(the setting of performance standards), and intrinsic rewarding. Often
intrinsic rewarding provides the most viable employee work incentive
source.[32]

Judicious time use is yet another characteristic of productive employees. Time effectiveness training, paperwork streamlining, and
form and material simplification increase work output.[33] Along with
effective time use, appropriate technology use can improve worker
output. "The origination, recording, transfer, acquisition, and in-
terpretation of information" is facilitated by computer technology.[34]
Library computing application, if harnessed in appropriate ways, will
enhance worker productivity.

Accountability

Organizational success and accountability are closely related. Library
staff accountability is the process by which employees can be required to
justify their actions and bear responsibility for reporting them to a
higher authority based on stated objectives.[35] Accountability emanates
from legislative and administrative sources. Legislative accountability is
derived from statute law, legal orders, court mandates, and hearings.
Administrative accountability is derived from superordinate-subordi-
nate relationships. Legislative accountability is external while administrative accountability is internal. Legislative mandates are imposed
and leave little room for collegial and collaborative effort; thus legislative accountability requires limited, if any, staff participative effort.
Administrative accountability involves the administrator's relationship
with allocated resources and the allocation's efficaciousness. Admin-

istrative accountability enhances superordinate and subordinate collaborative efforts and encourages joint goal setting and staff goal measurement. In any event, accountability is always a relationship between superordinate and subordinate, where superordinate has final decision-making authority and responsibility.[36]

As libraries attempt to cope with retrenchment effects, an increasing need arises for employee performance evaluation and measurement. Performance assessment is a method of improving the library's productivity by defining employee duties and responsibilities and developing standards congruent with library goals. As organization needs and user requests evolve, a corresponding library change develops and the need arises for new employee skills. The library manager in a changing environment must reallocate resources in creative ways while assisting staff personnel to acquire new skills.[37]

Effective and worthwhile accountability requires establishment of standards, methodology, and reporting systems for performance measurement and correction. Performance standards are criteria used to measure work and results. Performance standards are "continuing criteria used to measure and evaluate progress and results in achieving the key objective."[38] Employee standards must be specific, identify the tasks in each position, and measure performance.

A systematic approach is necessary to develop performance standards, reporting procedures, performance evaluation, and guidelines for corrective behavior. Accurate evaluation of employee effectiveness, as well as carefully planned corrective behavior activities, are also important. Taxpayer pressure in the public and board of trustees pressure in the private institution as well as faculty, student, university administrator, and other user pressures require that libraries be accountable in many ways. A systematic approach in task analysis development and a performance appraisal worksheet can be advocated.[39] The worksheet contains four major sections: task statement, performance expectations and standards, training and its effect, and performance rating. Employee-supervisor mutually developed task descriptions and performance standards can be stressed.

Performance standards relate closely to the performance evaluation process. Performance standards are impersonal and unbiased and should be diagnostic and indicate strengths and shortcomings. Duties, tasks, and responsibilities should be clear, coherent, and well-defined. A well-stated performance standard encourages employees to work harder and strive for greater productivity.[40] Performance evaluation is a measure of the employees' performance against collegially developed standards. Without clear standards, employees and employers do not know where they stand in terms of the systems and processes within the organization.[41]

Task analysis can be used to "provide performance evaluations based on specific tasks and standardized performance standards."[42] Establishing performance standards continues to pose problems for the library manager. Differentiating the professional and non-professional or the technical service and the public service employee are cases in point. Non-professional clerical and routine library tasks pose little problem in developing performance standard criteria. Axford suggested that technical service staff performance measurement was easily quantified; he used unit cost analysis for employee measurement.[43] A performance standard for a technical service card filer could be: an employee who will be able to "file one hundred cards per hour with an error ratio of less than five."[44]

Public service employees, given the nature of the duties performed, may be more difficult to assess and therefore performance standard development may be more complex. However, reference librarian performance may be assessed by discussing the quantity and quality of service rendered, service timeliness, complaints about service, and number of questions responded to.[45] Quality measurement is more difficult but the following may be offered: "To answer accurately reference questions received from the public or by telephone so that 80 percent of all questions received are answered to the satisfaction of the person."[46]

A reference librarian accountability model can be based on a number of activities and tasks. One is orientation/instruction presentations to faculty members. An accompanying performance standard would be to "personally contact twenty new faculty members and offer each a tour or orientation of the library this academic year."[47] This model addresses accountability by listing as an activity or task professional association activities with accompanying performance standards.[48] Once performance standards have been agreed upon and evaluation via analysis has occurred by measuring activities and tasks against standards, then procedural corrective action follows. Corrective action may include personnel reassignment, duty clarification, selection procedure improvement, and instituting staff development programs.[49]

If academic libraries become more accountable, several techniques can be utilized as controlling mechanisms. Perhaps the most popular one is program budgeting. As a controlling device the budget is the most important mechanism for program measurement and effectiveness studies. The relation of program costs to work performed and program budgeting has been described. A program budget is arranged according to library programs and activities and appropriations are correlated to work performed. Management can be more effective when program budgeting is employed, because budget cuts and changes can be explained in a clear and logical manner. Explicit relationships between services rendered and costs incurred can be more easily presented and defended.[50]

In a period characterized by decreasing expenditures and dwindling budget allocations, employee performance effectiveness must be demonstrated. In meeting retrenchment challenges, performance standards and measurement are critical. "Librarians have performed too long without established standards against which to measure the quality and quantity of their performance."[51] Employee accountability refers to duties performed, responsibilities accepted, and authority required in agreement with understood and accepted performance standards.[52] "Accountability is a factor of all administrative and professional work in that continued support for the activity must be justified" in terms of the quality and quantity of work performed by employees.[53]

Library Continuing Education Programs

A manager's administrative perspective which emphasizes productivity enhancement and accountability measures and promotes staff member creativity must consider continuing education programs that promote personal and professional growth. A widely accepted definition maintains that continuing education "consists of those learning opportunities utilized by individuals in fulfilling their need to learn and grow following their preparatory education and work experience."[54]

The major objectives of library continuing education are to improve staff quality and job performance, further capable and productive staff members' job advancement, and encourage leadership.[55] Globally, continuing education efforts strive toward increasing staff member knowledge and revising attitudes.[56] As accountability becomes more demanding, continuing education efforts related to employee job performance improvement must be developed and implemented.

Capable employees may be developed by collaborative efforts between employee and manager. When possibilities exist for future promotions, managers can, with employee input, propose a continuing education program which will provide the employee with the necessary skills, competencies, and knowledge required by the anticipated opening. Libraries need future leaders and the manager is responsible for assuring the field's future well-being. Continuing education should be used to promote future leadership.[57]

The organization of continuing education program responsibilities is varied and divergent. Certain libraries have a management person in charge of training and continuing education, full or part-time. The University of California at Berkeley has a training officer and a library committee to plan continuing education activities.[58] An employee committee can deal with training and continuing education programs. A conscious, systematized approach to continuing education program development where a staff committee and an administrator have final authority and responsibility must be a first step in tying continuing education offerings to job performance, organizational improvement, and the organization's response to change.

National efforts exist to provide an information exchange on continuing education. Continuing Library Education Network and Exchange (CLENE) provides program dissemination, a research center, tries to improve the providers' effectiveness, and tries to make continuing education part of career planning.[59] Continuing education programs may be internal or external. Internal programs are developed within an organization for its staff members. Instructors may be inhouse employees or outside consultants. External programs are developed at other sites and draw individuals from many organizations. The type of program selected is predicted on organizational needs and committee and administrative decisions. Course instructors may be found through CLENE which certifies instructors and providers. Other methods of locating instructors are through referral, neighboring research institutions, review of the relevant literature, and personal contact with field leaders.

Continuing education program participation can be encouraged by managers, but the initial desire to improve oneself must emanate from the staff member. Participation incentive may allow continuing education programs to occur during worktime (providing released time) and to provide fees, mileage, a luncheon or welcome party, and other participant inducements. Recognizing employee attendance can also promote employee well-being. A record of achievement and the grade or certificate awarded may be placed in the employee's personnel file. Program participation may be considered for promotion or tenure.

In times of economic belt-tightening, continuing education programs must be developed that are congruent with the public's demand for employee accountability and productivity. Only courses, workshops, or continuing education programs that foster creativity, accountability, and productivity are justifiable. Continuing education programs are often cut first in economic hard times, but if they can make the organization's employees more accountable, productive, and creative, then they must remain as serious and necessary tools.

Higher education institutions are concerned with library employee productivity and accountability. Few empirical studies have analyzed these two management subsets in austere times. California State University/Northridge (CSUN) carried out such a cost study, however. CSUN used a computer-based system to report, allocate, and analyze library labor costs. Services were broken down into functions, activities and tasks and their relationship to production units and employee productivity. CSUN attempted to relate productivity to dollars spent.[60]

Other analysis attempts within the California State University and Colleges System include the 1978 effort at California State University/Long Beach (CSULB), which undertook a self-initiated, six-month, task-analysis project to measure and evaluate library reference service. The statistical task analysis yielded data on the time spent on reference activities and provided parallels between staff use and stated objectives.

Areas for management and staff improvement were established and policies were instituted congruent with task-analysis findings. Columbia University, the Council on Library Resources, American Council on Education, and the Association of Research Libraries have cooperatively worked with Booz, Allen and Hamilton, Inc., in designing innovative organizational and staffing patterns for Columbia's library.[61] Business management strategies for organizational change in forming employee creativity and productivity improvement programs have been successfully employed at McGill University, University of Michigan, and University of California/Berkeley. At McGill, an institutional self-study generated numerous organizational changes, while Michigan's library planning committee developed and implemented long-range plans to improve management and organizational resources. At Berkeley efforts improved organizational communication vertically as well as horizontally.[62] The need is "for providing a work environment which builds a more effective organizational unit and which results in job satisfaction, mutual confidence and trust, personal motivation, and high standards of accomplishment."[63]

An innovative computer literacy program is currently being implemented at Pepperdine University. A one-year strategy development process seeks to use mini- and microcomputers in making libraries and learning resource centers more accountable and productive. Current plans call for each student soon to have her/his personal computer terminal. After training, each student will be able to access location information and eventually to secure hard copy through the terminal. All university community elements participated in outlining project goals, objectives, and implementation strategies, and this has stimulated creativity and spurred employee thinking on productivity enhancement and accountability. Where staff members think creatively and invent ways to make the library more productive and accountable, these tasks become a true part of the job.

At Stanford University a variety of staff development programs has been used. Certain programs attempted to institutionalize employee creativity. A seven-hour course presented in instructional modules entitled Career Exploration devotes several hours to self-assessment and creative process application to personal and job behavior. Other programs were aimed at management skill and stress humanistic and democratic decision-making as well as communication skill improvement. Staff development efforts with objectives of increasing employee productivity and improving library as well as employee accountability are currently in practice at Stanford.[64] A national need exists for research and program development to stimulate employee creativity and to correlate the creative process with academic library and employee accountability and productivity.

If libraries are to survive and deliver successfully the many services users demand, managers must develop systematic approaches and employ well-thought-out designs that enhance employee creative effort to make libraries more accountable and productive. As employees and managers become more personally accountable and productive, the organization becomes more accountable and productive, also. Virgo suggested that systematic approaches be used

> to cut personnel cost through appropriate technology; improve data collection and analysis; conduct fund-raising; stimulate and encourage staff in the face of modest salary increases and less turnover; . . . and be prepared to terminate the employment of the less productive.[65]

De Gennaro has described the academic library's future. They "have entered a new era of austerity in which the financial resources available will not be enough to enable them to continue to build their collections and operate as they did during the last two affluent decades."[66] Indeed, the manager faces the most important challenge that any administrator can face: scarce resources and unlimited wants and demands.

References

1. Richard De Gennaro, "Matching Commitments to Needs and Resources," *Journal of Academic Librarianship* 7 (March 1981), p. 11.
2. G. Edward Evans, *Management Techniques for Librarians* (N.Y.: Academic Press, 1976), p. 51.
3. Dale E. Shaffer, *Creativity for Librarians (A Management Guide to Encourage Creative Thinking)* (Bethesda, Md.: ERIC Document Reproduction Service, ED 082 798, 1973), p. 3.
4. Evans, *op. cit.*, pp. 52–55.
5. Shaffer, *op. cit.*, p. 5.
6. Ibid., pp. 16–21.
7. Ibid., pp. 12–13.
8. David Mars, "Developing a Climate for Creativity," *Public Management* 49 (March 1967), p. 59.
9. Evans, *op. cit.*, p. 60.
10. Ibid., p. 61.
11. Howard Samuelson, "Increasing Public Library Productivity," *Library Journal* 106 (February 1, 1981), p. 311.
12. Evans, *op. cit.*, pp. 55–58.
13. Ibid., pp. 58–59.
14. Ibid., pp. 59–60.
15. Nancy Wise Kalikow, "Recognizing the Outstanding Employee," *Show-Me Libraries* 31 (February 1980), pp. 23–24.
16. Carol E. Moss, "Bargaining's Effect on Library Management and Operation," *Library Trends* 25 (October 1976), p. 508.
17. Samuelson, *op. cit.*, p. 309.
18. Richard M. Dougherty, "Is Work Simplification Alive and Well Someplace?" *American Libraries* 1 (November 1970), p. 969.

19. Richard M. Dougherty and Fred J. Heinritz, *Scientific Management of Library Operations*, 2nd ed. (Metuchen, N.J.: Scarecrow Press, 1982), p. 149.

20. Ibid, 1966 edition, p. 169.

21. Evans, *op. cit.*, pp. 248–249.

22. Paul S. Strauss, "Is Job Enrichment Really the Answer?" in *Personnel Development in Libraries*, ed. R. Kay Maloney (New Brunswick: Rutgers University Press, 1977), pp. 27–44.

23. D. Dean Willard, "Seven Realities of Library Administration: Fear, Blame, the Productivity Obsession, Expediency, Management by Crisis, Bureaucracy, Management by Platitude," *Library Journal* 101 (January 15, 1976), p. 313.

24. Moss, *op. cit.*, p. 510.

25. Murray S. Martin, *Issues in Personnel Management in Academic Libraries* (Greenwich: JAI Press, 1981), p. 27.

26. Thomas W. Shaughnessy, "Redesigning Library Jobs," *American Society for Information Science Journal* 29 (July 1978), p. 187.

27. Rowena Weiss Swanson, *System Analysis + Work Study = Library Accountability* (Denver: Southeast Metropolitan Board of Cooperative Services Occasional Report No. 1, 1974), p. 17.

28. Timothy W. Spannaus and Joan E. Duryee, "Task Analysis: An Introduction and Practical Experience," *Media Spectrum* 5 (1978), p. 29.

29. Myrl Ricking, "Task Analysis in Libraries," in *Personnel Development in Libraries*, ed. R. Kay Maloney (New Brunswick: Rutgers University Press, 1977), p. 18.

30. Betty Jo Mitchell, Norman E. Tanis and Jack Jaffe, *Cost Analysis of Library Functions: A Total System Approach* (Greenwich: JAI Press, 1978), p. x (Foreword).

31. Strauss, *op. cit.*, pp. 37–40.

32. Jack L. Koford, "The Intangible Incentives," *Public Management* 61 (October 1979), p. 12.

33. Samuelson, *op. cit.*, p. 311.

34. Harold E. Bamford, Jr., "Assessing the Effect of Computer Augmentation on Staff Productivity," *American Society for Information Science Journal* 30 (May 1979), p. 136.

35. Martin, *op. cit.*, p. 124.

36. Evans, *op. cit.*, pp. 136–137.

37. Martin, *op. cit.*, p. 125.

38. Louis A. Allen, *Making Managerial Planning More Effective* (N.Y.: McGraw-Hill, 1982), p. 177.

39. Forest C. Benedict and Paul M. Gherman, "Implementing an Integrated Personnel System," *Journal of Academic Librarianship* 6 (September 1980), pp. 212–213.

40. Allen, *op. cit.*, pp. 48–49.

41. Evans, *op. cit.*, p. 206.

42. Benedict and Gherman, *op. cit.*, p. 210.

43. H. William Axford, "Performance Measurement Revisited," *College and Research Libraries* 34 (September 1973), pp. 249–250.

44. Benedict and Gherman, *op. cit.*, p. 212.

45. Donald E. Klinger, "Job Descriptions: New Uses for a Familiar Tool," *Law Library Journal* 72 (Winter 1979), p. 66.

46. Robert D. Stueart and John Taylor Eastlick, *Library Management* (Littleton: Libraries Unlimited, 1977), p. 95.

47. John W. Ellison and Deborah B. Lazeration, "Personnel Accountability Form for Academic Reference Librarians: A Model," *RQ* 16 (Winter 1976), p. 143.

48. Ibid., p. 144.

49. Stueart and Eastlick, *op. cit.,* p. 156.

50. Evans, *op. cit.,* pp. 228–233.

51. Stueart and Eastlick, *op. cit.,* p. 95.

52. Allen, *op. cit.,* p. 42.

53. Martin, *op. cit.,* p. 125.

54. Barbara Conroy, *Library Staff Development and Continuing Education: Principles and Practices* (Littleton: Libraries Unlimited, 1978), p. xv (Introduction).

55. Charles R. Martell and Richard M. Dougherty, "The Role of Continuing Education and Training in Human Resource Development: An Administrator's Viewpoint," *Journal of Academic Librarianship* 4 (July 1978), pp. 153–154.

56. Conroy, *op. cit.,* p. xi (Introduction).

57. Norman D. Stevens, "CE and the Academic Library Administration," *College and Research Libraries News* 41 (October 1980), pp. 277–278.

58. Carolyn A. Snyder and Nancy P. Sanders, "Continuing Education and Staff Development: Needs Assessment, Comprehensive Program Planning and Evaluation," *Journal of Academic Librarianship* 4 (July 1978), p. 145.

59. Elizabeth W. Stone, "Continuing Professional Education," *ALA Yearbook 1980* (Chicago: American Library Association, 1980), p. 122.

60. Mitchell, Tanis, and Jaffe, *op. cit.,* pp. ix–xii, 1–14.

61. Duane Webster and Jeffrey Gardner, "Strategies For Improving the Performance of Academic Libraries," *Journal of Academic Librarianship* 1 (May 1975), p. 14.

62. Webster and Gardner, *op. cit.,* pp. 14–15.

63. Ibid., p. 13.

64. Telephone interview with Marilyn Gilla, Stanford University, 24 August 1982.

65. Julie C. Virgo, Executive Director, Association of College and Research Libraries "Current Issues in Higher Education and Academic Librarianship," transcript of an address delivered at CSU Northridge, February 9, 1982, p. 12.

66. Richard De Gennaro, "Austerity, Technology and Resource Sharing: Research Libraries Face the Future," *Library Journal* 100 (May 15, 1975), p. 923.

14. Increased Productivity: Work Simplification and Its Heirs

Lloyd A. Kramer

NEARLY THREE DECADES of unparalleled academic library collection, staffing, plant and resources growth have recently come to a close. Most librarians practicing today have no memory of any other environment. Yet they must now shed the conditioning acquired during this remarkable period in order to cope with a kind of scissors action, consisting of one blade marked "declining resources" and another marked "rising costs." Thus, a college vice president saw "a black picture for the liberal arts college and its library in the years immediately ahead . . . libraries . . . will take a disproportionate share of the cuts. . . ."[1]

Concerning rising costs, an academic library report noted "the costs of running a highly labor-intensive operation are outpacing the general rate of inflation."[2] A Carnegie Commission report observed that "the cost of education has risen faster than the CPI. . . . Library and computer costs have been rising considerably more rapidly than other components of costs."[3] Thus, with resources in decline and costs rising, we stand on a collision course with serious financial difficulty.

The suggestion that industrial cost-cutting techniques be introduced by librarians is not new, nor are the techniques. An occasional work study method application has been reported, but general adoption of these techniques has not occurred. There is resistance and perhaps indifference to them. Librarians have been quite reluctant to introduce management techniques for improving operation, perhaps due to a "cottage industry mentality."[4] Early academic librarians were scholars, not managers; as late as the 1940's the Librarian of Congress was a poet. The marked individualism of such library leaders as Melvil Dewey exemplified the cast placed early on the field. No wonder that industrial models have been adopted slowly, if at all.

The situation does not remain static, however, Productivity increases in the economy as a whole create growing pressures on labor-intensive sectors. In this disequilibrium, as general productivity increases (associated primarily with improved technology and capital substitution for labor) the price of labor rises. As a result, higher production costs become increasingly evident in labor-intensive enterprises as compared with costs in other economic sectors. This increase, in turn, makes the labor intensive sectors increasingly vulnerable. Accordingly, it becomes increasingly urgent that certain scientific management elements be introduced into library operation. In addition, declining resources tend to stimulate the most able managers' departure from the sectors affected.[5]

Work Simplification

Work simplification, time-and-motion study, operations research and other methods of increasing productivity focus essentially on efficiency. However, efficiency is sometimes confused with effectiveness, and the distinction between them is important. Efficiency means performing a task economically; effectiveness means performing the right task. Efficiently performing the wrong task causes waste. Some time should be spent in reviewing goals and mission.

Serious challenges to traditional library goals are being heard now. For example, an author argued that traditional university library goals were obsolete. Instead of "to store and provide access to books, periodicals, etc.," it should be "to supply information," he said. This perspective shift should influence how one views networking arrangements, retention, and binding policies and storage.[6] Similarly, traditional collection development goals have been challenged.[7] Another author challenged the goal of organizing for economy of scale and found evidence of a threshold size for many functions where unit costs start to grow rather than decline.[8]

After reviewing goals and arriving at some confidence in them, the manager should consider ways of increasing efficiency as one response to declining resources. Work simplification embraces the earlier time (Frederick Taylor) and motion study (Frank Gilbreth) fields, but the insights which it affords can yield attractive cost savings. In applying work simplification, an activity's elements are broken down into process, delay/storage, transportation, and inspection. Process is the *only* element that adds value. The others may be necessary but add no value and are essentially waste. Anything that can be done to reduce or eliminate delay/storage, transportation, or inspection is pure savings. A further source of waste, in the work simplification lexicon, is failure to employ known faster devices. Transportation alone (moving objects around) is said to account for about 20 per cent of the economy's labor costs.[9]

Having charted an activity's elements (using symbols and formats found in work simplification guides), the manager explores ways to schedule the steps in a sequence that reduces delay/storage, transportation, or unneeded inspection. Sometimes the work area layout can be changed to reduce transportation or delay/storage. Similarly, a sequence change may make it feasible, through batching, to use mechanical or electronic equipment advantageously. Operations should be questioned and only essential ones retained. Combining or dividing operations and changing the step sequence can reduce non-productive elements. Inspection (what we call "revision") can be reduced by using sampling techniques.

Work simplification's relevance is universal, down to the details in form design. One author noted that "Motion and time study fits equally well when applied to the whole range of government activities. . . ."[10] Work simplification should not be confused with time management or speed up. It is not a question of working faster or taking shorter breaks, but of working smarter. A few technical services work simplification ideas in the literature may be interesting.[11] An account of a government-sponsored effort to introduce work simplification was reported.[12] Swedish public libraries identified and eliminated processes found not to be worth the cost and reassigned tasks to appropriate staff levels. Typically library labor discipline is not excessively rigid and individuals may slip into inappropriate "comfort zone" activities.

A text for applying scientific management to library work is available.[13] With illustrations it shows work simplification application techniques, flow process chart construction, and operations analysis application. It covers form design, work norms (standard times), sampling, cost analysis, and performance standards. A detailed case study applies these techniques to a circulation system. An aerospace library work simplification review of acquisitions, cataloging and circulation was reported.[14] It emphasized work measurement and production norm formulation and claimed substantial savings. A second Scandinavian contribution reported on comprehensive work surveys and sampling studies.[15] Work flow and cost analyses were completed. Many cost saving changes were reported in acquisitions, binding, and circulation. Another report appeared on work simplification analysis in cataloging. A 41 per cent transportation reduction was reported.[16]

An industrial engineers group reported studies undertaken in an academic library.[17] Book return and reshelving analysis resulted in saving ten hours per day. In the second study, a left hand-right hand flow chart recorded physical book processing, and resulting recommendations saved 52 per cent in labor costs. The third study saved cataloging costs by reassigning duties at more appropriate levels.

A recent article said "Increasing productivity—improving efficiency and effectiveness of a library employee's output—is one technique for successfully dealing with the budget crunch."[18] It reported substantial savings from a work simplification program and claimed that all library work aspects could benefit from work simplification review and analy-

sis. Suggestions included "Flow chart procedures . . . eliminate unnecessary or limited value services . . . ask employees for ideas . . . simplify
statistics . . . eliminate unneeded files and indexes . . . audit jobs for
appropriate classification . . . and increase automation and new
technology. . . ."[19]

Perhaps the most fruitful area for examination is delay/storage. In
technical services, turnaround time can be constrained by the sheer
quantity of material in process. In one work setting for which I had
responsibility, each work station along the route—receiving, bibliographic checking, card ordering/preparation, cataloging, processing,
and final revision—had at least one loaded book truck. Production was
speeded up by making the book the production unit and dispensing
with trucks. Work stations were attached to a single, long narrow table
which ran the length of the work area and functioned as an assembly
line. Staff were moved as needed to keep the work flow smooth.

In another illustration, at California State University/Long Beach, a
series of steps to arrange books for shelving by call number was reduced
to one step. Now, a truck is sorted at the initial return area and dis-
patched directly for shelving. In addition to excessive delay/storage, the
old method entailed unnecessary transportation. It is not unusual to see
excessive transportation problems in technical services because of
layout. By flow charting the step sequence such areas can be laid out
most efficiently. Of course, certain activities are concurrent and may
diverge or merge at certain points (e.g., serial and monograph cataloging merge for preparation for the shelves). The physical layout can be
designed to reflect departures from linearity.

While processing accuracy is important, a hierarchy of accuracy
urgency may be established. Thus, errors that bear on filing sequence
or result in disparities between volume and card call number may be
more significant than errors in the body of the card. The manner and
frequency with which inspection is done should reflect well-considered
policies. Repetitive steps require rapid devices. Thus, computer- or
copier-produced labels save typing for correspondence with principal
vendors.

Most reference departments show awareness of transportation costs
by having separate ready-reference collections close to staff work stations and service desks. Proximity to catalogs, terminals, and serial records should be considered, also. Excessive decentralization can result
in passing users from one service point to another, since few topics can
be fully contained in a single subject department. Circulation processes
are expensive, due primarily to the nature of shelving. Another difficulty is the scale of record-keeping required to track loans and delin-
quency, but automation is helping here. Transportation considerations
should influence circulation layout. Proximity of return book sites to
sorting areas and elevators and nearness of loan desks to security exit
points must be considered.

The above examples are illustrative; the important thing is the method. In addition to looking for excess transportation, storage/delay, and inspection, no more resources must be employed than are required to achieve objectives. Do not overdo contingency planning. Substantial investment in elaborate record-keeping, preparing for the unlikely, is poor resource use. Prefer simplicity to intricacy. Strive for uniformity and resist the psychic rewards of performing tasks a little differently each time.

Other Management Concepts

While work simplification remains a fruitful method of increasing productivity, several other useful management concepts have emerged since World War II. They include Operations Research, Systems Analysis, Cost-Benefit Analysis, Critical Path Analysis, and its close cousin PERT, and, simply, automation, although automation may more properly be seen as a systems analysis subset.

Operations research was developed to aid decision making in which models are built to test alternative solutions. A certain mathematical ability level is prerequisite to its use. Its basic analytical techniques have been described in a library context.[20] Operations research has been applied to collection building in which the model included levels of demand, number of copies, loan period, and immediate availability.[21] Another treatment included several case studies on loan policy and other issues.[22]

Systems analysis, another technique for studying and improving operation, is similar to operations research. It too involves several research methods, including probability theory and queuing theory, and requires mathematical knowledge.[23] Systems analysis can be applied at a simple level, however, and Chapman provided a step-by-step guide based on Rensselaer Polytechnic Institute experience.[24] Another case study collection provided an analysis leading to an optimal loan period, a sorting area layout and reshelving study, a flow charting illustration and a periodical replacement cost investigation.[25] Systems analysis application is prerequisite to automated system investment, also.

Systems analysis' objective is to increase efficiency. The method is to identify goals, consider alternate solutions, determine data needs and collection methods, develop findings, and prepare recommendations. Systems analysis uses many work simplification concepts, but while the latter uses an ad hoc approach, the former operates consciously in a systems context. A typical systems analysis study follows a perceived need for a policy decision in a situation where alternate solutions exist. Akin to these methods is cost analysis. In this technique, costs are used to evaluate alternate methods and technologies. Two useful library introductions were published a decade ago, one more entertaining and the other more technical.[26,27]

A final methodology, variously termed Critical Path Method, Critical

Path Analysis, or Program Evaluation and Review Technique, has a somewhat narrower focus. Large, one-time only projects, like a building move, construction, or new program installation with associated equipment, lend themselves to this technique. The basic concept involves diagramming anticipated events, from left to right, running those that are in a concurrent sequence in a parallel direction, with connecting links whenever an event in one sequence depends on an event in a concurrent sequence. The resulting network of interdependent events is then evaluated to see which path through this maze from start to finish takes the *most* time. This is the critical path.

The significance of the critical path is that the duration of the *total* project cannot be shortened without shortening events along the *critical* path. Efforts to expedite events *not* along the critical path cannot succeed in shortening the *total* project. With the critical path analysis in hand, the manager can sometimes reallocate resources in non-critical path areas to operations along the critical path areas to shorten the total project. There are many refinements, however, and they should be understood in order to use this planning tool. Horowitz covered both the Critical Path Method and PERT.[28]

Many techniques for evaluating work and improving productivity depend on quantitative data, particularly systems analysis, operations research, and cost analysis. Lynch noted, "A library, like most nonprofit organizations, does not have an overall measure of its success (such as profit) by which to evaluate itself."[29] Her work provides data categories and definitions and can serve as an initial data collection guide. Declining resources have created a need for data gathering to demonstrate accountability, also.[30]

It is reasonable to assemble data for accountability and operation study. Sampling methods applied to carefully considered activities can elicit much of the quantitative information needed.[31] Goodell explained sampling methods for measuring time use. A randomized clock time list for use with observations and tables to determine the number of observations needed were provided. These methods can be used to establish production norms, see how time is spent, and develop cost studies.

Libraries have been slow to realize the economies associated with standards and standardization. Fortunately, data processing has obliged them to adopt increased standardization. "Local" cataloging practices, for example, never economical, are now clearly impractical. The standards notion is pervasive in application. In terms of basic principles, standardization is a simplification process, the basis for interchangeability, fundamental to effective communication, including its technology, and to overall economy.

An early standardization example was the uniform interlibrary loan form. More recently, machine bibliographic data manipulation has made standardization essential. Performance standards can be applied in many library work aspects. Empirically derived mean shelving rates, for example, can be used to evaluate shelving performance and prepare a staffing budget. Form standardization is necessary to organize work and communicate information. Standards are vital to control variation in products and equipment, e.g., microfilm, fiche, print ribbons, copy paper, toner, etc. American National Standards Institute committees work on standards for photographic reproduction, audiovisual material information processing, library supplies and equipment, documentation, and publishing. Heightened consciousness of standardization is essential to cope with leaner budgets.

Work simplification, its heirs, and standardization are intended to aid work process study and increase productivity. In an austere era the prudent manager will use several techniques. We are accustomed to the idea that resources are allocated at a level sufficient to do the job properly. Evidently, this is no longer a reliable expectation. However, by taking seriously our managerial responsibilities to apply these techniques, we may have a reasonable hope of coping successfully in a time of declining resources.

References

1. *LJ/SJ Hotline* X (October 12, 1981), p. 33.
2. *New York Times Higher Education Supplement* (September 5, 1980), p. 4.
3. Carnegie Commission on Higher Education. *The More Effective Use of Resources; an Imperative for Higher Education* (N.Y.: McGraw-Hill, 1972).
4. H. William Axford, "American LIbrary Management Studies: From Games to Leadership," *Advances in Librarianship* (N.Y.: Academic Press, 1980), Volume 10, pp. 39–40.
5. K. E. Boulding, "The Management of Decline," *Change* VII (June 1975), pp. 8–9, 64.
6. Charles B. Weinberg, "The University Library: Analysis and Proposals," *Management Science* XXI (October 1974), pp. 130–40.
7. Daniel Gore, "The View from the Tower of Babel," *Library Journal* C (September 15, 1975), pp. 1599–1605.
8. A Graham MacKenzie, "Progress in Documentation: Whither our Academic Libraries? A Partial Review of Management Research," *Journal of Documentation* XII (June 1976), pp. 126–133.
9. W. Clements Zinck, *Dynamic Work Simplification* (N.Y.: Reinhold Publishing Corporation, 1962), p. 88.
10. Marvin E. Mundel, *Motion and Time Study* (Englewood Cliffs, N.J.: Prentice-Hall, 1978), p. 3.
11. Lloyd A. Kramer, "Work Simplification and Office Procedures," *Library Resources and Technical Services* III (Fall 1959), pp. 287–88.
12. Bengt Holmstrom, "Work Simplification in Swedish Public Libraries," *Library Journal* LXXXVIII (1963), pp. 4312–15.
13. Richard M. Dougherty and Fred J. Heinritz, *Scientific Management of Library Operations,* 2nd ed. (Metuchen, N.J.: Scarecrow Press, 1982).

14. William A. Kozumplik, "Time and Motion Study of Library Operations," *Special Libraries* LVIII (October 1967), pp. 585–88.
15. Danish Library Association. *Work Simplification in Danish Public Libraries* (Chicago: American Library Association, 1969).
16. Lawrence S. Aft, "Work Methods in the Library," *Industrial Engineering* V (November 1973), pp. 39–41.
17. Wayne C. Turner and others. "Library Methods Improvement," *Industrial Engineering* VII (January 1975), pp. 34–41.
18. Howard Samuelson, "Increasing Public Library Productivity," *Library Journal* CVI (February 1, 1981), p. 309.
19. See Samuelson, pp. 309–311 for these and other suggestions.
20. Jenny E. Rowley, *Operations Research, A Tool for Library Management* (Chicago: American Library Association, 1981)
21. Michael K. Buckland, *Book Availability and the Library User* (N.Y.: Pergamon Press, 1975).
22. Peter Brophy, Michael K. Buckland and Anthony Hindle. *Reader in Operations Research for Libraries* (Englewood, Colorado: Information Handling Services, 1976).
23. Philip M. Morse, *Library Effectiveness, A Systems Approach* (Cambridge, Mass.: M.I.T. Press, 1968).
24. Edward A. Chapman, Paul L. St. Pierre and John Lubans. *Library Systems Analysis Guidelines* (N.Y.: Wiley-Interscience, 1970).
25. Barton R. Burkhalter, ed., *Case Studies in Systems Analysis in a University Library* (Metuchen, N.J.: Scarecrow Press, 1968).
26. John Kountz, "Library Cost Analysis: A Recipe," *Library Journal* XCVII (February 1, 1972), pp. 459–64.
27. Donald W. King and Edward C. Bryant. *The Evaluation of Information Services and Products* (Washington, D.C.: Information Resources Press, 1971).
28. Joseph Horowitz, *Critical Path Scheduling, Management Control Through CPM and PERT* (N.Y.: Ronald Press, 1967).
29. Mary Jo Lynch, ed., *Library Data Collection Handbook* (Chicago: American Library Association, 1981).
30. Richard L. Alfred, ed., *Coping With Reduced Resources* (San Francisco: Jossey-Bass, 1978).
31. John S. Goodell, *Libraries and Work Sampling* (Littleton, Colo.: Libraries Unlimited, 1975).

15. Automation in Austerity

Hugh C. Atkinson and Patricia F. Stenstrom

IN 1952 WHEN RALPH PARKER wrote about library mechanization and automation, he anticipated a system which would not only improve service but also save money.

Whenever any discussion of the application of punched card methods to a new process is begun, one of the first points to be raised is that of cost. . . . [I]t should be understood at the outset that no installation of punched cards should be made unless the increased efficiency of operation will make the process at least as inexpensive as when done by the older method. Punched card installations are not an expensive luxury, and the manufacturers will not usually proceed with an installation until they are convinced of the economic soundness of the application.[1]

The dream of most early library automation commentators was certainly to reduce costs as well as improve service. The graph lines always seemed so clear. Computation costs were dropping and human labor costs were rising. Those lines seemed to meet about five years from the date of any particular study, but unfortunately, as each year went by, the lines still seemed to meet five years in the future. However, in an era with enormous and rapid higher education expansion, the climate was more favorable to system development to improve service, especially large volume manipulation, regardless of cost, than to cost-effective system development. In those days, we attempted to solve many national social problems by "throwing money at them." Higher education and libraries shared that attitude toward improving the quality of life.

As Fussler tactfully stated:

The cited literature tends to lack, in part for valid reasons, firm costs or objective performance data on both existing operations and new applications of technology. It is sometimes even difficult to tell what has been accomplished from what is being contemplated. Conventional library operating data also tend to be inconsistent and unreliable for careful economic or performance analyses, and are related primarily to inputs rather than outputs.[2]

Demands on automated systems grew faster than any possible savings could grow if they were successful, and if not, the failures were extraordinarily expensive.[3] The more realistic analysts agreed that no savings in actual dollar outlays would occur but rather that services would be improved.[4] Following the statement quoted above, Parker said:

It is often not desirable to reduce expenditures by an installation, if for no other reason than that the machines will open new areas for improved performance and better services. It is this overplus or results obtainable at the same cost through punched cards which has caused the greatest expansion in their use.[5]

Computer-based library system justification based on costs alone will continue to be difficult because machines not only replace manual systems but generally do more and different things. It is unsatisfactory to compare them with previous manual systems which frequently did the jobs inadequately and with unknown operating costs. In the short run, computer-based systems will not save money if all development and implementation costs are considered. They will provide better and more dependable records and systems, which enable libraries to cope with increased workloads, but they will cost at least as much as the inadequate manual systems replaced.

In the long run the picture may change, but it seems reasonable to expect that automation, in addition to changing profoundly the way in which the budget is spent, will increase service cost. However, that service will be pitched on a much higher level than today's library budget buys, and while certain jobs will be eliminated, others will be formed to provide new service, often at greater depth. As a library becomes increasingly responsive and successful the demands on it will increase. Such improvement comes from higher volume handling by both technical and public services, searching technique provision, and greater ease in bibliographic record error correction and data distribution. Data bases such as circulation files and serial holdings lists can be much more accurate than previous manual files.

Accuracy and service have improved and far surpass past manual system levels. However, to reach that point has been a twenty-year task, and the early automated systems were neither better nor cheaper than the manual systems they replaced. Kilgour provided an admirable summary of the library mechnization evolution.[6] Certain of the earliest computer applications were in indexing reports by subject. As early as 1954 through 1958, the U.S. Naval Test Station, China Lake, California and the General Electric Air Craft, Gas Turbine Division, Evandale, Ohio, used computers to provide document collection subject approaches.

The first large scale system was MEDLARS which produced not only the *Index Medicus* but the ability to search its journal articles and to retrieve specific medical literature citation bibliographies. MEDLARS be-

came operational in 1964. Continuing Boolean logic and machine
searching application, DIALOG (Lockheed Aircraft System) was applied
to NASA document subject searching and the SUNY Biomedical Communication Network developed—the predecessor of BRS (Bibliographical
Retrieval Services). The past fifteen years has seen development of the
Washington State Library Network, Control Data Corporation's ORBIT
and Northwestern University's NOTIS. They represent further development in applying both text searching and machine processing.

As Kilgour pointed out, almost concurrently with machine searching
system development, libraries began to produce catalog cards using
computer or computer-like devices. One of the most common card
production methods was to use a punched paper tape driven Friden
Flexowriter. At the same time computer produced book form catalogs
began to appear. The St. Louis Monsanto Information Center produced a computer-based book catalog in 1962. Two years later Florida
Atlantic University produced its first book catalog and the year after the
University of Toronto ONLUP catalog appeared. In 1969, Baltimore
County Public Library contracted with Documentation, Inc. to produce
a catalog similar in content to the early British Museum title catalogs, a
common nineteenth-century listing style. The Florida Atlantic and
Toronto catalogs were machine readable card catalogs reproduced in
book form.

Various specialized machine readable catalogs and SDI services appeared in the mid-1960s and continue to the present day. Kilgour
indicated that the Picatinney Arsenal in New Jersey was first to comput-
erize its circulation system in 1962 but certainly by 1964 and 1965
several academic libraries were using IBM data collection equipment in
circulation systems. This system attracted academic libraries because it
could read an IBM punched book charge card and a punched borrowers
card. Thus, combining book with user information produced an "items
out" circulation system. Southern Illinois University, Washington University, and the University of Missouri had similar systems. While they
were not on-line, they could print a daily books in circulation list. The
first real time on-line system was installed at Bell Laboratories Library,
Murray Hill, N.J. in 1968. It produced the same kinds of transactions
and querying ability associated with more recent CLSI, Data Phase, and
LCS circulation systems.

In 1965, an institution appeared which demonstrated that automation could effect true savings. The Ohio College Library Center, now
the Online Computer Library Center (OCLC), founded by Kilgour, had
as its stated goal, to "reduce the rise in costs of library activity."

Kilgour was convinced libraries could drastically improve productivity by adopt-
ing computerized cataloging. The phenomenal success of OCLC during the 70s
has confirmed Kilgour's faith in a library concept that was largely untested in
1969. In fact, a simple comparison of the period 1974–1980 between OCLC's

basic first time use (FTU) charges for a typical library in Michigan with the consumer price index (CPI) reveals the clarity with which Kilgour saw the future. In 1974 the OCLC FTU charge for a non-Ohio library was $1.87. By 1980–81 the comparable charge was $1.40, not an increase but an actual decrease, whereas the CPI for the comparable period rose 47% and the level of beginning librarians' salaries increased 31%.[7]

It is interesting to note that OCLC's first decade did not reveal so clearly the automated cataloging cost benefit. Stecher wrote a very critical and probably accurate OCLC experience survey and analysis in 1976 for his own institution, La Trobe University in Australia:

The crucial point which emerges from this exercise is that, even allowing for errors that might favor the use of the shared facility, in no way is it possible that a system such as OCLC would prove to be a windfall as far as cutting costs is concerned. At the same time it should be pointed out that, with a few somewhat aberrant exceptions, OCLC does not claim anything of the sort. Their objective is stated to be: to reduce the rate of rise of per-unit cost of cataloging, or, more simply and just as effectively, to increase the productivity of cataloging staff. In terms of our exercise this implies the assumption that unit costs are rising at a higher rate than is the figure for the OCLC costs, thereby giving a growing figure under net saving, with the percentage figure for gross saving remaining constant. The differential rate in the increases of the first two is crucial. Given that figures here are valid, the establishment of an OCLC-like facility would in fact represent an investment with benefits to be reaped some time in the future.[8]

Stecher criticized most of the literature published on OCLC prior to late 1975. He pointed out that many of the claims stated for OCLC suffered from the failing of *post hoc ergo propter hoc.* This characterization may not be entirely valid although it is an accurate description. An automated cataloging system requires rigorous analysis and management. This careful management may be the reason for the favorable cost-benefit. If automation makes one apply rigorous cost control then that is a real benefit.

The first study reflecting management's effectiveness appeared in the following year. A careful analysis of the Ohio State University Library experience demonstrated that cataloging cost increases were far less than inflation cost increases. In fact, if inflation had been factored in, a substantial unit cost decrease would have been found.[9] In sum, this pilot cost study demonstrated that OCLC use permitted OSU's cataloging production to increase, while unit costs rose but slightly even though inflation is ignored. In 1976, in what is probably the most careful automated cataloging analysis yet published, Ross noted that at Cornell University it "is obvious that the implementation of the OCLC cataloging support module has been cost beneficial."[10] Furthermore, in 1977, Spyers-Duran demonstrated a clear personnel and cost decrease as an effect of library automation in showing reduction of 103 full-time equivalent (FTE) positions from 46 libraries.[11]

An obvious problem is to reconcile the early unfavorable with the later favorable OCLC cost analyses. Apparently, 1970 brought a managerial perspective to new OCLC system application. That perspective which exercised cost control was probably the primary reason for Spyers-Duran's survey results.

Most managers are sympathetic to Ukeles' data processing attitudes in his study of governmental efficiency.[12] He recommended increased coordination, detailed planning, leadership in application development, personnel turnover reduction, and tight data processing control. The same attitudes and expectations might be applied to library management. The OCLC application studies should show that automation is in itself neither cost beneficial nor costly. What it will do and cost depends on the managerial skill with which it is applied. Well managed systems can be effective, poorly managed ones seldom are.

Of course, one overriding difference exists between the early 1970s and the early 1980s. The former was an expansion period and the latter is a retrenchment period. Recession has affected higher education in recent years, and it is seldom possible to obtain large dollar or people increments to implement new systems. They must be implemented within shrinking budgets. Thus, automation implementation as a parallel system with additional cost is likely to be bypassed. New technology application may be slowed but may also be better managed. OCLC and automated circulation demonstrated that automation may be applied with a reduced budget. Presently under development are the on-line catalog and serial control systems. Their literature stresses opportunities, not failures or costs.

The on-line catalog seems to us to have great cost effectiveness potential. We have very little published literature on functioning on-line system costs. There seem to be no such systems which have completely replaced library card or book catalogs. Some promise exists for cost effectiveness if the on-line catalog is integrated with an on-line bibliographic utility such as OCLC, RLIN, or UTLAS. With such integration the machine readable record production cost is concomitant with that of the cataloging itself. If the MARC format record can be placed in a computer with a searching system no more expensive than card or book catalog maintenance, then the effort will be both cost effective and service enhancing.

It is too early to see the cost of such systems but one can assume that the same problems will occur which slowed early OCLC applications. There will be enthusiastic proponents such as we, doubters who will point out salient economic facts, and managers who will insist that the application be done in a cost-beneficial manner. Most likely that will mean a personnel reduction elsewhere in the library system to pay for catalog transference to machine readable form. Since we have the circulation and cataloging experience, we can predict that the cost savings will not appear magically. They will have to be forced into existence by library managers. Raising the capital necessary to finance on-line systems presents a serious problem in austere budgets. Getting financing from the university or an outside agency, either a bank or foundation, is at best problematical.

Other factors may affect automation implementation, also. In an austere era, it may not be enough just to manage well. If the most pressing problems are external, real barriers may be provided to new technology use. The most obvious outside factor is the extrordinary telecommunication cost rise. It is not that the Bell System and its rivals are particularly rapacious but that their costs and necessary investment returns require a continuous price rise outside any administrator's ability to influence.

We depend on the existing telecommunication structure, and its costs are approaching those of the actual data processing itself. In Illinois when we pay through the Illinois Library and Information Network (ILLINET) $1.40 for an OCLC catalog card set, we also add 75 cents for telephone line use. Thus, over one-third of the total computational charge is spent for telecommunication. These charges have been rising at an annual rate above 15 per cent. OCLC's own costs are rising less than 5 per cent a year. If present trends continue, in a few years talking to the OCLC computer will cost as much as computer use itself.

Of course alternatives exist, not all of which are attractive. Certain technological solutions suggest switching away from standard telephone communication. One can change the organizational structure by moving the computer closer to the terminal or by sharing either the computer or the telecommunication system with a diverse user set. A technological solution greatly to be desired is one that reduces telephone line use by compressing and rapidly transmitting messages or by sharing use of already-in-place state or regional telecommunication networks. However, the most likely solution will involve moving away from the present telephone company configuration to a wide spectrum of communication devices including the microwave systems commonly used by such state agencies as the police and car license plate registration.

A telecommunication system alternative which strikes us as being fraught with complications is rapidly expanding mini-computer library use. Mini-computer system proponents are persuasive and seem to offer a low-cost alternative to the large traditional main-frame-based systems. It is true that advances in both storage and processing and continued miniaturization have been phenomenal. Certain mini-computers do more now than did the largest machines two decades ago.

The problem is that the libraries' perceived needs and the amount of data now deemed necessary have grown faster than the minis have shrunk. We now talk in terms of billions of characters to be stored and almost instantaneous response times. The mini-computer is self-limiting at the point where it becomes more costly to continue joining them together in series than to purchase a large machine. In fact, to access a reasonably large database, certain minis would use their whole power merely to form the series. We envision systems which not only display catalog data, holdings information, and circulation records but also title pages, indexes, and binding information. Until the technology develops much further, the mini-computer seems unlikely to be a promising alternative to the large main-frame machine. Even if a mini-computer cost breakthrough occurs, one must be extraordinarily careful to join the minis together so the data can be queried from all network points.

One design has appeared in the literature which seems to hold some degree of promise. IRVING is a Denver, Colorado area system design that has laid out an interconnected local area network configuration composed of smaller computers. If this design is implemented success-fully, it may be a future network model.[13]

Certain automation projects may be forced on us by users rather than our cost-efficiency analyses, regardless of the economic times. Two such projects are online bibliographic reference service and machine-stored aggregate data service. Online bibliographic reference service has achieved partial financing by requiring users to pay part of service cost. Use of databases and services has concentrated in the sciences, technol-ogy, and business. Clients have been willing to pay surcharges for quite fast or complete searches. Current service demand is high, and compet-ing agencies will offer these services if libraries do not. Thus, the library is forced into providing a service and financing it in a non-traditional manner.

Using aggregate data—voting records, census data, economic statis-tics, and the like—presents a future library material definition problem as much as an administrative problem of service finance. Traditional printing and publishing may be inappropriate or uneconomical forms for large knowledge storage of undigested data masses. The large mass and its unanalyzed nature are hallmarks of aggregate data. Researchers need both the data and the facility to manipulate it, so both the data and the statistical programs necessary to manipulate it must be provided.

We suspect that libraries will seldom store either data or statistical programs but rather will provide the nexus and computer to which the data are transmitted from a regional or national database. A locally stored offline statistical program will be added to facilitate manipula-tion. After data processing, the output will be delivered to the user, the statistical program returned to the computer program library and the raw data either destroyed or stored offline. Probably the library will store indexes of variables and programs which may either be printed or accessed via computer terminal. Libraries may be forced into such ser-vice which will be demanded by a user segment, and probably it will displace a lower priority activity. For either administrative or economic reasons, the aggregate database services initiated by non-library agencies may be serviced, also. They will take a place appropriate to demand in the library's priorities.

Another Ukeles management suggestion may assist in austerity automation project funding. He recommended avoiding duplication in a decentralized environment.[14] Most libraries have some form of decentralization. If certain decentralized costs can be recovered, they can be applied toward new technology implementation. Such may be the strategy employed to get through the implementation period to the period of integration into the general budget.

If automation is applied wisely, the catalog, check-in file, and serial record may provide a high likelihood of cost reduction by duplication elimination. For instance, Shoham analyzed the costs of obvious reader preference for branch libraries. One can estimate that an on-line serial system and an on-line catalog could save well over 10 per cent of public service costs.[15] That kind of saving could be close to the cost of on-line system implementation.

In most libraries, the serials department records the activities of all units and those same activities are re-recorded at the serials housing point. The farther from the serials department the unit is, the more likely and more extensive such re-recording seems to be. What we are suggesting is not centralization but rather decentralized on-line system use to eliminate duplicate costs and recover approximately the funds needed for central unit support. Since Shoham's study showed a decided user preference for decentralized service, on-line system implementation may have benefits beyond cost savings.

In discussing automation implementation in austerity, one must recognize that it will not be a library panacea. It may, if implemented well, reduce certain serious difficulties but probably will need to substitute for certain manual systems or printed material. In any case, some disagreement will exist about each implementation phase. Even in prosperous times one heard such disagreement continually. Library literature contains many warnings against automation as either a passing fad or a dead end. Both the over-enthusiastic and the detractors were wrong. Automation and mechanization are simply examples from a large spectrum of tools providing the library with the means to perform its educational mission more successfully.

References

1. Ralph H. Parker, *Library Applications of Punched Cards: A Description of Mechanical Systems* (Chicago: American Library Association, 1952), p. 71.
2. Herman H. Fussler, *Research Libraries and Technology* (Chicago: University of Chicago Press, 1973), p. 1.
3. H. William and Lavonne Brady Axford, "The Anatomy of Failure in Library

Applications of Computer Technology," In *Clinic on Library Applications of Data Processing, 1978: Problems and Failures in Library Automation* (Urbana: University of Illinois, 1979), p. 100.

4. Richard De Gennaro, "The Development and Administration of Automated Systems in Academic Libraries," *Journal of Library Automation* 1 (March 1968), p. 90.

5. Parker, *op. cit.*, p. 71.

6. Frederick G. Kilgour, "History of Library Computerization," *Journal of Library Automation* 3 (September 1970), pp. 218–229.

7. Richard M. Dougherty, "A Revisionist's View of Scientific Management," In Robert Stueart, *Academic Librarianship: Yesterday, Today and Tomorrow* (N.Y.: Neal-Schuman, 1982), p. 18.

8. G. Stecher, "Shared Cataloging: An Exercise in Costing OCLC," *Australian Academic and Research Libraries* 7 (March 1976), p. 11.

9. Ichiko Morita and D. Kaye Gapen, "A Cost Analysis of the Ohio College Library Center On-line Shared Cataloging System in the Ohio State University Libraries," *Library Resources and Technical Services* 21 (Summer 1977), pp. 286–301.

10. Ryburn Ross, "Cost Analysis of Automation in Technical Services," In *Clinic on Library Applications of Data Processing, 1976: The Economics of Library Automation* (Urbana: University of Illinois, 1977), pp. 10–27.

11. Peter Spyers-Duran, "The Effects of Automation on Organizational Change, Staffing, and Human Relations in Catalog Departments," in *Requiem for the Card Catalog: Management Issues in Automated Cataloging* (Westport, Conn.: Greenwood Press, 1979), pp. 29–39.

12. Jacob B. Ukeles, *Doing More With Less: Turning Public Management Around* (N.Y.: AMACON, 1982), pp. 201–211.

13. "IRVING Network Readies for Implementation Phase," *Advanced Technology Libraries* 11 (November 1982), p. 4.

14. Ukeles, *op. cit.*, p. 204.

15. Snunith Shoham, "A Cost-Preference Study of the Decentralization of Academic Library Services," *Library Research* 4 (Summer 1982), pp. 174–194.

Index

Notes on Contributors

HUGH ATKINSON is University Librarian and Professor of Library Administration, University of Illinois, Urbana. In 1959, he received an M.A. degree from the Graduate Library School, University of Chicago. He has been active in several American Library Association divisions—Resources and Technical Services, Library Information and Technology, and Library Administration and Management—in the Association of Research Libraries and OCLC (Online Computer Library Center, Inc.). Atkinson has written and spoken extensively on library automation and serves as an editorial advisor for four technical journals.

A former NDEA Fellow and academic library director, THOMAS C. HARRIS is now a higher education network employee, Associate Director, the State University Libraries, California State University, Long Beach. He has B.A. and M.L.S. degrees from the University of California, Los Angeles, and a Ph.D. in Higher Education Administration, Arizona State University.

JOHN F. HARVEY was educated at Dartmouth College, University of Illinois and University of Chicago, Ph.D. Previously Dean, School of Library and Information Science, Drexel University, he was later Dean of Library Services at the University of New Mexico and at Hofstra University, and Visiting Professor, Mottahedin University, Tehran. He was a board of directors member of three American Library Association divisions. Harvey founded the *Drexel Library Quarterly,* holds honorary life memberships in two national library associations, is listed in the who's who's of three countries, and serves as an international consultant.

EDWARD R. JOHNSON is Director of Libraries, North Texas State University. After a B.A., University of Colorado, he received two degrees from the University of Wisconsin, Madison, M.A.L.S. and Ph.D. Johnson has published *Organization Development for Academic Libraries,* Greenwood Press, 1980, as well as papers on library organization, management and objectives.

Former Administrative Vice President, College of St. Francis, LLOYD A. KRAMER is now Associate Director, California State University Library, Long Beach. Kramer holds three degrees: B.A. and B.L.S., University of California, Berkeley, and M.P.A., California State University, Long Beach.

THOMAS W. LEONHARDT has had a career in university library processing divisions and is now Assistant University Librarian for Technical Services at the University of Oregon. He is the author of a report on the Duke University Library Information System and on a library approval plan. Leonhardt has two degrees from the University of California, Berkeley: A.B. and M.L.S.

A former Council on Library Resources Fellow, FREDERICK CHARLES LYNDEN is now Assistant University Librarian for Technical Services, Brown University. His Fellowship Report was titled "Library Materials Budgeting in the Private University Library." Lynden graduated from Stanford University with B.A. in International Relations and M.A. in American History. His library science M.A. was received at the University of Minnesota.

A native of New Zealand, MURRAY S. MARTIN has three degrees or diplomas from the University of New Zealand: B.A., Bachelor of Commerce, and M.A., and one from the New Zealand Library School. He has contributed articles on New Zealand authors and literature to various publications. In addition, he has published *Budgetary Control in Academic Libraries*, JAI Press, 1978, and *Issues in Personnel Administration in Academic Libraries*, JAI Press, 1981. A past president, Pittsburgh Regional Library Center, Martin is now University Librarian, Tufts University.

GERARD M. McCABE is Director of Libraries, Clarion University, Clarion, PA. His degrees include a B.A. from Manhattan College, A.M.L.S. from the University of Michigan and M.A. in English, Michigan State University. McCabe had a Library Service Fellowship and a Scholarship, University of Michigan. He is senior editor of the new *Advances in Library Administration and Organization* series published annually by JAI Press.

ROBERT J. MERIKANGAS has four academic degrees: B.A. from Tulane University, M.A. from Catholic University, M.L.S. from the University of Maryland, and Ph.D. from Catholic University. He is Head, Reference Services, Hornbake Library, University of Maryland. Merikangas presented papers at both the First and Second ACRL National Conferences.

A winner of awards for outstanding papers, in the 1969 *Journal of Library History* and *Library Lit: The Best of 1979*, JOSEPH Z. NITECKI has made numerous contributions to the theory of librarianship and library management. He has two master's degrees, one from Roosevelt University in Philosophy and one from the University of Chicago in library science. He is Director of Libraries, State University of New York, Albany. Nitecki's B.A. in Philosophy is from Wayne State University.

GLORIA NOVAK is both a university administrator and a private library architecture consultant. Her job title is Library Space Planner, University of California, Berkeley, and she has both B.A. and M.L.S. degrees from that university. On three recent occasions Novak has chaired American Library Association conference programs on library architecture.

Director of Libraries, Miami University, Ohio, DONALD E. OEHLERTS has published in several librarianship fields. He has also taught part-time in several library schools. Oehlerts' bachelor's degree is from the University of Wisconsin, Madison, in American Studies; his master's degree from Wisconsin is in library science as well as his doctorate from Indiana University.

A Phi Beta Kappa graduate of the University of Missouri, THEODORE SAMORE has M.A. and M.A.L.S. degrees from the University of Michigan. He has spent two decades collecting, analyzing and writing about American academic library statistics, most recently for the *Bowker Annual*. Samore is Professor, School of Library and Information Science, University of Wisconsin, Milwaukee.

PETER SPYERS-DURAN has an M.A. from the University of Chicago Graduate Library School and an Ed.D., Nova University. He is Director of Libraries, Wayne State University. Formerly the Executive Director, California State University Library and Learning Resources, Long Beach, he has consulted and taught library science and is a former President, University of Chicago Graduate Library School Alumni Association. In the past seventeen years, he has made numerous contributions as an author or editor to the literature of collection development and library management. He is an active member of ALA. In addition, Spyers-Duran is a Standing Committee member, International Federation of Library Associations and Institutions' Section on University Libraries and Other General Research Libraries.

The Library and Information Science Librarian, University of Illinois, Urbana, is PATRICIA FITZGERALD STENSTROM. She is a University of Illinois B.A. and M.S. graduate with previous library experience in serials and cataloging who also produced a survey of social science faculty serial use.

Reference Librarian, California State University, Long Beach, DONNA BELLI YGLESIAS has three academic degrees: B.A., California State University, Long Beach; M.P.A., and M.L.S., University of Southern California. Ms. Yglesias has published two books: *Dissertations in Urban History: The Historical Dimension,* Ann Arbor, UMI, 1976; and *Minorities and Women: A Guide to Reference Literature in the Social Sciences,* Los Angeles, Reference Service Press, 1977, selected by *Choice* as an "Outstanding Academic Book." In addition, she was one of the planners of the "Even the Odds; Women in Library Management" seminar in 1981.

DATE DUE